REMEMBER
THE AMERICAN WAY

# REMEMBERING WAR
# THE AMERICAN WAY

## G. KURT PIEHLER

SMITHSONIAN BOOKS
WASHINGTON

Copy Editor: Karin Kaufman
Production Editor: Jenelle Walthour
Deisgner: Alan Carter

Library of Congress Cataloging-in-Publication Data
Piehler, G. Kurt.
Remembering war the American way / G. Kurt Piehler.
p.   cm.
Includes bibliographical references and index.
ISBN 1-56098-461-9
1. United States—Social life and customs. 2. Memory—Social aspects—
United States—histroy. 3. Historic sites—United States.
4. United States—History, Military. I. Title.
E161.P52 1995
973—dc20                                                    94—10755

British Library Cataloguing-in-Publication Data is available

A paperback reissue (ISBN 1-58834-145-3) of the original cloth edition

Manufactured in the United States of America
10  09  08  07  06  05  04     5  4  3  2  1

∞The paper used in this publication meets the minimum requirements of the American National Standard for Permanence of Paper for Printed Library Materials Z39.48–1984.

Photographs credited to the Smithsonian Institution Archives are from the Smithsonian Instution Archives, Record Unit 377, Eisenhower Institute for Historical Research, Records, circa 1946–1984, Box 12. For permission to reproduce illustrations appearing in this book, please correspond directly with the owners of the works, as listed in the individual captions. Smithsonian Books does not retain reproduction rights for these illustrations individually, or maintain a file of addresses for photo sources.

FOR

VINCENT AND ISOLDE CLARK

JOHN WHITECLAY CHAMBERS II

SUSAN G. CONTENTE

# CONTENTS

# PREFACE TO
# PAPERBACK EDITION

On September 11, 2001, Americans were stunned by the terrorist attacks on the World Trade Center and the Pentagon. Two commercial airliners struck the twin towers of the World Trade Center and sparked massive fireballs that engulfed both buildings. Despite the heroic efforts of rescue workers, especially those from the New York Fire Department, the twin towers collapsed and killed over 2,500 men and women. Another commercial airliner crashed into one wing of the Pentagon and produced a fire that left a gaping hole in the Defense Department headquarters. Over 100 active-duty military personnel and civilian workers were killed in the attack, but at least the fire departments from northern Virginia were able to extinguish the fire.

Mourning and memorialization began almost immediately in the wake of these assaults, which were deemed to be acts of a terrorist war against the United States. In the initial hours after the attack on the Trade Center, New Yorkers created homemade memorials of flowers and candles near the smoking hole in the ground that marked the collapsed twin towers. Relatives posted signs with pictures of their missing loved ones and placed them around the city hoping someone could provide word of their whereabouts. Survivors were reunited, but as hope gradually dimmed for others, these posters became icons of remembrance. Firehouses across the city emerged as places of mourning as New Yorkers placed wreaths and flowers at their doors.

Soon the funerals began for those who had been killed. It took months to sift through the wreckage of the World Trade Center in search of the dead. Despite advances in forensic anthropology and the tireless work of the scores of men and women who sifted and removed the rubble from the World Trade Center, some bodies were never recovered. Sadly, in many cases they had been vaporized by the intense inferno. In others cases, some human remains were found, but could not be identified.

Even as the rubble was being removed from the World Trade Center and the Pentagon, questions began to emerge over how Americans should preserve the memory of those who were killed in these grievous attacks. In the case of the Pentagon, the undamaged parts continued to function as the headquarters of the Defense Department. Within days, efforts began not only to remove the wreckage, but to start the process of rebuilding the damaged parts of this World War II–era building. In contrast, many questioned whether the World Trade Center should be rebuilt or the site turned into a memorial park. Despite the wishes of some family members who lost loved ones in the attack on the World Trade Center, city and state officials as well as the Port Authority of New York and New Jersey owners of the land for the World Trade Center made it clear that financial considerations made it impossible to leave the site vacant. At the same time, public officials in charge of the reconstruction of lower Manhattan also made it clear that any rebuilding on the World Trade complex had to include a fitting memorial to those who were killed on September 11. A growing consensus emerged that no building should be placed on the actual footprint of the twin towers at the World Trade Center site.

There are strong elements of continuity between how Americans mourned the dead of September 11 and the way Americans have memorialized past wars. Perhaps the most striking pattern is the emphasis placed on remembering the name of every individual who died in these attacks. At memorial services on the first and second anniversaries of the attacks on the World Trade Center, the names of every individual killed in the attack were read aloud. Further reflective of this pattern of remembrance is the efforts of the *New York Times* to write a short obituary of every single individual killed in the terrorist attacks of September 11. All the designs proposed in November 2003 as a permanent memorial on the World Trade Center site have several features in common, including a list of all the names of those killed in the attack.

Families wanted to know what happened to their loved ones and have their bodies recovered. Their expectations were no doubt encouraged by advances in forensics that enabled the Defense Department in 1998 to identify the remains of the

Unknown Soldier from the Vietnam War. Nearly 40 percent of the human remains recovered from the World Trade Center could not be positively identified. As a result, the World Trade Center memorial will become a burial site until there are further advances in science.

There have been other acts of commemoration. Across America in the days and months after the attacks of September 11 there were local memorial services to mourn the victims of the attack. Countless memorials have sprung up in communities across Greater New York memorializing those who died in the attacks of September 11. Often these local memorials incorporate portions of the ruins from the World Trade Center site. Moreover, a number of oral history projects have been sponsored by universities, historical societies, and others to not only preserve the history of what happened on September 11, but also to serve as a memorial to the victims.

There have also been controversies over remembrance. For example, should the civilian workers killed at the Pentagon be granted burial rights at Arlington National Cemetery? In building permanent memorials on the World Trade Center site, should separate monuments be commissioned marking the deaths of rescue workers? Who should be the custodians of the memory of the events of September 11? Political leaders, especially President George W. Bush and former New York Mayor Rudolph Giuliani, have sought to play a decisive role in shaping the public memory of these tragic events. Their efforts, however, have not been uncontested, and survivors, especially family members, have tried to assert a decisive role.

Can any memorial do justice to the memory of those who died in the attacks of September 11? Many victim's families have been reluctant to defer to the expertise of architects and other professionals who are competing to design the memorial. Although many have accepted the idea that much of the World Trade Center site will be redeveloped, they are determined to preserve the remnants of the Twin Tower's "basement" walls as a memorial to their loved ones. Will the political, business, and cultural leaders selected by the Lower Manhattan Development Corporation decide on an acceptable aesthetic that honors the memory of those who died? Will any consensus be reached in the end? One simple effort to memorialize September 11 may offer some hints at what might prove meaningful to the families of the victims as well as the general public. In late winter and early spring 2001, two memorial beams of light were sent into the night sky from the original World Trade Center site each night for several weeks. Both editorial writers and average citizens on the street applauded this simple, but moving memorial that was initially conceived by a small group of New York City architects, artists, and designers.

Although there is a long history of domestic terrorism in the United States, the events of September 11 inaugurated a new decisive turn in American foreign policy. President Bush led the United States into war against Afghanistan after the Taliban regime refused to turn over Osama bin Laden and other members of the Al Qaeda regime who masterminded the attacks of September 11. Despite considerable debate at home and abroad, in March 2003, President Bush sent massive U.S. forces into Iraq arguing in part that Iraqi dictator Saddam Hussein had links with the Al Qaeda terrorist organizations. Although the United States along with coalition forces contributed by Great Britain, Poland, and several other nations managed to quickly overthrow the Iraqi regime, it took eight months to capture Saddam Hussein. Even after President Bush declared an end to major hostilities ended in May 2003, the fighting did not end. Sadly, my book continues to be relevant not only to scholars, but to those Americans who mourn the dead from both recent acts of terrorism, and the over 400 war dead from these two overseas wars.

When I first began *Remembering War the American Way* in 1987, there were few scholars who had examined how Americans commemorated past wars. George Mosse had studied the question of war and memory in the European context with a special emphasis on Germany. Historians of the American Civil War examined the significance of the Lost Cause to southern history. Art historians had begun to write about the history of war memorials, but their analysis focused primarily on aesthetic questions. As my book was nearing publication, the scholarship on memory and history in the U.S. context started to burgeon, most notably with the publication of Michael Kammen's *Mystic Chord of Memory: The Transformation of Tradition in American Culture* (1991) and John Bodnar's *Remaking America: Public Memory, Commemoration, and Patriotism in the Twentieth Century* (1992).

Since my work appeared in 1995, there has been an explosion of scholarship dealing with memory and war. There have been a number of more specialized studies that focus on American efforts to commemorate individual conflicts or the role of memory in specific periods. Several examining the memory of Revolutionary War are especially noteworthy, including David Waldstreicher's *In the Midst of Perpetual Fetes: The Making of American Nationalism, 1776–1820* (1997) and Sarah Purcell's *Sealed with Blood: War, Sacrifice, and Memory in Revolutionary America* (2002). Kirk Savage's *Standing Soldiers, Kneeling Slave: Race, War, and Monument in Nineteenth-Century America* (1997) as well as the anthology edited by Cynthia Mills and Pamela H. Simpson entitled *Monuments to the Lost Cause: Women, Art, and the Landscapes of Southern Memory* (2003) are essential works for anyone seeking to understand the memory of the Civil War. Another valuable contribution with a broader focus is Cecilia Elizabeth O'Leary's *To Die For: The Paradox of American Patriotism* (1999). There is a growing history of the memorialization of the Holocaust, and in the American context the most significant work is James Young's *The Texture of Memory: Holocaust Memorials and Meaning* (1993) and Edward T. Linenthal's *Preserving Memory: The Struggle to Create America's Holocaust Museum* (1995).

Despite this new scholarship there remains no major work that has offered a fundamentally different interpretation of how Americans have sought to remember war from the Revolutionary War to the first Persian Gulf War. One of the strengths of the present study is the broad sweep of time covered. It analyzes the major shifts in the American pattern of remembrance, especially the successful efforts to create national cemeteries and monuments after the Civil War and the two world wars. As this book will show, those in positions of national power have sought to use the federal government and other institutions to shape the public commemoration of war, their efforts have often been contested. In my view, much of the recent scholarship only serves to buttress my contention that various groups—ethnic, racial, political, and religious—often forced authorities to adopt more pluralistic monuments and other forms of public commemoration.

Since this book first appeared in 1995 there has been a significant reawakening of the interest in the American experience of World War II and a major trend toward lionizing the servicemen and women in that conflict as the "Greatest Generation." The years around the fiftieth anniversary of the end of the war sparked a remarkable interest in this conflict by veterans and also by their families. International ceremonies marking both the anniversary of D-Day (June 6, 1994) and V-E Day (May 8, 1995) were aired on network television. Tom Brokaw's book, *The Greatest Generation,* soared to the top of the bestseller lists and featured oral histories with members of the World War II generation. Movies such as *Saving Private Ryan* by director Stephen Spielberg attracted both critical acclaim and large audiences at the box offices. This resurgence of interest in World War II also sparked a surprising resurgence of interest in building memorials to this conflict. As *Remembering War the American Way* will show, Americans, especially in the immediate aftermath of the Second World War, had shown little interest in building traditional monuments and tended to favor "living memorials" such as hospitals, parks, stadiums, auditoriums, and schools.

This new interest energized efforts to build a national memorial to the Second World War in Washington, D.C. In 1993 Congress authorized a national memorial on the Mall in Washington, D.C., and the campaign to raise the necessary funds from private donations allowed construction to begin in 2001. This monument, which was placed between the Lincoln and Washington Memorials, also had its share of detractors. Some thought the memorial should be built, but argued against placing it on the Mall out of fear it burdened this public space with one too many memorials. In contrast to Maya Lin's innovative design for the nearby Vietnam Veterans Memorial, the American Battle Monument Commission selected a more traditional neoclassical design, which some critics criticized on aesthetic design. Other major memorials were also dedicated in this period. In 2000 a national D-Day museum opened in New Orleans, and the following year the first part of the D-Day memorial in Bedford, Virginia, was dedicated by President Bush.

How will the war against terrorism and the wars in Afghanistan and Iraq affect the memory of past wars, especially World War II? At the same time it is clear that memory of the Second World War has shaped not only public debates, but also the iconography and commemoration of these more recent conflicts. Immediately after the attack, many journalists, politicians, and citizens wondered about the parallels between September 11 and the Japanese attack on Pearl Harbor. To symbolically link the two events, the Pacific Command sent the flag that flew over the USS *Arizona Memorial* and placed it over the Pentagon. One of the most representative images that emerged from the aftermath of September 11 was a photograph of a group of New York firemen raising an American flag on the World Trade Center site reminiscent of an earlier flag raising at Iwo Jima in 1945.

As Americans grapple with how to memorialize September 11 they should bear in mind that some wars have faded in the public memory. For complex reasons, the War of 1812, the Mexican American War, the Spanish American War, and the First World War have not endured in the popular consciousness. Other wars, especially the American Revolution, the Civil War, World War II, and the Vietnam War have not been forgotten. Can we build memorials to the attacks of September 11 that not only offer healing to the victim's families, but are also are embraced by future generations? As this book will show, this will not be an easy task.

No generation of Americans has managed to avoid fighting a major war. How we have remembered these conflicts have played a crucial role in shaping the American national identity over time. Most significantly, we have used memorials and rituals to define who is a good citizen. As we enter a new century, can Americans in the aftermath of the attack of September 11 and the wars that followed continue to embrace a pluralistic identity? I am hopeful that Americans in remembering our current war against terrorism will continue to forge a national memory of war that embraces religious, ethnic, racial, and gender diversity.

# INTRODUCTION

Each year millions of Americans view the Vietnam Veterans Memorial in Washington, D.C., and few are left unmoved by the experience. The stark black granite wall bearing the name of every American killed in Vietnam from 1959 to 1975 evokes powerful emotions of pain, grief, and awe. Many of the survivors—widows, orphans, and Vietnam vets—come as mourners and often break down in tears. In gestures of reconciliation and recognition of the American dead, many visitors leave tokens of affection for lost family members and comrades. Each day the National Park Service collects and stores in a warehouse thousands of articles left by mourners— flags, medals, cigarettes, clothing, books, letters, and poems. Often visitors make tracings of the etched names as a keepsake, taking part of the Wall with them and thus making it a moveable and more accessible memorial.

The national Vietnam memorial attracts intense interest and has gained almost universal acceptance largely because it indeed offers emotional catharsis. Providing a symbolic common ground for both supporters and opponents of the war, it allows Americans of disparate views to cast aside their differences and unite in their grief. On the one hand, former hawks can see the memorial, especially with the addition of an American flag and a "traditional" statue in 1982, as a fitting tribute to those who died for their country in a noble cause. On the other hand, former doves can view the memorial as an "antimonument" that marks the war as tragedy and those killed in the war as victims. Above all, it allows loved ones and friends to mourn the dead and seek a meaning for their loss.

The tremendous power of the memorial is all the more remarkable given the barrage of criticism it produced when first proposed in 1980. Critics, mostly from the political right, found fault with the design of Maya Lin, a twenty-one-year-old architectural student from Yale University. To conservatives, who maintained that the United States had fought a noble struggle to preserve freedom in Indochina, the monument smacked of dishonor and defeatism; an editorial in the *National Review* branded it "Orwellian glop." James Watt, secretary of the interior under President Ronald Reagan, refused to approve construction of the monument unless it included a traditional heroic statue. Some on the left attacked it for ignoring the tremendous destruction inflicted on the Vietnamese people by American involvement.[1]

The political and aesthetic controversy that surrounded the establishment of the Vietnam Veterans Memorial was not unique—it had ample precedents. Every American war has evoked similar debate. Americans have disagreed over the design and even the wisdom of erecting war memorials, clashed over what holidays and ceremonies should be observed to remember past conflicts, and even questioned where the war dead should be buried. Those who create war memorials have often wanted them to serve as a source of unity and symbolic resolution to the tensions that exist within society. Often they have been disappointed to find that symbolism alone falls far short of their goal. The Vietnam Veterans Memorial, however, remains remarkable for the degree to which it has bridged the differences and divisions within the nation.

The federal government, by creating and preserving the memory of past wars, has played a crucial role in defining the national identity and the obligations of citizenship. Since 1783 individuals and special interest groups, most notably veterans and their families, have campaigned and lobbied the government to build monuments, create official holidays, and sponsor rituals designed to ensure that Americans remember their military conflicts as instances of national unity. Other Americans have insisted that commemorations respect individualism and local traditions.

War has played a decisive role in shaping the development of American society. The United States gained its independence from Great Britain through the force of arms, and every generation of Americans has seen its

country engage in a major conflict. The War of 1812 secured the legitimacy of the nation against Britain. The Mexican-American War expanded
our national boundaries and aspirations. The Civil War was fought to preserve the Union and evolved into a war of liberation that led to the destruction of slavery. In the Spanish-American War and the Philippines
Insurrection, the country acquired a taste for empire and realized the cost
of such ambitions. The First World War enhanced the international power
and prestige of the nation while polarizing society at home. The Second
World War catapulted the United States into the position of a superpower,
and the limited wars of Korea and Vietnam underscored the burdens of
such a responsibility. Even the end of the cold war has not led to peace for
American forces. In the early 1990s, American troops engaged in conflicts
in Panama, Iraq, and Somalia.

Almost as important as the fighting itself is how Americans have assimi-
lated the experiences of particular wars into their national consciousness
and culture. The American national identity remains inexorably inter-
twined with the commemoration and memory of past wars. From the very
beginning of the Republic, the American Revolution served to explain how
the nation began and the basic principles it espoused. In the late eigh-
teenth century and throughout the nineteenth century, Americans remained divided regarding the proper role of the central government in the
political, economic, and cultural life of the nation and these tensions were
reflected in how Americans commemorated the Revolution and succeeding wars. This book shows how the efforts of the federal government
to create national war memorials in the early national and antebellum periods often failed or were forced to embody a vision of nationalism that
stressed local autonomy.

In the aftermath of the Civil War, the federal government, its power
and authority vastly expanded by the conflict, undertook an activist role in
creating monuments and national holidays to foster the memory of that
war and previous wars. Although the government played an increasingly
important role in shaping the national memory of war, its vision of nationalism continued to reflect an amalgam of local, state, and regional interests.
For instance, Congress established for the first time an elaborate system of
national cemeteries to commemorate the sacrifice of individual soldiers in
the struggle to maintain the Union. Although these burial grounds were
intended to symbolize the paramount authority of the federal government,
they also represented concessions to local traditions, because state and
local veterans' organizations were allowed to erect monuments commemo-

rating the service of specific units. Eventually, even the Confederate dead and their war memorials were placed in federal cemeteries. The deference paid to local traditions after 1865 often strengthened efforts to create national monuments, rituals, and veterans' organizations. In many cases the federal government co-opted individual, local, and even regional patterns of remembrance, particularly the rituals honoring the war dead on Decoration Day. Often at the behest of local interests, the government nationalized battlefields and other historic sites associated with the American Revolution, the War of 1812, and the Civil War.

The First World War marked a watershed in attempts by the federal government to encourage a national pattern of remembrance that minimized or ignored the ties of class, ethnicity, region, and race. At the same time, the government wanted to foster a memory that minimized the divisions created by the war. To this end, it created a series of national monuments in Europe and the United States, encouraged the formation of a national veterans' organization, the American Legion, and fostered the commemoration of a new holiday, Armistice Day.[2]

This study will make clear how difficult it is for the federal government or any group in America to manipulate the memory of this pluralistic society. In World War I, for example, controversy dogged every attempt by political and cultural elites to foster an official and consensual memory of the war. Crude attempts to promote a narrow vision of nationalism, particularly by a strong nativist movement, provoked a sustained challenge from the excluded groups. The debates surrounding the entrance into and the prosecution and settlement of the First World War could not be ignored and were reflected in the national monuments built and in the ceremonies commemorating the conflict. In the end, the official repositories of national memory represent a far more ambiguous interpretation of the war and a vision of nationalism more inclusive than many political, economic, and cultural elites initially wanted.[3]

Some wars have produced few war memorials and little interest in commemorating them with holidays. In the 1940s and 1950s, Americans were generally reluctant to build monuments to the Second World War and in many cases simply "updated" their memorials to the First World War. To a large extent, this absence of memorialization reflected a high degree of consensus in regarding the Second World War as the "good war." President Harry S. Truman and his successors exhorted Americans at the dedication of national war memorials and cemeteries to remember the lessons of the Second World War and to continue the struggle against Soviet totalitarianism. Americans, however, often proved reluctant cold war warriors and responded with little enthusiasm to efforts to create brashly militaristic memorials, such as a national military museum. Decades elapsed before the federal government started planning a national monument to the Korean War. Only after the Vietnam War did Americans again engage in a flurry of monument building, and these memorials tended to reflect Americans' deep misgivings and ambiguity regarding the nature of the conflict.[4]

The varying receptions and shifting attitudes of Americans, both individuals and groups, over the past two centuries have ensured that the manner in which they remember war remains anything but fixed and have demonstrated that rituals and traditions are not immutable. Immortal heroes from the American Revolution and the War of 1812 have slipped into obscurity. No longer do Americans drink ritualistic toasts on Independence Day to military leaders such as Generals Warren and Montgomery and Commanders Decatur and Perry. Few Americans remember the USS *Maine,* and to most Americans the First World War—the war to end all wars—is not even a distant memory. Armistice Day has become Veterans Day. Although monuments are built and dedicated with great enthusiasm, interest in them frequently diminishes rapidly. In many places, monuments are not adequately maintained, and they deteriorate from the continual assault of pigeons and acid rain.

There are, nevertheless, important elements of continuity in how Americans remember war. Certain conflicts, for example, continue to strike a responsive chord in the national consciousness. More than any other conflict in American history, the Civil War arouses deep passions, and as long as racial divisions rend this society, it can be expected to remain a vivid conflict for most Americans. In international affairs, the Second World War, even more than the Vietnam War, explains the role and responsibilities of the United States.

American society, of course, is not the first to commemorate war with memorials. In ancient Greece, the importance of burying and mourning the dead surpassed even the enmity of war. After battle, the victors not only buried their own dead but also allowed the vanquished to carry off and bury their fallen. Monuments to fallen Greek warriors still endure. In the Roman Imperial army, all soldiers paid into a burial fund to ensure that they would receive proper funeral rites. Monuments and tombs honoring the service of officers, and sometimes of common soldiers, still survive in what was once the Roman Empire. In several pathbreaking books,

George Mosse has shown how, beginning with the French revolutionary government of the 1790s, European nation-states in the nineteenth and twentieth centuries actively worked to create elaborate war memorials and ceremonies in order to legitimate their existence.[5]

Until the First World War, European nations did not routinely mark and permanently maintain the graves of combatants. When built, permanent graves and monuments tended to be reserved for dynastic rulers and members of the officer corps. Like Europe, the United States has not always centered the commemoration of wars on the common soldier. After the American Revolution, the burial places of enlisted men killed in battle often went unmarked for decades. During the early national period and antebellum era, war memorials usually honored the service of officers, particularly generals and naval commanders, but the Civil War fostered an enduring shift in the way the United States preserved the memory of past conflicts. Although Americans continued to offer homage to heroic officers, the federal government went to great lengths to locate and permanently mark the graves of all who died in service of the Union cause. This book seeks to examine why the American pattern of remembering war, most recently reflected in the Vietnam Veterans Memorial, has since the antebellum era emphasized memorializing the sacrifice of the average soldier.

The U.S. pattern diverges from that of other societies in the relative importance of political and cultural pluralism. Those with political, economic, and cultural power in American society have usually sought to use their influence to shape a vision of the past that bolsters their authority. I examine this phenomenon and show how rituals, holidays, monuments, and cemeteries, and also veterans' organizations, have been used to advance the agenda of dominant, if often competing, elites. There have been, however, sharp limits to how much any one group can shape the national memory of war, and delineating those limits is also part of this study. Often those who sponsor rituals and design memorials are explicit in demonstrating the ideas they hope to foster. The more difficult task I undertake is to examine what rituals and symbols meant to different individuals and groups.[6]

Why have rituals and monuments remained so important not only to American society but also to other modern nations? I believe that through a predetermined set of ceremonies they invoke symbols and symbolic action in order to convey and represent ideas. For example, by means of a carefully prescribed order of marchers, parades have been used to demarcate the status of different groups in American society, and religious services and the laying of wreaths on Memorial Day have served to reflect the grief experienced by individuals and communities for their war dead.[7]

Rituals have a history. Sometimes their origins are murky, but often their history can be carefully delineated. In the case of Armistice Day ceremonies, for instance, it is possible to chart the efforts of the American Legion to create a series of ritualistic observances to perpetuate the memory of World War I. In the 1920s the legion urged all Americans to pause for two minutes of silence on the eleventh hour of the eleventh day of the eleventh month to mourn the fallen. In many communities the legion sponsored memorial services and parades. On the national level, it succeeded in convincing Congress to make 11 November an official holiday. After the Second World War, which ended the special significance of the 1914 conflict as a "war to end all wars," many of the rituals from the interwar period faded and the observances increasingly emphasized honoring the veterans of all wars. In 1954, after the Korean War, Congress contributed to this trend by renaming the holiday Veterans Day and calling on Americans to remember the service of combatants from all previous conflicts.[8]

War memorials also share a history that reflects changing attitudes toward war and culture. Americans have often defined war memorials as permanent statues or other sculptural forms. Frequently, memorials have been distinguished by aesthetic qualities and by their separateness from the profane and mundane aspects of life. But in the twentieth century, many have argued that a whole range of utilitarian structures and objects—from auditoriums to trees—should serve as war memorials.

How will Americans view the Vietnam Veterans Memorial one hundred years from now? Will the Persian Gulf War even be remembered by the average American? What may be commemorated and considered important by future generations is that both the Vietnam War and Persian Gulf War expanded the definition of who is an American. After both wars, for example, American society recognized, in rituals and monuments, the integral part African Americans played in the conduct of these wars, and the Persian Gulf War was the first war commanded by an African American general, Colin Powell.

Finally, a word about context and the limits of this book is in order. There is a rich body of scholarship that examines how literature, art, and the visual mass media have been used in contrasting and reflecting the memory of war. Although this study focuses on the lesser-known history of rituals, memorials, and activities of veterans' organizations, I sought to draw on the existing scholarship to show how monuments and rituals have often reflected dominant literary and cultural patterns. For instance, the emphasis placed on reconciliation in Decoration Day ceremonies and in memorials commemorating the Civil War in the late nineteenth century mirrored similar patterns in literature and historiography.[9]

This study does not examine how Americans have remembered the wars waged against Native Americans. In large measure this subject must be studied in the context of the "winning" and settlement of the West. The federal government fought scores of battles and even several sustained wars against Native American tribes, from the Seminole to the Sioux. Nonetheless, in the "conquest" of the continent, the boundaries between peace and war remain in the Indian conflicts more problematic. In short, the fur trader, the railroader, the cowboy, and the pioneer proved equally decisive in eventually reducing Native Americans to wards of the federal government.[10]

Although I argue that the memory of war remains central to the creation of the national identity, the federal government and other groups in American society use more than war rituals, memorials, and organizations to shape this identity. The government maintains a vast array of historic sites designed to commemorate events and individuals not associated with the nation's military past. Holidays centered on the founding of America— most notably Thanksgiving and Columbus Day—have been used to explain the origins and purpose of the American Republic. And controversies in the late 1960s and 1980s surrounding the honoring and safeguarding of the American flag suggest how important at least one symbol is in defining American nationhood.[11]

The existence of other important sources of tradition and memory attest to an ambivalence toward war. Americans have often viewed war as an anomaly, and they have never defined themselves as servants of the state. Efforts by military and political leaders to institute universal military training at various times in the twentieth century have been met by opposition and apathy, and war memorials have frequently acknowledged the inevitable loss of life and destruction caused by war.[12]

A growing number of studies examine specific memorials, holidays, and veteran organizations, but by focusing on a narrow time span or on a specific battlefield, statue, or organization, they fail to place them in a larger context.[13] Art historians, for example, have long studied individual war memorials, but they have usually failed to place them in a broader political perspective. The great advantage of a study with a broad chronological focus is that it helps to illuminate and clarify change over time. Moreover, it can highlight certain cultural patterns and ideas that permeate society in a particular period. For instance, war monuments and holidays follow distinctive patterns. After the American Revolution, most communities chose obelisks to commemorate the war and usually built them over the neglected graves of the war dead. In the aftermath of the Civil War, monuments, such as bronze statues of lone sentinels, increasingly moved out of the cemeteries and into the town squares, thereby emphasizing the service of the common soldier.

Americans remain troubled and divided over the most appropriate way to remember and commemorate the past, particularly armed conflicts. This book offers a larger context for understanding these difficulties and debates. It shows that citizens in this Republic have continually disagreed over how to commemorate wars, and that debates surrounding Vietnam and other wars are very much within the American pattern.

# 1

# THE MEMORY
# OF A NATION
# FORGED IN WAR

In 1776, many Americans greeted the Declaration of Independence with joy. In cities and towns and throughout the countryside, crowds assembled and marched through the streets led by government officials, clergy, and militia officers. Underneath liberty trees in town squares or inside churches, Americans heard the Declaration of Independence read aloud, and orations were delivered praising the event of its signing. Prayers and sermons were offered on behalf of America. Dignitaries and notable citizens attended lavish public dinners and offered long series of toasts celebrating independence, the Continental Army, and the new nation. Cannons and firearms boomed salutes. At night fireworks lit the sky and many people placed candles in the windows of their homes.[1]

In successive years Americans continued to commemorate the anniversary of American independence. Even before victory had been achieved against Great Britain, Independence Day had become a national holiday. It served many civic, social, and cultural functions for a country fighting to become a nation. Tories and neutrals who refused to illuminate the windows of their homes on the Fourth were in danger of having stones thrown through their panes. Parading and mustering the militia on this day improved the readiness and morale of these citizen-soldiers. The long, ordered processions that marked most celebrations recalled the crowd activity of the early stages of resistance in the 1760s and 1770s. Invariably these celebrations featured the firing of thirteen guns and the drinking of thirteen toasts to honor the number of states in the Union. Orations, prayers, and sermons urged Americans to sacrifice their lives and fortunes on behalf of the cause.[2] Above all, the Fourth provided the new nation with a symbol that pointed to a common source of unity.

Independence Day served to remind Americans that they had forever broken their ties to King George III and Great Britain. Drafted by Thomas Jefferson, the Declaration of Independence condemned the king and blamed him for a series of tyrannical measures that had forced the United States to sever it ties. In July 1776, a crowd in New York City, upon hearing the Declaration of Independence for the first time, destroyed an equestrian statue of King George III and made bullets out of the metal. Elsewhere, crowds had to satisfy themselves with burning effigies of George III or destroying his royal seals.[3]

From the beginning Independence Day offered Americans a broad set of ideals that established the purpose and meaning of the new Republic. The Declaration of Independence was more than simply a laundry list of grievances against the British imperial system. In justifying the Revolution, the declaration began with a statement of principles that maintained that government existed to promote the common interests of "life, liberty, and the pursuit of happiness." Moreover, it insisted that whenever a state failed to serve the governed, the people had the ultimate right to address these grievances through revolution. Early Independence Day processions often symbolized the ideal of freedom by including a marcher who held aloft a cap of liberty and a woman frequently dressed in a costume depicting her as the embodiment of liberty. Orations and toasts often dwelt on the blessings of a government based on the consent of the governed.

After eight years of warfare, Great Britain finally acknowledged the United States as a free and independent nation. The length and nature of this struggle ensured that the memory of the Revolution would remain both ambiguous and contradictory. The revolutionary generation drew on the ideas of republicanism, the Enlightenment, and the Great Awakening to challenge British rule. Crowds spawned the American Revolution, but a regular army under George Washington secured it. Although many Americans acknowledged Washington as the preeminent leader of the struggle, Congress jealously guarded its authority over the cause.[4]

After the American Revolution, Independence Day quickly developed into one of the most enduring and widely celebrated holidays on the civic calendar. Perhaps only Thanksgiving has come close to rivaling the Fourth of July in the degree to which it has been observed in the twentieth century. To successive generations of Americans, Independence Day remained central to explaining the genesis and ideals of the nation. Reflecting an American nationalism that emphasized strong localist traditions, the Fourth had no prescribed official ceremonies, and even in the nation's capital, the federal government usually passed to private citizens' committees responsibility for organizing rituals to mark the day.

Profound changes in the commemoration of this holiday marked important ideological shifts in American society. In the early Republic, ceremonies marking the Fourth mirrored many of the partisan differences left over from the Revolution. With the passing of the revolutionary generation, the holiday began to portray the founders as heroes worthy of imitation. Also in this period, particularly in the 1820s and 1830s, Americans began to shed earlier republican fears about the suitability of monuments as a means of commemorating the Revolution.

There were other ways to preserve the memory of the American Revolution during the early Republic. Even before the Revolution had ended, George Washington served for many Americans as a symbol of national unity and a focus of adulation. Although Washington had opponents within the army and later in civilian life, he emerged as the central figure in the War of Independence. His popularity stemmed from his decision to follow and advance the path of the noble Cincinnatus and his ability to serve first as a general and later as a civilian leader. In contrast to countless other revolutionary leaders who came before and after him, Washington did not make himself into a dictator, whether serving as commander of the Continental Army or as president.[5] The American Revolution remains exceptional in the degree to which it became linked to the persona of Washington. No other American war leader, not even Abraham Lincoln in the Civil War, is as important to defining the memory of a conflict. As early as 1783, Congress planned a permanent monument to preserve Washington's reputation and to mark his role in the Revolution.

From the beginning, Washington served as a contested symbol. In the 1790s, Federalists took the lead in creating rituals to honor Washington and to monopolize his fame in order to legitimate their policies; their efforts had only limited success. Diverse groups of Americans, ranging from nativists to women's organizations, sought to claim and shape the memory of Washington by building a suitable national monument to him. Most portrayed Washington as a symbol of unity, avoiding the strife of partisanship and sectionalism, but the various efforts could not escape controversy as they reflected the fragile and ambiguous state of American nationhood in the early Republic and in the postrevolutionary period.

The differences surrounding the celebration of the Fourth of July and the commemoration of Washington echoed important disagreements regarding the nature of a republican society. Often the divisions centered on the degree to which Americans viewed the Revolution as creating a new social order. Some, like the participants in Shays's Rebellion in 1786 and the Whiskey Rebellion in 1794, viewed the Revolution as an ongoing process that granted them the continued right to rebel against the central authority. In contrast, many federalists and retired officers of Washington's army, fearing disorder and continued upheaval, considered the War of Independence a singular affair.

During the final winter encampment of the Continental Army at Newburgh, New York, in 1783, Henry Knox and a group of several dozen officers formed the Society of Cincinnati in order to perpetuate into peacetime the fraternal bonds that had developed among them. Because Congress had failed to make good on promised pensions even after the implied threat of a coup d'état during the Newburgh Conspiracy, the society was also expected to serve as a vehicle to continue pressing these claims. At the same time, members of this organization declared that the memory of the American Revolution should not be centered on the part played by civilians or on the service of the common soldier, but on the activities of the officer corps. Because the premise of the Society of Cincinnati remained self-consciously elitist, only officers from the Continental line or the militia who served a requisite numbers of years could join. Like a hereditary order of knighthood in Europe, membership in the society was to be passed on to the eldest son. To symbolize their special status, a distinctive badge was created for members of the society to wear on special occasions.[6]

During the 1780s the Society of Cincinnati, along with the Confederation Congress, became one of the few truly national organizations in the United States. Every three years representatives from each of the thirteen state chapters gathered for a convention on the anniversary of the Battle of Lexington and Concord. Although a secret society, its public celebrations on Independence Day garnered significant public attention. In New York City the entire Congress attended the oration sponsored by the society's New York branch, and in Philadelphia members of the Society led the annual Fourth of July procession and sponsored an orator for the day.[7]

Society of Cincinnati claims over the Revolution's legacy aroused fear, apathy, and satire. Thomas Jefferson and several others feared that the organization was nothing less than a thinly disguised attempt to foist an aristocracy on the new nation. Even worse, some suspected that members of the society would conspire in their secret triennial national meeting to install a king on an American throne. Others wondered whether the officers wanted to make themselves into a class of pensioners who merely raided the public treasury. Benjamin Franklin, in a letter to his daughter-in-law, noted that the Articles of Confederation banned Congress and individuals from establishing ranks of nobility and that the Cincinnati remained in "direct Opposition to the solemnly declared sense of their Country!" In his critique of the "Absurdity of *descending Honours*," he ridiculed the notion that the Society of Cincinnati could pass to the next generation the honor they had won during the Revolution, and he pondered whether it might not be more appropriate for the parents, instead of the sons, to wear the society's medal. He offered the following mathematical proof that mocked the patriarchal assumptions of the society:

A Man's Son, for instance, is but half of his Family, the other half belonging to the Family of his Wife. His Son, too, marrying into another Family, his Share in the Grandson is but a fourth; in the Great Grandson, by the same Process, it is but an Eighth; in the next Generation a Sixteenth; the next a Thirty-second; the next a Sixty-fourth; the next an Hundred and twenty-eighth; the next a Two Hundred and Fifty-sixth; and the next a Five hundred and twelfth; thus in nine Generations, which will not require more than 300 years (no very great antiquity for a Family), our present Chevalier of the Order of Cincinnatus's Share in the then existing Knight, will be but a 512th part; which, allowing the present certain Fidelity of American Wives to be insur'd down through all those Nine Generations, is so small a Consideration, that methinks no reasonable Man would hazard for the sake of it the disagreeable Consequences of the Jealousy, Envy, and Ill will of his Countrymen.[8]

Although only circumstantial evidence supports the suspicion that the founders of the Society of Cincinnati wanted to establish an American nobility or a monarchy, the widespread anxieties regarding the order reflected deep tensions over the memory of the Revolution. As the first president general of the society, George Washington sought unsuccessfully to allay public fears by abolishing hereditary memberships, triennial national meetings, and a number of other features deemed subversive. Nonetheless, the officer corps of the Revolution had an important impact on the political life of the young Republic. Continental officers almost uniformly favored scrapping the decentralized government under the Articles of Confederation and remained the most vigorous supporters of the new Constitution of 1787. George Washington and Alexander Hamilton drew on these same retired officers to fill an array of executive and judicial positions in the new government.[9]

The creation of the Constitution of 1787 also affected the way the nation memorialized the Revolution. The debates surrounding the drafting and ratification of this new blueprint of government underscored the divisions that existed within American society regarding the role and purpose of central authority and the question of revolution. The Federalist Party of the 1790s and supporters of the new Constitution in general, believed that the political pendulum had swung too far in the direction of disorder and anarchy. They were embarrassed by the inability of the national government to meet its financial obligations to creditors and former soldiers. Also, Federalists were upset that state militia units had failed to deter the British from violating U.S. territorial sovereignty in the Northwest, and they feared that an internal revolt such as Shays's Rebellion could easily be repeated. In their view, the national government needed the power to tax and to maintain a standing army.[10]

To anti-Federalists, and, later, Jeffersonian Democratic Republicans, the great lesson of the struggle against Britain had been the need to remain vigilant to ensure the power of the central government always remained in check. Both groups believed that a national government with unlimited authority to tax and to maintain a large standing army would again threaten liberty. Tyranny could only be prevented by vesting political authority primarily in the states and requiring the national government to depend largely on the militia for its defense.[11]

After a long struggle, Federalists were able to win ratification of the new Constitution, which vastly increased the power of the central government. Celebrating its adoption by state conventions in 1787 and 1788, Federalists sponsored ceremonies that stressed how the Constitution fulfilled the aims of the Revolution. In the largest celebration, in Philadelphia, more than five thousand marched on Independence Day 1788 to commemorate the ratification of the Constitution by Pennsylvania. But not everyone was convinced.[12]

Ratification of the new Constitution failed to end the debate over how to commemorate the American Revolution and over the role of the military in American society. At the semiofficial Independence Day ceremonies in New York City in 1789, two members of the first federal Congress reacted differently to the celebrations. Senator William Maclay of Pennsylvania recorded with approval in his famous diary that the "Anniversary of American Independence" in the city had been "celebrated with much pomp" by the local branch of the Society of Cincinnati, but he emphasized the need to strike a balance in remembering the character of those who fought in the Revolution. In his view the oration, sponsored by the society and delivered by Alexander Hamilton in honor of the late General Nathanael Greene, should have emphasized Greene's virtues "as a Citizen as well as a Warrior" because this late hero had lived after the war as a farmer. On the other hand, Representative Aedanus Burke took such offense at Hamilton's characterization of the militia as the "the mimicry of soldiership" that he delivered an intemperate rejoinder on the House floor that almost led to a duel between the two men.[13]

Some Americans refused to accept the new constitutional order and maintained that the powers newly granted to the federal government violated the principles of the American Revolution. Efforts to place an excise tax on whiskey in the early 1790s aroused intense dissent in large sections of the frontier, particularly in western Pennsylvania. In the eyes of many on the frontier, an excise tax levied by the national government would be no different from one that had been levied by the British government a generation earlier. As during the Stamp Act crisis, protesters met and passed resolutions that denounced taxes as oppressive. Liberty poles, with messages of defiance attached, were erected. Tax collectors and other federal officials who tried to enforce the excise laws were on several occasions physically intimidated, and in some cases tarred and feathered.[14]

During the Whiskey Rebellion the crowds that gathered in western Pennsylvania used the symbols and rituals of the American Revolution against the federal government. To suppress the rebellion, Alexander Hamilton called for the deployment of the new national army to establish order. Instead, Washington collected more than thirteen thousand men from several state militia who, in the summer of 1795, marched into western Pennsylvania. With this decisive show of federal force, opposition to the whiskey tax completely collapsed. Several "ringleaders" were arrested, tried for treason, and sentenced to death, but to avoid creating martyrs around which subsequent dissatisfaction could coalesce, Washington commuted their sentences.[15]

Washington's adept handling of the Whiskey Rebellion helped ensure the authority of the federal government. His use of the militia made it difficult for opponents to liken his actions to those of the British a generation earlier. In using the citizen-soldiers of the militia, Washington symbolically declared that the new national government rested on the consent of the governed and need not rely on a regular army to maintain domestic tranquility. When his successor, John Adams, called out army troops in 1799 to suppress the Fries Rebellion, a similar insurrection against unpopular direct taxes in rural eastern Pennsylvania, his action engendered fierce criticism in Congress and in the press. Jeffersonian Republicans insisted that the use of regulars against common citizens provided glaring evidence of a betrayal of the Revolution's legacy.[16]

Although the federal government easily suppressed the internal rebellions of the 1790s, divisions over the power and authority of the federal government remained, leading to sharp differences over how to remember the American Revolution and who should be the rightful guardians of its memory. Many Americans became suspicious of the motives of the Federalists and suspected the worst in their domestic and foreign-policy agendas. The French Revolution and the wars that followed placed the United States in an awkward and difficult position. Should it view the French Revolution as akin to its own struggle for liberty? Did it have an obligation, legally or morally, to come to the aid of France in its struggle with Great Britain?[17]

Federalists, for pragmatic and ideological reasons, believed it essential that the United States maintain a policy of neutrality. Alexander Hamilton wanted rapprochement with Great Britain and argued that the new nation could not risk alienating the most powerful nation on earth in order to aid the French. Over the course of the 1790s many Federalists maintained that the French Revolution not only failed to advance the cause of liberty but also threatened the security of the United States. During the Adams administration, disagreements with the French government led to the outbreak of naval hostilities, and the United States raised a new provisional army to meet the crisis.

Jeffersonian Republicans saw the worst in Federalist policies and believed that they threatened the gains of the Revolution. They deplored concessions made to Great Britain in Jay's Treaty of 1794 and believed that the United States should use economic sanctions to pressure their former enemy into recognizing American rights. Jeffersonian Republicans believed that, even worse, Federalists sought to risk war with France, a former ally and sister republic. In countless pamphlets and newspaper pieces they compared Federalist actions to those of the British government before the American Revolution. By maintaining a large standing army and creating a navy to meet the alleged French threat, Federalists ensured that the American people would be burdened with high taxes. This military establishment would not only cost a great deal of money and create a myriad of parasitical officeholders but also potentially abridge the liberties of the people.

Jeffersonian Republicans feared the standing army and embraced the common militia, believing the militia to be a more cost effective and efficient means of defending the country. But they also favored the militia because it served as a means of preserving a memory of the American Revolution that emphasized the struggle for independence as a localist battle against tyranny. The common militia served for the enlisted ranks several of the same functions as the Society of Cincinnati did for the officers. In the early Republic, the bulk of those who served in the militia were veterans of the Revolution. When these veterans attended militia muster days or marched with their units in Independence Day ceremonies, they proclaimed that they continued to serve as custodians of the spirit of '76.[18]

Political differences led over the course of the 1790s to the splintering of Independence Day ceremonies, and in many communities Federalists and Jeffersonian Republicans marched in separate parades, listened to different orators, and in some cases even erected opposing liberty poles. The more partisan of both sides wore different cockades to symbolize their respective loyalties and their different interpretations of the legacy of the American struggle for independence: Federalists donned a black cockade, and their Jeffersonian Republican opponents wore a tricolored one.[19] To warn Americans of the perceived threat to their liberties, Jeffersonian Republican orators stressed the revolutionary character of the war for independence and often linked it with the French and other European revolutions of the 1790s. They placed great emphasis on liberty poles and, especially, liberty caps as symbols of the ongoing struggle for freedom. In 1798, Federalists in one New Jersey town stole the liberty cap from atop the liberty pole and placed it over a judge's seat in the local courthouse. The editors of the local Jeffersonian Republic paper cried out against this "Felonious Act" and warned their neighbors that "the men who will pilfer from you the *Emblem of Your Freedom* would, were it in their power, rifle from you the SUBSTANCE!"[20]

Federalists ignored, mocked, and denounced Jeffersonian Republicans in their Independence Day ceremonies. In order to minimize Thomas Jefferson's contribution to the American Revolution, especially his writing of the Declaration of Independence, they ignored the document on the Fourth. In the late 1790s, Federalist orators railed against the French Republic and questioned its commitment to advancing the cause of freedom, finding few links with the American Revolution. Moreover, they used this occasion to remind Americans of the ongoing danger the French Republic posed to national security. The French not only seized American merchant ships and extorted bribes from U.S. diplomats but also, through their allies in the Jeffersonian Republican Party, threatened to spread anarchy, disorder, and atheism at home. The differences between Federalists and Jeffersonian Republicans over the memory of the Revolution are best displayed by the differing toasts each offered on Independence Day. In one toast in 1798, a Federalist in Boston declared, "John Adams—may he like Sampson slay thousands of Frenchmen with the jawbone of Jefferson"; a Jeffersonian Republican in Morristown, New Jersey, remarked, "May the British party in the State of New Jersey, be banished from its peaceful shores."[21]

Despite their differences in emphasis and interpretation, certain common themes run through both Jeffersonian Republican and Federalist celebrations of the Fourth. For both, the pattern of ceremonies remained, with variations, the same and usually featured parades, orations, toasts, and the firing of cannons or fireworks. Toastmasters in both camps remembered the fallen heroes—Warren, Montgomery, and De Kalb. Both praised the militia, but Federalists tended to also salute the army and the new navy. Above all, both groups yearned to win the other side to their point of view.[22]

In the 1790s Federalists began to supplement Independence Day ceremonies with celebrations of George Washington's birthday. When Washington served as president, they commemorated his birth in a manner befitting an English monarch. In Philadelphia, militia units paraded, churches held special services, the wealthy sponsored balls, and people built bonfires in his honor. To many Federalists, then, Washington remained the embodiment of the revolutionary struggle and the resultant nation, and they wanted to link him with their political party.[23] Of course, even some Federalists thought there should be limits placed on the adulation accorded to Washington. In the first year of the Adams administration, the president and many other "low" Federalists refused to attend a birthday ball in honor of Washington.

Federalists were not alone in claiming Washington as their hero. Even at the height of the partisan rancor of the 1790s, Jeffersonian Republicans continued to toast Washington. They refused to concede the symbol of Washington—the father of the country—to the Federalists.[24] When Washington died in 1799, Jeffersonian Republicans joined Federalists in mourning his passing and claiming his mantle. Although within days of Washington's death, Congress unanimously called for the removal of his body to a public tomb to be erected in the new Capitol, his body was never entombed there. Plans to build a monument to Washington floundered for decades. The fate of early attempts to memorialize Washington suggests how strong partisan and cultural differences remained over the memory of the Revolution and demonstrates how many Americans recognized the fragile nature of the young Republic. Architect and engineer Benjamin H. Latrobe urged the congressional committee charged with planning a permanent memorial to Washington to build a huge outdoor mausoleum topped with a pyramid instead of a modest indoor tomb in the Capitol. To Latrobe, only a massive structure had any chance of surviving and preserving the memory of Washington. In explaining his plans to committee member Robert Goodloe Harper, Latrobe offered little hope that a statue to Washington would survive for more than a few years. Latrobe noted how the statue to Norborne Berkeley, Baron de Botetourt in Williamsburg, Virginia, had survived the American Revolution but had been thoughtlessly "mutilated, and decapitated by the young collegians, in the first frenzy of French revolutionary maxims, *because it was the statue of a Lord.*" He described how the recently installed Houdon equestrian statue to Washington in the Virginia state capitol had already lost a spur. Moreover, Latrobe mused, even Washington's virtues "are hated, by fools and rogues, and unfortunately that sort of animals crawl much about in public buildings."[25]

Agreeing with many of Latrobe's arguments, a number of Federalists and some Jeffersonian Republicans embraced the idea of a mausoleum. Roger Griswold urged his colleagues to support a mausoleum because a statue would easily be "destroyed by a lawless mob or by a set of schoolboys." But a number of congressman, especially Jeffersonian Republicans, remained skeptical of a mausoleum and supported earlier proposals for a marble monument and simple tomb. According to Republicans, Federalist proposals remained far too lavish and ostentatious for a republican society. One Jeffersonian representative characterized the proposed mausoleum as nothing more than a "huge, ugly mass of stones heaped upon one another" and insisted that a plain tablet would be more appropriate because it would allow every man to "write what his heart dictated." Nathaniel

The creator of this embroidery is unknown, but its theme, women mourning
before the tomb of Washington, is common to a number of paintings and
illustrations from the early 1800s. (Embroidery courtesy David Library of the
American Revolution, Washington Crossing, Pennsylvania; photograph by
Gordon Miller)

Macon of North Carolina insisted that in lieu of a monument, money should be spent on educating poor children in order to extend "the empire of his [Washington's] virtues, by making those understand and imitate them, who, uninstructed, could not comprehend them." During the waning months of John Adams's administration, Federalist majorities in both houses of Congress passed different bills authorizing a pyramid. The two chambers never reached an agreement, however, and plans for any federal tomb for Washington faded with the inauguration of Thomas Jefferson. Washington's body remained interred in a modest family vault at Mount Vernon.[26]

Although both Federalists and Republicans hailed Washington as a symbol of the nation, he remained a contested one. The reluctance of Jeffersonian Republicans to embrace the mausoleum is not surprising. To begin with, they remained far less fearful of the dangers posed by upheaval from below. John Randolph of Virginia took umbrage at the suggestion by supporters of the mausoleum that public statues in his home state were vulnerable to mob attack. In addition, Republicans' concerns with cost and suitability reflected a strict constructionist view of the Constitution that limited the power of the federal government to undertake a wide range of cultural and educational initiatives. For example, in 1802 Jefferson turned a deaf ear to appeals by the artist Charles Willson Peale for federal patronage of his famous Philadelphia museum because Jefferson believed that under the Constitution the support of learning and culture remained outside the powers of the national government.[27]

Even some Federalists expressed misgivings regarding the place of monuments in a Republic and federal patronage of the arts. In 1799 one Federalist newspaper declared its opposition to monuments and observed that their creation in ancient Rome heralded the decline of republican virtue and the arrival of imperial rule. In retirement John Adams urged caution regarding efforts by the federal government to build monuments or to support the arts, insisting that both forms of cultural expression remained too closely associated with decadent European government. In 1817 Adams congratulated John Trumbull, the Connecticut artist, on winning a commission to paint a series of historical paintings in the rotunda of the Capitol. At the same time, Adams urged Trumbull to remember "that the Burin and the Pencil, the Chisel and the Trowell, have in all ages and Countries of which we have any Information, been enlisted on the side Despotism and Superstition."[28]

Nevertheless, war memorials were built in the early years of the republic.

Virginia and several other states erected statues to celebrate Washington's heroic exploits. Many of the earliest memorials built to remember the Revolution marked the graves or otherwise commemorated the war dead. In 1794 a Massachusetts masonic lodge erected a monument to Joseph Warren on the spot where he fell at the Battle of Bunker Hill. The reburial of Anthony Wayne's body in 1809 from an isolated grave site to a cemetery in Radnor, Pennsylvania, led the state chapter of the Society of Cincinnati to place an obelisk over his grave. Also in 1808, a citizens' committee in New York City collected and placed in a crypt some of the bones of American soldiers who had died on British prison ships and had been buried in shallow graves near the water's edge.[29]

The first national war memorial in Washington, D.C., however, commemorated neither the American Revolution nor George Washington. In 1806 naval officers who participated in the undeclared war against the Barbary powers commissioned the Italian sculptor John Charles Micali of Leghorn to carve a monument for their comrades who died in the attack on Tripoli. This elaborate monument served, in part, a funerary function as it included an urn containing the ashes of those killed in action. It featured a host of statues resting on large pedestal that signified ideas such as Union, Victory, and History, as well as a column topped by an American eagle to represent the United States. In addition, four lamps of "black Marble & vase of Gilt bronze [gave] heat round the tomb as the breasts of Citizens should be warmed by the love of their Country." The base of the pedestal bore the names of the officers who had died in the battle as well as those who had contributed to the monuments and officers.[30]

Although the federal government did not provide financial support for the Tripoli monument, Congress allowed the capital's first public monument to stand on the Capitol grounds, establishing in the process a precedent for the creation of future national war memorials. Despite this development, and even as the power of the federal government increased dramatically in the twentieth century, Congress remained reluctant to use public funds to build national monuments. Invariably, Congress allowed private individuals or organizations to erect national war memorials and legitimized their activities by granting them federal charters, often allowing their finished monuments to rest on public land. Commemorating the American Revolution and all future wars, then, remained a haphazard endeavor dependent on the initiative of individuals, private societies, and local and state governments. For instance, work began on a huge monumental obelisk marking the site of the Battle of Bunker Hill decades before the nation's capital acquired a completed monument to George Washington.[31]

The triumph of Thomas Jefferson in the election of 1800 failed to end partisan conflicts regarding the nature of the American Revolution. In many communities both Federalists and Democratic Republicans continued to hold separate Independence Day celebrations offering sharply divergent interpretations of the holiday's significance. By 1807 Democratic Republicans were viewing the struggle against Great Britain as continuous and, therefore, used Independence Day orations and toasts to protest British impressment of American sailors and the confiscation of American ships. Conversely, Federalists wanted to avoid war with Great Britain and stressed the need for reconciliation and negotiation. They argued, for instance, that the reading of the Declaration of Independence should be ended because it encouraged continued animosity against the British.[32]

Despite the vigorous opposition of Federalists, the United States again went to war with Great Britain in 1812 over the question of neutral rights, impressment of American seamen, and the desire of many southerners and westerners to acquire Canada. Few wars in American history have been so marked by disaster as the War of 1812. Most confrontations with the British on land ended in defeat, and efforts to invade Canada proved embarrassing to the Madison administration. Federalist New England refused to provide financial loans for the war, and on several occasions state governors from this region refused to allow the president to exercise full authority over the militia. By the end of the war, many in New England talked openly of secession, no longer wishing to be part of a federal government that could not prevent the destruction of its own capital.[33]

The War of 1812 destroyed the Federalist Party. The stunning victory of Andrew Jackson in 1815 against British forces at New Orleans made the meeting of New England Federalists at the Hartford convention appear at best ill-advised and at worst treasonable. The collapse of the party granted Republicans a virtual monopoly of power. Still, the Republican Party that ruled during the Era of Good Feelings had been one chastened by the experience of war; they remained more willing to support a standing army and navy and accepted the need for a national bank.[34]

The demise of the Federalist Party and the ascendancy of the Republican Party profoundly altered the public memory of the American Revolution. No longer would the reading of the Declaration of Independence have the same partisan connotations. The erection of liberty poles and the type of cockade a man wore ceased to provoke violence. In 1818, a Democratic Republican president, James Monroe, proposed, and a Republican Congress adopted, legislation granting a lifetime pension to all destitute veterans of the Continental Army who had served for at least nine months. Moreover, the fall of the Federalist Party helped ensure that the War of 1812 was portrayed and remembered as an American triumph, characterized as a second American Revolution.[35]

With few exceptions, the militia had not fared well during the War of 1812, and this altered republican thinking regarding its future. Both proponents of a more effective military and workers who resented the burden muster or training day placed on them called for its elimination. In the 1820s and 1830s a number of states abolished militia duty or failed to collect fines for non-attendance. The gradual demise of the common militia coincided with the passing of the soldiers of the revolutionary era. In Independence Day parades, the aged and gray veterans of the Revolution increasingly gained for themselves a distinct and separate place in the line of march. To a degree, Americans, by granting the fast disappearing survivors of the War of Independence a special place of honor, acknowledged their unique sacrifice in founding the nation. However, when viewed in the context of the increasingly successful attack on and demise of the common militia, it represented an acknowledgment that the republican ideal of the citizen-soldier had become anachronistic.[36]

The thinning ranks of the veterans marching in Independence Day ceremonies was one of several signs that the revolutionary generation was passing away. Lafayette's grand tour of the United States in 1824 and 1825 as a guest of the nation produced an outpouring of interest in the Revolution and a recognition of the need to mark its passing. Countless communities showered Lafayette with honors, and many speeches dwelt on his relationship with Washington, which bordered on the filial. During his visit to New England, Lafayette participated in the laying of the cornerstone for the Bunker Hill Monument and was received at Harvard. In New York City, the Society of Cincinnati and a host of other organizations entertained the nation's guest, and a crowd became so enthralled with his presence that they flocked around him, seeking articles of his clothing and other tokens of remembrance. His visit to Philadelphia prompted the city to save the Old State House from destruction; this building became increasingly known as Independence Hall to emphasize its association with the revolutionary struggle.[37]

Americans' genuine affection for Lafayette was evidence of a vision of nationhood that was both inclusive and exclusive. Orations applauded the fact that as a French noble Lafayette fought for the cause of freedom in America and then returned to his home in order to continue the struggle there. In other ways, however, Lafayette's visit underscored how much of the revolutionary egalitarianism on the question of slavery had faded. Lafayette continued to voice his opposition to the institution of slavery, viewing it as incompatible with the principles of liberty. His sentiments stood in sharp contrast to a growing number of white southerners who no longer viewed the slave system as an embarrassment to the nation but as a positive good. Reflecting this shift in attitude, a number of southern communities decided to ban African Americans from attending ceremonies in Lafayette's honor out of fear his words or gestures would foment a revolt.[38]

On 4 July 1826, the fiftieth anniversary of the Declaration of Independence, both Thomas Jefferson and John Adams died. President John Quincy Adams, along with other Americans, saw the hand of divine Providence in the twin demise of these great statesmen. He was not alone in seeing great symbolism in the timing and coincidence of their deaths. In the outpouring of eulogies and other ceremonies, Americans focused on the contribution both had made to the cause of independence and dwelt only in passing on their strained relationship and on the partisan enmity that existed between them in the 1790s. To orator and politician Edward Everett and others, the friendship that had developed between the two statesmen in retirement remained emblematic of the growing sense of common purpose and unity in the Union. The deaths of Jefferson and Adams enabled Americans to develop and embellish a myth that saw the founders as models of virtuous behavior and the Revolution as a heroic age.[39]

The demise of those who had participated in the Revolution helped erode earlier misgivings expressed by Jeffersonian Republicans, and even Federalists, regarding the suitability of monumental art in a republican society. Most early memorial markers tended to memorialize Washington and other prominent heroes of the Revolution. Except for officers or militia men killed close to their homes, the burial of the war dead during the Revolution had been a haphazard affair. In many cases only crude and hastily erected markers were placed over their graves. The remains of the victims of the Paoli Massacre, for example, had to wait until 1817 before the heap of stones over their common grave was replaced with a formal monument.[40]

Obelisks became a favored grave marker in the new public and private cemeteries that replaced church burial grounds in the 1830s. They even gained favor where war memorials did not directly mark the graves of the fallen. The simplicity of their design made obelisks desirable, particularly for smaller monuments. Good portraiture or memorial structures remained out of the reach of many monument associations as they were perennially short of funds. There were simply too few sculptors available and the work of European sculptors was often prohibitively expensive. Ease of construction was not the only reason for the popularity of the obelisk. To a large degree, the association that the obelisk had with death and classical antiquity was a central, if not underlying, reason for its selection by monument committees. Americans were well aware of the great age of the ancient Egyptian obelisks and pondered the perishability of statues. In selecting an obelisk for the Bunker Hill Monument, some openly expressed the hope that these structures would endure long after American civilization had vanished.[41]

Several communities began building elaborate monuments imbued with a spirit of nationalism. In the aftermath of the victories of 1814 against British forces, Baltimore constructed massive memorials to Washington and to the defenders of Baltimore. On 4 July 1815, the Washington Monument Association in Baltimore laid the cornerstone and began work on a massive structure designed by American-born architect Robert Mills. This monument featured a statue of Washington atop a column that rested upon a trophy room. A few weeks later, on 12 September, a large procession of Baltimore residents turned out for ceremonies marking the start of work on another memorial, designed by French-born architect Maximilian Godefroy, to those who had died in the defense of the city. In 1818, the Washington Monument Association of Massachusetts finally secured the necessary funds to commission British sculptor Sir Francis Chantrey to complete a statue of Washington for placement in the State House in Boston.[42]

The federal government continued to provide only lackluster support for the commemoration of the Revolution. Artists and sculptors pleaded with Congress for money to build monuments they had designed. Local communities petitioned the national legislature for grants-in-aid to help them mark battlefields and commemorate local heroes. Occasionally House and Senate committees offered a ringing endorsement of these requests, but few appropriations ever made it through the full Congress.[43]

Congress provided some direct financial support only for monuments or art work that embellished the Capitol. In 1817, Congress made its first

*Gen. Washington Resigning his Commission to Congress. Annapolis, Md. Dec. 23d, 1783.* Copy of painting by John Trumbull, 1822–24. Trumbull's series of paintings for the Capitol rotunda provoked a firestorm of criticism in Congress and among the public. (Reprinted from J. Heller, *War and Conflict,* National Archives, 1990, 34; original source, Department of Agriculture)

significant expenditure on public art when it commissioned Connecticut artist John Trumbull to complete four murals for the Capitol rotunda depicting key events in the Revolution. In what some viewed as an unseemly act, Trumbull charged admission to a series of public exhibitions of the paintings before their installment in the rotunda. Trumbull's work was widely lambasted by the public, fellow artists, and congressmen when it was finished in 1825. In private John Quincy Adams mused that Trumbull's works were "immeasurably below the dignity of the subject." Representative John Randolph offered more caustic comments on the floor of Congress that berated Trumbull's work as an embarrassment to the nation and assailed *The Declaration of Independence* as a "*Shin-piece*," declaring that "surely, never was there, before, such a collection of legs submitted to the eyes of man."[44]

It was not until the centennial of Washington's birth in 1832 that Congress finally funded a monument to his memory. Instead of following earlier proposals for an equestrian monument or pyramid, Congress commissioned Horatio Greenough to complete a colossal statue of the war hero and first president. After its unveiling in 1841, Greenough's statue provoked a flurry of controversy. The sculptor had portrayed Washington in a seated pose reminiscent of the Roman god Jupiter and showed him nude from the waist up. Many viewed the partially naked statue of Washington as tastelessly inappropriate and the complex classical allusions as unnecessary. Critics soon demanded that the statue be banished to the Capitol basement or to some other out-of-the-way place. One congressman wanted the head of the statue saved and the rest of it thrown into the Potomac.[45]

The firestorm of criticism these handful of commissions engendered served to further dampen congressional interest in funding monuments. Efforts to build monuments, even in the nation's capital, remained largely the domain of private groups or local governments, ensuring that interpretation of the Revolution would continue to be both diverse and contested. To be built, monuments had to attract the support of a small number of wealthy donors, local or state governments, or a broad range of small contributors. As a result, public support for monuments, even for George Washington, proved fickle and unpredictable.

In the 1830s, however, a private society founded by a group of civic leaders took upon itself the task of raising money for a huge outdoor monument to Washington. Although Congress offered no direct support, it provided the Washington National Monument Society with a federal charter and a grant of public land in the nation's capital. Under the terms of the charter, contributors who purchased memberships in the society were to annually elect a board of managers to oversee the enterprise.[46] The goals of the society were anything but modest. In 1836 it called on individuals to submit designs that would cost at least one million dollars. Nine years later the society adopted a design by the architect Robert Mills. It called for a decorated obelisk five hundred feet high encircled by a one-hundred-foot Doric colonnade containing a rotunda filled with murals and sculptures of revolutionary heroes.

On 4 July 1848, an impressive array of dignitaries and a huge audience attended the cornerstone-laying ceremony. Over the next several years state, and even foreign, governments contributed specially carved stones that were incorporated into the structure. Although these stones added little bulk to the monument, they proved a rich source of publicity and added further legitimacy to the project.[47] Although the Washington Monument Society maintained a national network of agents, support for the monument proved spasmodic. A *New York Home Journal* article in 1848 decried the poor record of Brooklyn and New York City residents in fulfilling their obligations to the memory of Washington. The article noted that in the 1830s the two cities together contributed less than two hundred dollars to the monument, and it urged residents to be more generous in the latest fund drive. Four years later the monument society suspended construction because of a lack of funds. To bolster contributions, the society announced that any donor who offered twenty-five dollars would be made an honorary member of the board of managers; for one hundred dollars, the donor would be granted the title of honorary vice president. Larger contributors were to have their name and place of residence inscribed on one of four marble tablets to be placed in the completed structure.[48]

Lack of funds was not the only problem hindering efforts to finish the Washington Monument. One night in 1855 a nativist mob seized and removed a stone donated to the monument by the papal states. Nativists also packed the annual meeting of the monument society and replaced the board of managers with a nativist-controlled one. Because the old board refused to accept the nativist takeover, for several years two competing boards claimed control of the monument society. By seizing control of the society, the nativists hoped to advance, by means of the monument, a less-inclusive vision of nationhood, one that specifically excluded the newly arrived Irish and German immigrants, who were mostly Roman Catholics. They insisted that the United States had been and must continue to be a homogeneous, English-speaking, Protestant nation. To ensure that the monument be associated with that vision, the board of managers decreed that only members of the Know-Nothing Party could contribute to its construction.[49]

Nativist efforts to finish the Washington Monument proved a dismal failure, and they eventually lost control to the original board of managers. But this did little to revive public support for the project, and efforts by the Ladies's Washington National Monument Society also ran into problems. In one appeal issued in 1860, the ladies' society called on all Americans to remember Washington's "virtues," "sacrifices," and "devotion to the cause of human liberty" by offering contributions to finish the monument. To aid in the solicitation of donations, the society asked election inspectors to place donation boxes next to ballot boxes in polling places. Through these and other means, the ladies' society succeeded in raising some money, but Margaret C. Brown's letter, dated April 1861 to the treasurer of the society, explains why the society's efforts were doomed. In it, Brown reported forwarding $23.51 raised over the past few months in Florida, but asked: "Does not the secession of our States, cause me to loose my office as Vice President of Fla.?" It did, and not until the 1880s, when the federal government finally took charge of the project and provided the necessary funds, would a finished obelisk rise to the memory of Washington.[50]

Although women proved unable to rescue the Washington Monument on the eve of the Civil War, they proved in other cases far more successful in completing monuments and in staking out a role for themselves as interpreters of the American Revolution. When the federal government or a private group failed to complete a proposed monument, women frequently stepped in to finish it. In Boston, women held a fair to raise the money necessary to complete the obelisk to the Battle of Bunker Hill and then turned the funds over to the all-male corporation charged with building the monument. In other cases, women established completely separate organizations that took full responsibility for building and for safeguarding memorials of the Revolution and other wars.[51]

When George Washington's heirs put the general's Virginia home up for sale in the early 1850s, Congress refused by a narrow vote to purchase it. Some members voted against it because they believed it would establish an unwise precedent. As one congressman declared, if Mount Vernon became federal property, why not Monticello next? There would be pressure to purchase not only the homes of other presidents but also battlefields. Strict constructionists insisted that the Constitution did not grant the national government authority to make such purchases. In fact, the resolution authorizing the purchase of Mount Vernon required that the state of Virginia first grant the federal government permission to take such an action. In voting against the resolution, one Virginia representative insisted his state would never cede "jurisdiction over any part of her soil to the General Government, except for those purposes which the Constitution provides."[52]

Mount Vernon was rescued in 1856, however, when a group of women organized the Mount Vernon Ladies' Association of the Union to buy and maintain Washington's home. Although the effort to save Mount Vernon became a national one, it originally began on a regional basis. Ann Pamela Cunningham, daughter of a wealthy South Carolina planter, was a driving force behind the association and had initially directed her appeal on behalf of Mount Vernon to the "Ladies of the South." Cunningham, in an 1853 appeal, urged that patriotic southern women save Mount Vernon out of a "sense of national and, above all, Southern honor."[53]

Women's involvement in the preservation of Mount Vernon and in other similar efforts led them to move beyond some of the boundaries set by a male-dominated society. Through incorporated societies, women exercised legal rights ordinarily denied them. Monument associations allowed them to enter the public arena to a degree matched only by their work in benevolent organizations. In such societies women corresponded with government officials, gave public speeches, raised and managed money, and held offices.[54]

The role of women, particularly in the case of Mount Vernon, served in part to feminize the memory of the American Revolution. In making Washington's home a patriotic shrine, women were able to draw attention to the domestic life of the American Cincinnatus. The increasing interest in venerating the memory of Washington's mother led the residents of Fredericksburg, Virginia, to begin constructing, in 1833, a tomb to mark Mary Washington's grave. During ceremonies dedicating the cornerstone, President Andrew Jackson stated that he envisioned this monument becoming a symbol of religious inspiration. He further hoped that the "American pilgrim" would "in after ages, come up to this high and holy place, and lay his hand upon this sacred column, . . . [and] recall the virtues of her who sleeps beneath, and depart with his affections purified, and his piety strengthened, while he invokes blessings upon the memory of the mother of Washington."[55]

Women nevertheless remained subordinate to men. Generally, women built monuments commemorating the war service of men, improving their status by praising and supporting a sphere of activity largely closed to them. By and large men applauded their activities. As one observer noted, "In all benevolent or patriotic enterprises the services of one woman are equal to those of seven men and a half."[56]

How important were monuments to postrevolutionary Americans? Decades elapsed before the monuments to Washington and his mother were finished. In his 1851 account of his travels to revolutionary battlefields, Benson Lossing chastised communities that failed to protect adequately their war memorials. Unfinished monuments, he observed, were particularly prone to destruction by relic-seeking vandals who took pieces of them home as souvenirs. Even the creators of monuments often remained aware that alternative sources of memory could undermine their

A. C. Howland's *Fourth of July Parade* (c. 1886) depicts the fading ranks of revolutionary veterans in the early 1800s. (Painting in a private collection; photograph courtesy George Gurney)

efforts. When the aged survivors of the Battle of Bunker Hill gathered for the laying of the cornerstone of the monument to their battle, the Bunker Hill Monument Association asked them to record their accounts of the battle. After collecting them, the association decided that the veterans' accounts were so contradictory that they must remain private and available for "inspection of the Directors exclusively." In short, the association wanted to suppress sources of memory that could be used to call into question their portrayal of the battle and of the American Revolution.[57]

The passing of the revolutionary generation led to a cycle of interest, apathy, neglect, and often renewed concern regarding Independence Day. An individual community would in some years stage elaborate Fourth of July ceremonies that included a parade, oration, fireworks, and even a public dinner, but in other years they would completely neglect the holiday. As in the case of monuments, the federal government did little to promote the commemoration of Independence Day, except on army and naval bases. One small diplomatic incident near the close of the Madison administration illustrates aptly the reluctance of the federal government to interfere in local Fourth of July ceremonies.

In 1816, John Stuart Skinner, a federal postmaster and local politician

The top half of a membership certificate of the Bunker Hill Monument Association. Most monuments built in the early revolutionary and postrevolutionary periods depended on private contributions from such members. (Courtesy American Antiquarian Society)

in Baltimore, offered an Independence Day toast criticizing the restoration of Louis XVIII to the throne of France. Hyde de Neuville, the French minister to the United States, filed a formal protest and demanded Skinner's removal. The Madison administration refused to remove Skinner and informed Neuville that such an action would be, in the American view, inappropriate. In writing to Albert Gallatin, the new minister to France, regarding the incident, Secretary of State James Monroe made clear the official administration policy regarding the affair:

The Anniversary of our Independence has been always celebrated as a day of festivity throughout the U. States. Our citizens have been accustomed on that day, to relax from their ordinary avocations, to assemble in their respective circles, and to express without reserve their sentiments on all public subjects. Public officers, ought it is true, to be more guarded, at all times, in their language, than private citizens, but it is equally true, that in this great national festival, their official character is lost in that of the citizen.[58]

In the face of American intransigence and the relatively weak position of France, the French government dropped its demands and both sides soon forgot about the incident. But the Skinner affair illustrates the role the federal government, especially in the postrevolutionary period, played in shaping the public memory of the Revolution and other wars. In short, the government would accept, and at times assist and even defend, the right of Americans to create their own rituals and monuments to remember these conflicts. Although there would be an "American" pattern to how Americans commemorated past wars, by design and default, it remained one that stressed pluralism.[59]

In larger cities new types of celebrations, representing a variety of political parties, ethnic groups, and causes, multiplied. By the late 1830s the Democratic and Whig Parties in many communities held competing ceremonies and used the occasion to bolster their own position. For instance, Davy Crockett in 1834 used his oration in Philadelphia to deliver a blistering attack on Andrew Jackson for betraying the democratic principles of the American Revolution by his arbitrary actions against the Second Bank of the United States.[60]

In the 1830s temperance advocates began to sponsor their own parades and orators in order to link their cause with that of the American Revolution. Although they continued the long tradition of offering toasts in their ceremonies, they substituted "cold water" for alcoholic beverages. In many northern and southern cities, artisans and mechanics, proudly attired in their crafts' distinctive clothing and carrying the tools of their trade, marched with elite volunteer militia companies on the Fourth. By parading, workers declared that they remained important custodians of the memory of the Revolution. At the same time, the parade, particularly in the 1830s and 1840s, served to encourage solidarity among workers and provided them with an opportunity to voice their grievances against their employers.[61]

Independence Day ceremonies were only one of the forums workers used to link their cause with that of the American Revolution. Trade unions and workingmen's charitable societies named themselves after Washington and other leaders of the Revolution. Among trade unionists, free-thinking skeptics, and utopian socialists, Tom Paine remained a central figure in the revolutionary pantheon of heroes. Modest gifts from them in the 1830s paved the way for a monument to Paine's memory on the site of his former burial spot in New Rochelle, New York. Celebrations and banquets were from time to time organized in several cities to commemorate the anniversary of his birth.[62]

The influx of new immigrants to the major urban centers did not dampen enthusiasm for Independence Day, but served to heighten it. Irish and German militia companies and other ethnic organizations marched in Independence Day parades. In 1845 the *New York Herald* recorded with pleasure the participation of the Italian Guards, Shamrock Benevolent Society, the Laborer's Union Benevolent Society, and other ethnic organizations in the Independence Day ceremonies. It recorded that the "Declaration of Independence was read by Mr. John Collins, in a rich Irish accent, and with heartfelt emphasis."[63]

Over the course of the nineteenth century, abolitionists used the occasion of the Fourth of July to denounce the institution of slavery. Frederick Douglass, Wendell Phillips, Henry David Thoreau, and others attacked the hypocrisy of the festivities.[64] Douglass, in an Independence Day oration delivered in 1852 before a Rochester, New York, audience, asked how white Americans could celebrate this day as a jubilee of freedom without extending that freedom to those who remained in chains? To a slave held in bondage, Douglass declared, the Fourth meant nothing more than a day that

reveals to him, more than all other days in the year, the gross injustice and cruelty to which he is the constant victim. To him, your celebration is a sham; your boasted liberty, an unholy license; your national greatness, swelling vanity; your sounds of rejoicing are empty and heartless; your denunciations of tyrants, brass fronted impudence; your shouts of liberty and equality, hollow mockery; your prayers and hymns, your sermons and thanksgivings, with all your religious parade, and solemnity, are, to him, mere bombast, fraud, deception, impiety, and hypocrisy—a thin veil to cover up crimes which would disgrace a nation of savages.[65]

That Douglas could use an Independence Day oration to denounce slavery points to the malleability of both the holiday and the American national identity. Even in the postrevolutionary period, the Fourth offered a haven in some locales for abolitionists and those of other dissenting traditions. The same applied to the Declaration of Independence itself. Throughout American history, workers, farmers, and dissenters have not only debated the meaning of this document but also promulgated alternative declarations based on the original. In the most famous and enduring of these, Susan B. Anthony and other participants in the 1848 women's rights convention at Seneca Falls, New York, offered a "Declaration of Sentiments" that proclaimed equality between men and women and called for an end to the long "history of repeated injuries."[66]

The Revolution had a deep and abiding impact on American society. It endured in the nation's memory despite the federal government's reluctance to promote official observances of Independence Day or to build monuments. In fact, the government's deference to localist traditions helped create the ambiguity that permitted both dominant and dissenting voices to claim the memory of this war as their own.

Perhaps more than any other conflict in American history, the War of 1812 demonstrated the selective nature of public memory. In the aftermath of this conflict Americans remembered a few great exploits and a handful of victories the navy and army managed to win. On Independence Day, toasts saluted Decatur, Perry, Scott, and Jackson. A poem celebrating the successful defense of Baltimore, "The Star Spangled Banner," became the national anthem in the twentieth century.

The War of 1812 provided Americans with a new living hero, Andrew Jackson, who symbolized his age in much the same way as George Washington had embodied the revolutionary era. In New Orleans and many other cities, Jackson's triumph against the British would be commemorated annually by parades and orations. Victory at New Orleans eventually propelled Jackson to the White House in 1828, and his supporters likened him to Washington and to the noble Cincinnatus. But they also styled Jackson as a man of the people, the voice of a rising democracy. Despite his personal wealth, Jackson was portrayed as a common frontiersman whose native genius made up for his lack of formal education.

Jackson was a controversial symbol who did much to spark the partisan division of the postrevolutionary period. Although opponents hailed his victory at New Orleans, they remained suspicious of him and his motives. His critics found little in his character to compare with Washington or Cincinnatus. Instead, they feared that Jackson would become another Napoleon, a despot who used military forces to subvert the Republic. Jackson's occasional arbitrary exercise of military and, later, presidential authority only served to fuel this opposition.[67]

Nonetheless, Jackson's triumph at New Orleans led to grudging admiration, even from his critics. Although Democrats tended to take the lead in holding ceremonies on 8 January, the anniversary of his victory, Whigs often saw merit in honoring the date. Although politicians had become more comfortable with political partisanship, they continued to view the military fame acquired by heroic commanders of the Republic as a superior virtue standing above narrow differences. In 1841 Abraham Lincoln called on his colleagues in the Illinois legislature to support a resolution calling for a half-day adjournment on January 8 in honor of Jackson's victory. Lincoln declared that "he was proud of the victory of New-Orleans, and the military fame of Gen. Jackson, though he could never find in his heart to support him as a politician." He further observed that for the last six years the legislature had observed the day "as a matter of course, with no view whatever to politics."[68]

Although it took years before a national monument rose to the memory of Washington in the nation's capital, the death of Jackson in 1845 prompted quick action. President James K. Polk, an ardent expansionist, convened a meeting in the White House to organize efforts to build a monument to Old Hickory. John L. O'Sullivan, a notable York City newspaper editor and leading proponent of Manifest Destiny, proposed forming a central committee to raise $100,000 to build a monument to the memory of the late general. Polk offered a contribution of one hundred dollars to the project and considered lending his name and that of his entire cabinet to it. George Bancroft, secretary of the navy and noted historian, and several other advisers convinced Polk that his role must not be prominent because their efforts "might be attributed to a desire on their part to appropriate the great popularity of General Jackson for the benefit of the Administration and for party purposes."[69]

In three years the Jackson Monument Committee raised sufficient funds to commission the self-trained American sculptor Clark Mills to design an equestrian statue commemorating Jackson's victory at New Orleans. Controversy and partisanship soon emerged when the committee petitioned Congress for permission to melt for the statue several British canons captured by Jackson. Whig Congressman objected because they feared the committee wanted to melt down the "precious trophies of the Revolution." The assurance that only the cannon captured by Jackson would be used did not quell dissent. One congressman insisted that these "trophies of the valor of our ancestors" be passed down to succeeding generations and argued that no man, "however distinguished, patriotic, or brave" deserved such an honor. Another noted efforts by the House to defeat attempts to build a monument to Washington.[70]

Defending donation of the cannon, John Alexander McClernand, a Democratic congressman from Illinois, insisted that it was not "a misapplication of national trophies to devote them to the perpetuation of the names of the heroes whose valor and patriotism had won them." After all, the "brave, the wise, and incorruptible" Jackson remained inseparably "blended with the glory of his country." To bolster his argument, McClernand noted that the French had built a column to Napoleon from the cannon captured at Austerlitz and that the English had used brass pieces taken at Waterloo for an equestrian statue of Wellington.[71]

McClernand's use of European precedents suggests how earlier republican misapprehensions regarding the suitability of monuments had faded. The Jackson Monument Committee prevailed, and work proceeded on the first equestrian statue designed by an American. In 1853 Mills completed his work and Congress placed the monument in Lafayette Park, across from the White House. A Democratic Congress was so pleased with Mill's finished statue that they voted him twelve thousand dollars for his labors and commissioned him to build a similar statue of Washington for the capital.[72]

The growing acceptance of equestrian monuments, which traditionally had smacked of royalty and aristocracy, coincided with the high point of Manifest Destiny and the increased willingness of the United States to resort to war in order to expand its borders. Territorial expansion, even when accomplished through diplomatic means, has always provoked debate within American society. Federalists challenged Jefferson's decision to purchase Louisiana in 1803 on the grounds that it overstepped the constitutional authority of the federal government. The cry of war hawks for Canada added to the unpopularity of the War of 1812 among many Federalists, particularly in New England. The Missouri Compromise of 1820 made the issue of territorial expansion inseparable from the question of slavery.[73]

The federal government did not always take the lead in expanding the nation's boundaries. For instance, settlers in Florida, Texas, and California helped pave the way for the eventual acquisition of these lands. In the case of Texas, Americans in 1836 started a successful rebellion against the Mexican Republic that eventually led to the creation of the Republic of Texas. American settlers in Texas rebelled out of fear that their religious and political liberties would be subverted by Santa Anna's rise to power and his determination to limit regional autonomy. At the same time, a number of Texans wanted to keep their slaves and sought to halt any efforts on the part of Mexico to abridge their property rights. After several defeats, most notably at the Alamo, the Texans under Sam Houston succeeded in winning their revolt. Soon after achieving independence, the Lone Star republic sought annexation to the United States.[74]

Slavery proved to be the crucial stumbling block in delaying the annexation of Texas. Soon after the United States acquired Texas in 1845, it found itself at war with Mexico, largely as a result of the Polk administration's controversial deployment of the U.S. Army in disputed territory. Abolitionists expressed fierce opposition in 1845 to "Mr. Polk's War" and believed that the United States had gone to war with Mexico in order to advance dubious territorial claims. Abolitionists were not alone in their dissent. Free-Soilers, opponents of the spread of slavery, joined the Whig Party in their opposition to this conflict. In Congress Whigs questioned the justice of the war and claimed that President Polk could have avoided it. Opponents of the Mexican-American War insisted that the United States had engaged in a conflict that betrayed the principles on which the nation was founded. Charles Sumner, in an 1845 Independence Day address before the assembled units of the Massachusetts militia, railed against the use of force to settle disputes among nations. Albert Gallatin, in a widely circulated pamphlet to protest the war, argued that the founders of the Republic would not condone an offensive war fought for greed.[75]

Supporters of the war and of the principles of Manifest Destiny did not ignore the ideological challenge posed by their opponents. In justifying territorial expansion and Manifest Destiny, they claimed that the United States could best promote the principles of liberty and democracy by annexing more territory. In the case of Mexico, they maintained that the United States had been provoked into war by that nation and must revenge the unjustified attack on American forces along the Rio Grande. As for the question of slavery, northern Democrats remained indifferent to this matter and believed it to be an issue outside the domain of the federal government. Many southern Democrats favored the acquisition of new territory and viewed it as essential for the survival of the institution.[76]

The Mexican-American War marked an important watershed in the American pattern of making warfare. In contrast to earlier conflicts, professional journalists reported the exploits of the army in a growing number of newspapers. Americans were aware that they were engaged in a conflict with another culture and society. The war with Mexico, led by a professional officer corps trained at West Point, remains among the most militarily successful conflicts fought by the United States. With the adept leadership of a Whig general, Winfield Scott, American forces managed to defeat a Mexican army twice its size. The capture of Mexico City by Scott in 1847 forced Santa Anna to make huge territorial concessions to the United States.[77]

In some ways, the pattern of remembrance for the Mexican War followed the pattern established by earlier conflicts. To preserve the ties of comradeship and the memory of the conflict in which they fought, the officers established the Aztec Club. As with the Society of Cincinnati, enlisted personnel were barred from membership. The conflict produced two hero generals, Zachary Taylor and Winfield Scott, both of whom ran for the presidency. Only Taylor succeeded in winning the office, in large part because like Jackson before him, "Old Rough and Ready" projected an image of a heroic military leader who remained in touch with the common man. Ironically, Scott, the far better general and strategist, acquired a not-undeserved reputation as "Old Fuss and Feathers," which contributed to his defeat in the presidential election of 1852.[78]

In contrast to the American Revolution and even the War of 1812, decades did not elapse before the graves of this conflict's common soldiers were marked. In 1847 the state of Kentucky built and dedicated a cemetery to its Mexican-American War dead. Those killed in Mexico were returned to Kentucky at state expense. The state legislature commissioned Robert Launitz to design a statue to honor common soldiers who died in this war, and in earlier conflicts as well. A few years later the federal government established a permanent cemetery in Mexico City for the bones of the American soldiers who had fallen there. The bones of the officers and common soldiers who had died in battle were removed from the vicinity of the Mexico City garbage dump and buried in a permanent mass grave marked by a monument.[79]

Volunteers who returned home from the Mexican-American War received far more generous land bounties than granted to veterans of either the American Revolution or the War of 1812. Each returning volunteer who served for at least a year received a 160-acre land warrant. In contrast, veterans of the War of 1812 had to serve for at least five years or die in the conflict to receive a comparable land warrant. The generosity accorded to the veterans of 1847 proved decisive in spurring the veterans of the War of 1812 to further democratize the memory of war.[80]

During the 1850s, veterans of the War of 1812 began to form state societies and outline a national organization in order to preserve the memory of their conflict and to assert their claims for more generous land bounties. Unlike the Society of the Cincinnati or the Aztec Club, the War

A simple obelisk marking the graves of American Mexican-American War soldiers buried in Mexico City is an example of one of the first efforts by the federal government to maintain the burial places of the common soldier. (Photograph courtesy National Archives, 92-CA–30A–1)

A view of the outside of the American cemetery in Mexico City, photographed in the early 1900s. (Photograph courtesy National Archives, 92-CA–30A–2)

of 1812 societies declared that all veterans were the proper custodians of the war's memory. Moreover, they were far from reluctant to praise their past services and to demand they be compensated for them. At the first national convention for the War of 1812 veterans, held at Philadelphia in 1854, one participant observed that "many of the officers and soldiers of the Revolution suffered seriously from not keeping a *perfect record* of their services before the national eye."[81]

To bolster their claims to more generous benefits and to link them to a higher good, the veterans of the War of 1812 proclaimed their desire to strengthen the ties of the Union by fostering a remembrance of their own conflict as well as of the Revolution. On repeated occasions the 1812 veterans made explicit the continuity they believed existed between the two conflicts. For example, when the New York state veterans of 1812 gathered in 1856, they met in Saratoga on the anniversary of Burgoyne's surrender. In their speeches they dwelt at length on the glorious struggle waged in 1777. They urged Congress to appropriate money to mark the battlefields at Saratoga and Yorktown and called on the state of New York to settle their outstanding salary and pension claims from the War of 1812.[82]

Despite the growing democratization of the memory of war and the early attempts to commemorate the Mexican-American War, this conflict remains one of the most "forgotten" in American history. To a certain extent, the Revolution and the Civil War overshadowed the exploits of both the generals and the common soldiers. In other ways, the neglect of this conflict can be explained by Americans' reluctance to view the United States as fighting a war of conquest. This explains in large measure why the Texas rebellion, particularly the fall of the Alamo, looms so large in the American imagination.[83]

Although Americans have placed the Mexican-American War in the deep recesses of public memory, they have remembered the Alamo. The defeat of a small band of mostly American-born revolutionaries fighting for an independent Republic of Texas burns bright in the national memory, particularly in the twentieth century. Why do Americans commemorate a defeat and largely ignore the successful campaigns of Scott a decade later? To a degree, the Alamo proved easier to remember, because it sits on American soil. Initially, the Alamo developed as an important regional symbol used to define an Anglo-Texan identity. In 1883, the state of Texas began acquiring the surviving structures associated with the Alamo and gave custody of it to the city of San Antonio. After completing the purchase of the remaining structures in 1903, the state allowed the Daughters of the Republic of Texas to administer the site as a shrine to Texan and American patriotism. Fictional accounts in the nineteenth century and in Hollywood films in the twentieth century proved crucial in making the Alamo into a regional and national symbol that often emphasized the role played by Davy Crockett in the struggle.[84]

The Alamo has served to justify for Americans the Texas revolution and the Mexican Revolution. The refusal of Santa Anna and his army to grant quarter to the brave defenders of the Alamo offers convincing evidence of the barbarous nature of the Mexican regime. The courageous stand at the Alamo allowed its defenders to become martyrs and ennobled the Texas revolution as a struggle for freedom against tyranny. What is usually forgotten is the role slavery played in the rebellion and the annexation of this republic by the United States.

Slavery proved to be the central barrier to national unity in the postrevolutionary period. It intruded into almost every federal action and shaped the way Americans remembered the American Revolution, the Texas revolution, and the Mexican-American War. On the centennial anniversary of the birth of George Washington, several Virginians in Congress argued against entombing his body in the Capitol because they were not sure if the Union would endure and did not want their native son interred in alien soil. To defend slavery, southerners had to rely on racism to explain why the principles of the Declaration of Independence did not apply to African Americans, but they had to accept its principles to support their right to leave the Union. They understood the Constitution as a compact of sovereign states that limited the power of the federal government, particularly with regard to the issue of slavery.[85]

Many northerners and southerners expressed alarm at the divisions within American society over slavery and the proper role of the federal government. Some yearned for rituals and monuments that would remember the American Revolution and ameliorate sectional divisions. In a long essay on American holidays in an 1857 issue of the *North American Review*, H. T. Tuckerman, a Boston-born literary critic, remained disappointed at the lack of interest Americans displayed in holidays and civic rituals. Other than the Fourth of July, Americans did not celebrate a national holiday, although a multitude of holidays were celebrated in different regions and by various ethnic groups. For instance, citizens of Charlestown, Massachusetts, annually commemorated the Battle of Bunker Hill, and New York City residents celebrated "Evacuation Day" to mark the departure of the British in 1783. Although widely observed, Tuckerman sadly noted that the Fourth of July had become a holiday marked by "bursting cannon, draggled flags, crowded steamboats, the disgust of the educated, and the uproar of the multitude" instead of a day of rededication commemorated with "a sacred feast, a pious memory, a hallowed consecration, a 'Sabbath-day of Freedom.'"[86]

To heal sectional divisions, the United States vitally needed what Tuckerman called a "common shrine, a national feast, a place, a time, or a memory sacred to fraternal sympathies and general observance." Although pessimistic and critical throughout his essay, Tuckerman did not despair. Instead, he applauded efforts to venerate the memory of Washington in "literature, art and oratory." The time was right for an institution of "solemn national festival" centered on the birthday of Washington; if properly carried out, it would "fuse and mould into one pervasive emotion the divided hearts of the country, until the discordant cries of faction are lost in the anthems of benediction and of love, and, before the august spirit of a people's homage, sectional animosity is awed into universal reverence."[87]

In his first inaugural address, Abraham Lincoln appealed to Americans to take heed of the "mystic chords of memory" that stretched from "every battle-field, and patriot grave" in order to avert the impending crisis of disunion. In a sense, Lincoln should not have been surprised that the bonds of nationhood remained so brittle in 1861. After all, Americans frequently neglected the graves of fallen soldiers. The federal government made only scattered efforts to mark the battlefields of the Revolution or the War of 1812. It even refused to pay for a national monument to Washington or to acquire Mount Vernon. By the end of Lincoln's first term in office, the United States would acquire a host of new battlefields and scores of freshly sown graves.[88]

# 2

# THE DIVIDED LEGACY
# OF THE
# CIVIL WAR

The American Civil War was marked by paradoxes and contradictions. Initially, most Northerners marched off to war to crush a rebellion—not to abolish slavery, but to preserve the Union. Military and diplomatic advantage eventually encouraged Abraham Lincoln to issue the Emancipation Proclamation in 1862, thus turning the conflict into a war of liberation. Each side had gone to war in 1861 with the expectation that one decisive battle would bring an end to the conflict. Instead, it turned into a brutal war of attrition, ultimately costing the lives of more than a million soldiers.

Civil wars often end in a bloodbath, as the victors execute, exile, or dispossess the vanquished. Despite the harshness of the American Civil War, the North remained exceedingly magnanimous in victory. No Confederate leader was ever tried for treason, and captured Rebel soldiers were allowed to return to their homes after surrendering in 1865. Southern planters lost their slaves, but most were allowed to keep their land and other property.

In a sense, the North could be gracious because it had won a total victory. The armies of the South had been crushed and the entire region occupied by Federal troops. Slavery, the underlying cause of sectional divisions during the postrevolutionary period, had been ended as a result of a constitutional amendment. Still, it remained a triumph tinged with loss and uncertainty. The war had exacted a terrible price in lives lost and shattered. And on the eve of complete triumph, President Abraham Lincoln was struck down by a Confederate assassin.

In the wake of war, northern leaders and public opinion remained divided over what should be the future of the South and of the emancipated African Americans. President Andrew Johnson joined northern Democrats in supporting a federal policy that called for the rapid reintegration of the South into the Union and opposed citizenship for freed male slaves. But to many abolitionists and African Americans, the reunited nation finally had the opportunity to fulfill the ideals set forth in the Declaration of Independence, including liberty and freedom as the birthright of all men. On more pragmatic grounds, many Republican leaders thought that by extending political and legal rights to the former slaves, they could assure their future political dominance of the South.

Supporters of radical Reconstruction, particularly abolitionists and African Americans, emphasized the need to remember the Civil War as a struggle waged against slavery. In their view, blame for causing the war rested squarely on the greed, sinfulness, and arrogance of southern slaveholders. Ceremonies and memorials commemorating the conflict, therefore, had to remind Northerners of the terrible price paid in defense of the Union and for the cause of liberty, and were designed to inspire patriots to oppose Southerners' efforts to undermine the fruits of victory.

The majority of white Southerners accepted defeat and the supremacy of the federal government; however, many remained defiant. Although Southerners proved willing to accept the abolition of slavery, most opposed efforts by the federal government to extend full legal and political rights to former slaves. Through the ballot box and by extralegal means, many former Confederates challenged federally sponsored Reconstruction governments.

In remembering the Civil War the white South mourned its tremendous loss and suffering, and most secessionists refused to admit that it had been wrong to leave the Union. By honoring the Confederate dead with memorials and ceremonies, these Southerners, although not flinching from the view that slavery was the principal cause of the war, declared that the fallen had died for a just and noble cause.

During the Reconstruction era, sectional, party, and racial divisions led to divergent ways of commemorating and remembering the Civil War. At the same time, there emerged a distinctive American pattern that frequently crossed these divisions. In both the North and the South, for

Union army burial place, Fredericksburg, Virginia. The Civil War was the first war in which the federal government took responsibility for maintaining permanent cemeteries for the war dead. (Photograph courtesy Brady Collection, National Archives, 111-B–4817)

example, a distinctly new holiday, Decoration Day, or Memorial Day, emerged to commemorate the sacrifice of the common soldier, regardless of whether he had worn blue or gray.

Shortly after the first battle deaths of the Civil War, the War Department announced that the graves of Union soldiers would be properly marked and registered by the federal government. The *New York Times* welcomed this action declaring that "those left behind will find consolation in the fact that the tenderest humanities are to be observed towards the graves of their loved ones." In 1862 Congress formalized this executive action and authorized the secretary of war to maintain permanent cemeteries for the Union war dead. However, not all cemeteries were established by the national government. After the Battle of Antietam in August 1862, a cemetery for the Union war dead of this engagement was built and maintained by a private association of Maryland Unionists. A year later, after the greatest battle of the war, Pennsylvania and several other states established, with the blessing of the Lincoln administration, a cemetery for the Union dead killed at Gettysburg.[1]

The efforts of the federal and state governments, as well as private groups, to mark the graves of all soldiers reflected a dramatic departure from earlier practices and mirrored a wider cultural shift in American attitudes toward the dead. Before the Civil War, civilian cemeteries had become more elaborate and had taken on the characteristics of gardens, especially as the final resting places for members of the middle and upper classes. Urban workers created mutual-aid societies in order to ensure that they received proper funerals and avoided burials in potter's fields. The federal government, because it initially raised its army through voluntary enlistments during the Civil War, could ill afford to ignore the changing expectations of northern-born Americans regarding burial of the dead.[2]

Abraham Lincoln elevated the war dead and Union military cemeteries as foremost symbols of the struggle to preserve a united and democratic nation. In November 1863, Lincoln and other leading officials of his administration participated in elaborate ceremonies dedicating the Gettysburg soldiers' cemetery. Edward Everett, the scholar-statesman of Massachusetts, delivered an oration to an audience of more than twenty thousand, linking the burial of the Union dead at Gettysburg to the ancient Greek tradition of mourning the fallen warrior. He recounted the causes and course of the rebellion and provided a detailed report of the fighting that had taken place on each of the three days of battle in July 1863. In the remainder of his address, this former president of Harvard and former secretary of state explained at length the terrible crime of rebellion, although still offering the promise of eventual victory and reconciliation. To bolster his belief in a Union victory and to put an end to Confederate resistance, Everett closed his address by noting how the deep animosities aroused in a number of European civil wars had faded over time.[3]

Lincoln spoke near the end of the ceremonies, delivering in two minutes an address that would become his most famous. In ringing terms, he defined the nature of American democracy and nationhood, declaring that the national government at its creation gained its authority directly from the people and that the nation rested upon the "proposition that all men are created equal." Moreover, he insisted that the "honored dead" remained emblematic of a larger struggle to ensure "that this nation, under God, shall have a new birth of freedom; and that government of the people, by the people, for the people, shall not perish from the earth."[4]

With the coming of peace in 1865, the war dead and their cemeteries continued for the North to be important symbols of victory and nationhood. In an 1866 issue of *Harper's New Monthly Magazine,* James Russling described the efforts by the U.S. Army to create a series of permanent military cemeteries for fallen Union soldiers. To Russling, the task of burying the Union dead remained so important that he urged Congress to pass additional legislation to clarify the authority of the War Department in this area. Russling observed that in contrast to aristocratic or monarchical governments, a "Democratic republic . . . based on the equality of the race" cannot neglect those who defended it. Honoring the common soldier with a proper burial indicated that the Civil War marked the dawning of a new age in which "narrowness and bigotry, of class and caste, seems [to be] passing away."

To ensure that Civil War military cemeteries embodied the "might and majesty of the Union," Russling cautioned the federal government not to turn responsibility for them over to the states, as it had done at Gettysburg, or to a private association, as at Antietam. He applauded the decision of one Union general at Chattanooga to bury soldiers in a way that minimized state affiliation. Russling welcomed the sentiments of this unnamed major general, who explained his decision by declaring that there had been "quite enough of *State Rights;* that these soldiers had died fighting *for* the Union, *against* rebellious States, and now we had better mix them up and *nationalize* them a little."[5]

As a result of lobbying by Russling and others, Congress authorized in 1866 the creation of an extensive system of permanent national cemeteries for the Union war dead. In addition, the Quartermaster Corps of the army conducted an elaborate search for isolated graves in order to ensure that each one was properly marked and maintained. In the South, the U.S. Army frequently decided to remove bodies from scattered locations and reburied them in larger cemeteries surrounded by stone walls so that they would not be desecrated by Southerners. To further protect the graves of Union soldiers, Congress made it a federal crime to vandalize a national cemetery.[6]

Union cemeteries mark a dramatic departure in the federal government's role in commemorating past wars. They also represent the first major effort by the government to build national memorials outside of the nation's capital. Most of these were constructed and maintained by the army's Quartermaster Department, but state governments and private groups were allowed to erect suitable memorials marking the service of a particular regiment, state, or individual hero on these sites.[7]

Monument in Memory of the Patriots Who Fell in the First Battle of Bull Run. This lithograph by L. Prang & Co., Boston, is based on a photograph by A. Gardiner. Even before the conflict had ended, Americans began commemorating battle sites of the Civil War with monuments. (Courtesy American Antiquarian Society)

One of the first national cemeteries established by Union forces was created, in part, as an act of vengeance against Robert E. Lee. In 1862 General Montgomery C. Meigs of the Quartermaster Department, with the consent of Abraham Lincoln, established a cemetery at Lee's planation at Arlington, Virginia, which became Arlington National Cemetery. But in many ways this act was an exception, and after the war the federal government compensated Southerners when their property was expropriated for national cemeteries. Moreover, the quartermaster general and the attorney general, and eventually Congress, determined that the Constitution required the federal government to request permission from a given state to build a national cemetery within its borders. As a result, the War Department officially petitioned southern state officials, asking them to approve national cemeteries already built, all of which were duly approved.[8]

Even before victory had been assured, some communities and groups considered erecting memorials to the conflict. In June 1861, a citizens' committee met in Detroit and announced its plan to erect a monument to those who died in defense of the Union. The regular officers of the army did not wait until the end of war to build a memorial to their fallen at West Point. In June 1864, General George B. McClellan delivered an oration at the monument's dedication praising the service of the volunteers and regulars who fought for the Union. McClellan declared that he expected each state to create memorials to remember the "services of its sons" who "abandoned the avocations of peace and shed their blood in the ranks of the volunteers." Because the regulars belonged to no one state but served the entire nation, McClellan declared it imperative that memory of the "sacred brotherhood of arms" be preserved with a fitting memorial.[9]

Within a decade of Grant's triumph at Appomattox, dozens of monuments appeared in towns and cities across the North. In contrast to the national cemeteries, these efforts to commemorate the Civil War remained largely the domain of private individuals, communities, and states until the 1890s. These memorials, like the national cemeteries, commemorated the service of the common soldier and sailor. In most places, especially in small towns, the typical memorial featured a realistic bronze statue of a lone soldier. Usually placed in town squares or in city parks, these memorials frequently listed the names of those from that community who had died in the war.[10]

The soldier monuments of the North proclaimed victory and marked a departure from the "funerary" character of the typical postrevolutionary war memorial, most of which represented a belated effort to mark the graves of fallen, usually revolutionary, heroes. Although the obelisk did not entirely disappear, far fewer communities selected them as memorials. Stylistically, northern soldier monuments, particularly in larger cities, used realistic and allegorical imagery that underscored the themes of loss, struggle, and triumph. The more elaborate ones featured common soldiers and sailors, but also bas-reliefs and a host of additional statuary depicting famous events, leaders, or allegorical figures, such as those of History, Peace, or Justice. The feminine figures of Liberty and Victory proved the most popular allegorical figures provided by patrons of soldiers' memorials. For instance, the Worcester, Massachusetts, soldier monument, which was completed in 1874, included a winged figure of Victory on a globe, with one raised hand holding a sword and the other a palm branch symbolizing peace.[11]

The Civil War became the first major conflict in American history to create a large number of photographic images and this new form of representation served to encourage the creation of cemeteries and monuments. Mathew Brady, Alexander Gardner, James F. Gibson, and other photographers offered the public enduring and haunting images of the war. For technological reasons photographers could not record actual battles, but they could capture a wide range of poignant and striking images. Frequently, before a soldier, Northerner or Southerner, left his hometown, he posed for a photograph in his new uniform as a way of preserving his memory for his family. Northern photographers followed armies during their campaigns and provided the public with photographs of camp life, generals, escaped slaves, and the dead of the battlefield. The Union army, especially the engineers and medical corps, used photography to aid and document their work.[12]

Photographs themselves took on a memorial character. For a widow or family, a photograph was an enduring image of a loved one killed in battle. In the fall of 1862, scores of prominent New Yorkers flocked to view Brady's pictures of the war dead at his public gallery in the city. Lincoln's death prompted photographers to reproduce for sale earlier photographs of him and to document the journey of his funeral train from Washington, D.C., to Springfield, Illinois. Soon after the war, expensive photographic histories chronicling the course of the struggle appeared.[13]

Photographs offered a selective and partial history of the war, of course, and not all of this incompleteness stemmed from the technological or logistical limits imposed by photographic equipment. For instance, the successful blockade of the South vastly limited the number of Confederate photographs available. Moreover, both photographers and the public wanted photographic images to combine both realistic and aesthetic qualities. Photographers thus had preconceived notions of what pictures they wanted to take, and in some cases they even created contrived images. For example, Alexander Gardner moved and rearranged the bodies of the Confederate dead at Gettysburg before photographing them.[14]

The existence of photographs may explain why decades elapsed before monuments to the most successful and popular northern generals were created. Widely circulated images of these military heroes served to record and publicize their fame. No doubt this delay in building monuments also reflected the fact that most successful military leaders survived the conflict and went on to prominent postwar careers. Not until their deaths in the 1880s and 1890s would monuments appear to Grant, Sherman, Sheridan, and other prominent northern generals and admirals. But above all, none of the prominent commanders of the North approached the fame of Lincoln.

Lincoln, more than any general or common soldier, personified the Civil War, and his assassination made him a martyr for the Union cause. In contrast to the handful of memorials to George Washington, which went up decades after his death, only a decade elapsed before scores of statues—in San Francisco, Washington, D.C., Brooklyn, and New York City—were built to Lincoln's memory. In 1874, a private association dedicated an elaborate tomb to Lincoln in a Springfield, Illinois, cemetery that featured a huge obelisk and a series of statues depicting images of the late president and allegorical figures of Civil War soldiers.[15]

Even more than their counterparts in previous wars, the fallen president and heroic Civil War generals were portrayed as reflecting the interests and aspirations of the common citizen-soldier. For instance, General George B. McClellan's concern for the welfare of the average soldier and his desire to avoid high casualties contributed to his popularity among the rank and file. Despite Grant's victories, his casual dress and humble background hardly conformed to the martial image of a conquering general. In contrast to the image of Washington, the gentlemen planter, Grant had failed at everything before winning fame on the battlefield. Washington's presidency only served to heighten his fame, whereas two terms as the nation's chief executive managed to sully Grant's reputation. The public viewed Grant as an indecisive and inept president who allowed corruption to flourish. Unlike Washington, who left the presidency voluntarily, Grant had wished to seek a third term. In short, Grant remained in the popular imagination, both in life and after death, not a demigod, but a too-human hero who triumphed in war but in little else.[16]

Lincoln represented the common man as hero even more than his generals. As a candidate and later as president, Lincoln cultivated an image of himself as a man who embodied the common sense, simplicity, bravery and wit of the frontiersman. Although a successful railroad lawyer in the 1850s, Lincoln's presidential campaign literature in 1860 featured an image of him as a rail splitter. His assassination only served to reinforce the image of him as a noble son of the frontier. Early partisan criticism of the late president, particularly regarding his conduct during the war, was forgotten.[17]

Lincoln's posthumous reputation rivalled, and to some degree surpassed, that of Washington. Washington helped to create the Republic; but Lincoln saved the Union and freed the slaves. In 1867 Congress granted a charter to the Lincoln Memorial Association to erect a memorial "commemorative of the Great Charter of emancipation and universal liberty in America." Three years later an association member, Dr. Henry W. Bellows, former president of the United States Sanitary Commission, offered a detailed description of a proposed seventy-foot triangular memorial. The design called for equestrian statues of the six greatest Union generals, and above them, around the base of the second level, twenty-one bronze statues of the leading civilian leaders of the war. At the peak of the monument would be a huge statue of a seated Lincoln signing the Emancipation Proclamation. In addition, there would be a series of allegorical figures and bas-reliefs documenting the institutional history of slavery and the central events of the war, such as the firing on Fort Sumter and the congressional enactment of a constitutional amendment outlawing slavery.[18]

The Lincoln Memorial Association never raised enough funds to realize its grandiose vision. The lack of public resolve mirrored northern ambivalence about the role slavery and race played in the Civil War. If Bellows and others had been successful in building such a monument on the scale proposed, they would have created a permanent symbol in the nation's capital commemorating the Civil War as preeminently a military and civilian struggle for freedom and liberation.

In the end, African Americans built a smaller memorial in a Washington, D.C., park that portrayed Lincoln as an American Moses setting the people free. Although the statue was funded by African Americans, the U.S. Sanitary Commission assumed responsibility for raising the necessary monies and selecting a sculptor, Thomas Ball. The symbolism of this monument, by failing to commemorate their service in the Union army or to acknowledge the massive flight to freedom when given the chance to escape, served to minimize the role played by African Americans in bringing about their own liberation. Instead of depicting an African American soldier, Ball, a New England–born and European-trained sculptor, created a monument that showed a standing Lincoln granting freedom to a kneeling slave.[19]

In 1876, Frederick Douglass, the prominent African American abolitionist, delivered the principal address at the memorial's dedication before an audience that included President Ulysses S. Grant and a host of federal officials. Despite his reservations about the design of the monument, Douglass applauded efforts to venerate the memory of Lincoln and called on white Americans to "multiply his statues" and build them of the "most costly material, of the most cunning workmanship; let their forms be symmetrical, beautiful, and perfect; let their bases be upon solid rocks, and their summits lean against the unchanging blue, overhanging sky, and let them endure forever!" To this former slave, the martyred president must be remembered as a statesman who both saved the Union and led a cause that lifted African Americans "from the depths of slavery to the heights of liberty and manhood." Douglass recounted with pride how Lincoln presided over an army that eventually included two hundred thousand former slaves who had laid aside the "rags of bondage" for the "blue uniforms of the soldiers of the United States."[20]

Northerners differed over what the fate of the South should be. Democrats wanted to integrate the South quickly back into the Union. Many Republicans, however, especially those within the radical wing of the party, insisted that the federal government reorder southern society and end the power of the secessionist planter class. Beginning with the 1866 congressional campaign, Republicans sought to preserve the memory of Civil War divisions in order to garner northern votes. In the "bloody-shirt" campaigns developed in the 1860s and used intermittently until the 1880s, Republicans associated both Democrats and the South with rebellion and disloyalty. During many campaign rallies, a blood-soaked shirt was waved in the air to symbolize the northern lives lost in the war. For several presidential campaigns, Republicans formed veterans into "Boys in Blue" organizations and had them march in distinctive blue uniforms in huge torchlight parades.[21]

Republican leaders also played a decisive role in the creation of the largest and most successful organization of Union veterans, the Grand Army of the Republic (GAR). Ostensibly founded as a nonpartisan society in 1866, the GAR rendered invaluable service to the Republican cause. Under the leadership of John A. Logan, a U.S. senator from Ohio and a former Union general, the GAR solidified support among Union veterans for the party and kept the memory of war before the public's eye. Over the course of its existence, a majority of Union veterans never joined this society, even when its membership peaked in 1890 at slightly over four hundred thousand members. Moreover, membership in the GAR fluctuated greatly, particularly in the late 1860s and 1870s, with the membership in 1876 standing at only 26,899. Furthermore, the GAR was by no means the only organization to attract the allegiance of Union army veterans. Former officers created a number of exclusive societies, most notably the Loyal Legion, that excluded enlisted men.[22]

The importance and effectiveness of the GAR stemmed from its ability to play a decisive role in shaping the commemoration of the Civil War in the larger society. Soon after the war ended, the GAR began to encourage the commemoration of Memorial Day, a day dedicated to remembering the war dead. To a certain extent the GAR had merely standardized and formalized an increasingly common observance. In the South, as early as 1865, groups of women decorated the graves of Confederate soldiers and held memorial services in the spring. This custom spread north in 1866 and 1867 and was celebrated on a wide variety of spring days. The GAR played a crucial role in turning Memorial Day into a widely observed holiday in the North and in eventually making it into an official federal holiday. In 1868 Logan directed GAR posts to decorate the graves of Union soldiers and to hold memorial ceremonies on 30 May in honor of the fallen. The "heroic dead," Logan declared, had made themselves into a "barricade between our country and its foes." They had served as the "reveille of freedom to a race in chains," and their deaths were "the tattoo of rebellious tyranny in arms." Logan charged GAR posts to guard their "graves with sacred vigilance," so that coming generations would know the "cost of a free and undivided Republic."[23]

In response to Logan's call, GAR posts throughout the nation held ceremonies featuring prayers, hymns, patriot anthems, and dirges. Although most ceremonies had a decidedly Protestant cast, in some cities Catholic priests presided or participated. Orators, usually former generals or members of the clergy, described how the sacrifice of the dead had paved the way for a united nation and brought the blessings of liberty. Many saw the results of the war as a fulfillment of the promise of the Revolution and the Declaration of Independence. Frequently, the names of the community's war dead were read aloud. At the end of a ceremony, participants generally placed flowers, wreaths, and, in some cases, small American flags on the graves. At the conclusion of the program at Arlington National Cemetery in Virginia, children orphaned by the conflict scattered flowers over the twelve thousand graves as two future presidents, Ulysses S. Grant and James Garfield, together with other invited dignitaries, watched. As Logan had hoped, Memorial Day became an annual and widely observed holiday in much of the North, and even in parts of the South.[24]

Although often breached, the GAR's policy of political neutrality proved essential to its success in sponsoring Memorial Day. Logan and other GAR leaders wisely refrained from overtly partisan orations and symbols. Still, the holiday bolstered the Republican cause by reminding Americans of the tremendous losses incurred during the war, and most orators made it clear that responsibility for beginning the war rested with the

Memorial Day ceremonies in Morristown, New Jersey, in the late 1890s reflected a pattern of remembrance common to both the North and South. (Courtesy of Morristown/Morris Township Library, New Jersey)

South. In the South, Memorial Day observances indicated who among the community supported congressional Reconstruction and the Republican Party.[25]

Early Memorial Day ceremonies and Republican campaign rhetoric declared that continued vigilance was needed to protect the fruits of Civil War victory. Logan and other Republican leaders considered the GAR more than just an organization created to preserve the memory of the Civil War and to bolster the party's electoral chances. During the impeachment crisis of 1868, for example, Logan developed plans to mobilize the GAR in order to check any effort by Andrew Johnson to use the regular army to evict Secretary of War Edwin Stanton from his War Department offices or to dissolve Congress.[26] The feared military coup never materialized, and the GAR did not have to take up arms again to preserve the Constitution and the Union victory. Johnson successfully fought his impeachment in the Senate, not in the streets. The incident, however, highlights how tenuous the boundaries between peace and war remained during the Reconstruction era. Throughout this period, congressional Republicans, and later the Grant administration, used the regular army in the South to assist Reconstruction governments and to protect the rights of African Americans. At the same time, Republicans believed the threat to the Republic remained so great under Johnson that it might warrant the possible use of extralegal force.[27]

During the 1870s, membership in the GAR declined as Republican concern over a threatened Reconstruction faded. Although its posts dissolved in several parts of the country, the GAR survived. Even if only thinly cloaked, nonpartisanship proved crucial to the durability of the GAR because Americans still had a lingering distrust of political parties. Overtly partisan veterans' organizations had brief life spans. Moreover, the organizational independence of the GAR allowed its membership to play a role in shaping the goals and purposes of the society. As a result of pressure from members, the GAR downplayed its ties with the GOP and, instead, placed greater emphasis on securing better pensions for disabled Union veterans. Consequently, although always a minority, Democrats joined the GAR in order to counter the strong Republican bias of the society.[28]

Although northern Democrats found it difficult to challenge the bloody shirt in presidential elections, they refused to concede all symbols of the Civil War to the Republicans. During several presidential campaigns, Democrats sponsored their own society of Union veterans, the "White Boys in Blues," to counter the "Boys in Blue." The Democrats often flirted with the idea of nominating a Democratic Civil War general for the presidency and actually did so in 1880, when they selected the hero of Gettysburg, General Winfield Scott Hancock, as their candidate. This tactic failed, however. Republicans insisted that although Hancock had personal integrity, he would quickly become a dupe to southern interests. Above all, northern Democrats appealed to the racism and ambivalence many, if not most, northern whites felt regarding the new status of African Americans.[29]

For white Southerners the Civil War was a defeat that had turned the social order upside down. Former slaves were not only free but many had served in the Union army—the ultimate insult to southern sensibilities. Radical Republicans had passed statutes and constitutional amendments in the 1860s that legally elevated African American slaves to citizenship. The Union army, with its many black regiments, served as an occupying force in the South.

Despite the upheavals caused by the war and its aftermath, most former Confederates refused to admit that secession had been a mistake. Privately, and often publicly, they made clear their displeasure at being forcibly returned to the Union. They shunned GAR-sponsored celebrations on Memorial Day and the Fourth of July, allowing both of these ceremonies to become the domain of black and white southern Republicans. Most Southerners built monuments, created holidays, and even formed organizations dedicated to preserving the memory of the "lost cause."[30]

Although they suffered enormous economic losses during the war, Southerners, like Northerners, quickly set out to build monuments to the conflict. Whereas citizen groups, state or local governments, and veterans organizations built the majority of Union monuments, "ladies' memorial associations" sponsored most of the early Confederate ones. The first wave of monuments to the Confederate cause differed from their Union counterparts in both location and design. Unlike northern monuments, most southern memorials tended to be obelisks, usually placed in cemeteries.[31] In explaining the preference for the obelisk, one ladies' memorial association observed:

As it is a memorial of a lost cause, it should not be a triumphal memorial. Placed in the City of the Dead, and near the entrance, the sight of it cannot fail to call back the memory of the sad history which it commemorates. A splendid monument in the city would be only an ornament to be gazed on with listless and indifferent eyes; and, instead of being a memorial of the dead, would be only the object of cold, art criticism.[32]

As in the North, the common soldier remained at the center of southern memorial efforts. Women's memorial associations undertook massive efforts in 1865 and 1866 to locate the Confederate dead and to create permanent cemeteries for them. In this effort, Southerners displayed their continued sense of alienation. Confederate soldiers buried in the North, even in important national battlefields such as Gettysburg, were returned to the South for reburial.[33]

Southerners honored the Confederate war dead in their own Memorial Day ceremonies, commemorated on a variety of dates. Confederate Memorial Day, as it would eventually be called, included ceremonies similar to those of the GAR, but there were important differences. Naturally, instead of praising the Union victory, southern orators predicted the eventual vindication of their cause. In selecting the date of commemoration, states expressed symbolically their continued adherence to localism. Generally, communities in the Deep South held ceremonies on 26 April, the day General Joseph E. Johnson surrendered his army. But in the Carolinas, they chose 10 May, the anniversary of the death of Thomas "Stonewall" Jackson. In Virginia, local communities honored the war dead on a wide variety of dates, from mid-May to mid-June.[34]

White Southerners actively resisted efforts by the federal government to grant southern African Americans political and economic rights. To ensure the continued subjugation of African Americans, white southern Democrats frequently resorted to extralegal violence. In the opening years of Reconstruction, many Confederate veterans joined the Ku Klux Klan (KKK), which conducted a campaign of terror against newly freed slaves. In an elaborate initiation ritual, members pledged themselves to secrecy, vowed to protect the widows and children of Confederate veterans, and declared their opposition to the GAR and a variety of other groups supporting Reconstruction. To keep the "Negro in his place," KKK chapters assaulted, robbed, and lynched African Americans.[35]

The KKK was not in the traditional sense a formal veteran's organization. As it spread throughout the South in 1868, membership was extended to any white male who accepted the goals of the society, and many of its rituals had more in common with the Greek letter fraternities of the college campus and other secret male-bonding societies of the nineteenth century.[36] Yet the KKK was also a nontraditional veteran's organization. Despite important differences, there were striking similarities between the GAR and the Klan. Civil War generals played a crucial part in the early development of both societies. In the case of the Klan, General Nathan Bedford Forrest served as the first and only grand wizard. Circumstantial evidence suggests that Forrest carried out a somewhat successful campaign to enlist support for the Klan among former Confederate comrades. Although the GAR never resorted to extralegal violence, it had been ready to march on Washington in 1868. Both organizations started out as secret societies. Originally, the GAR began as a secret society whose elaborate initiation ritual called on veterans to remember the war dead. In one initiation ceremony, for example, a prospective member was required to enter a room blindfolded and kneel, and when the blindfold was removed, he saw a coffin with the name of an Andersonville victim written on it, two crossed swords, an American flag, and an open Bible. Taking their oaths, prospective GAR members promised never to reveal the secrets of the society and pledged loyalty to his fellow comrades and organizational leaders.[37]

Initially, when the Klan perpetrated its violence, members clad in white

costumes declared themselves to be the ghosts of dead Confederate soldiers. In part, Klansmen hoped this disguise would hide their identity as
well as frighten African Americans. But the use of white costumes, along
with many of the Klan's rituals, had a deeper symbolism that represented
an effort among Southerners to cope with the reality of defeat by appealing
to magical forces. In one sense, Klansmen conjured up these rituals and
the images of ghosts in order to counter the real power of the North. Of
course, to a larger degree, the Klan's claim that it resorted to violence to
protect southern women was simply a self-serving attempt to justify un-
warranted attacks on African Americans and other supporters of Republican Reconstruction. But their claim also may have reflected a perceived
need among many white southern males to redeem their honor and to
reinforce their sense of masculine prowess deemed lost as a result of their
surrender to the Yankees.[38]

The concern with preserving southern honor helps to explain the success of the ladies' memorial societies. In many places wealthy males served
as the chief financial backers of these associations, as southern men deemed
the commemoration of the Confederate dead a proper sphere of activity
for women. By showing their fidelity to the dead and by honoring the
Confederate cause, southern women, in a sense, served to reassure living
southern males that they continued to value their male identity. By joining
the Klan and by opposing Reconstruction, southern men assumed for
themselves the role of protector of women and children in order to buttress
their own sense of manhood, at the same time pursuing their goals of political and racial superiority.

Federal intervention in the early 1870s helped eliminate the Ku Klux
Klan until it reappeared in the early 1900s. But the Klan's initial success
proved to be a terrible omen of the fate that would befall Reconstruction.
Although many white Southerners accepted the end of slavery, they stub-
bornly resisted efforts to grant African Americans any political rights. One
by one, white southern Democrats managed to topple every Republican-
controlled state government through a combination of bullets and ballots.

The North won the war and the nation would no longer be burdened by
the question of slavery, but in 1877 the Civil War produced an ambiguous
peace settlement that profoundly shaped the legacy of the war. Inconsis-
tent Republican efforts to reshape the South politically through force of
arms and empowerment of African Americans collapsed with the end
of Reconstruction. Indeed, southern African Americans eventually had

most of their political and economic rights stripped away. The rise of tenant farming and the crop-lien system of agriculture eventually reduced many African Americans, as well as large numbers of poor whites, into debt peonage.[39]

Eventually, the majority of northern Republicans bade farewell to the bloody shirt and joined Democrats in urging sectional reconciliation. This abandonment stemmed in part from a frustration with continued southern intransigence and in part from a desire for economic stability. Business interests found in the New South an excellent source of raw materials and cheap labor, particularly because of its depressed wage scales. To a large degree, white Southerners had met business leaders' conditions for reunion by allowing them to exploit the economic resources of the region. In the 1870s and 1880s, a new southern elite, favoring commercial and industrial development, emerged. As the federal government stopped its periodic intervention on behalf of African Americans, white Southerners moved to embrace the nation. Although supporters of a New South wanted reunion, they did not ignore the old Confederacy. Instead, they joined southern veterans in forming organizations, building monuments, and organizing massive ceremonies to the Lost Cause.[40]

During the last two decades of the nineteenth century, former Confederate soldiers displayed increased interest in veterans' organizations. The United Confederate Veterans (UCV), founded in 1889, attracted the largest number of veterans. According to one estimate, by the early 1900s as many as one in three living Confederate veterans had joined the UCV. In a number of ways the UCV paralleled the GAR in organization and purpose. Members belonged to local units called *camps,* which were largely autonomous. Above the camp, there were several layers of hierarchy on the state, regional, and national level. As in the GAR, officers in the UCV bore military titles and usually were former officers. Also like the GAR, the UCV acquired an auxiliary organization for women and later one for the sons of veterans.[41]

To a large degree the UCV took responsibility for building monuments and organizing Memorial Day ceremonies separate from the ladies' memorial associations. The monuments built by the UCV and their women's auxiliary, the United Daughters of the Confederacy, as well as other citizens' committees and governmental bodies, differed from their Reconstruction era counterparts. Cemetery obelisks gave way to soldiers' monuments placed outside county courthouses or in city squares, just as had happened in the North. These statues, often mass produced by commercial monument firms, usually featured a lone Confederate soldier with his musket standing at parade rest. In larger communities scores of monuments went up to the memory of commanders such as Robert E. Lee, Stonewall Jackson, and even President Jefferson Davis.[42]

Monuments and ceremonies dedicated to the Confederate cause took on a celebratory cast. Even Confederate Memorial Day, although focusing on the dead, had a less-than-melancholy air about it. Instead of emphasizing defeat, orators focused on the bravery, courage, and tenacity of the average soldier. The UCV annually sponsored widely attended national conventions that featured scores of speeches, social events, and a huge parade with the Confederate and American flags displayed prominently side by side.[43]

As did the leaders of the New South, veterans' organizations came to minimize the importance of slavery in leading to the Civil War, emphasizing instead constitutional issues involving state sovereignty and opposition to federal intervention. Although veterans and New South leaders insisted that the South had no reason to apologize for defending their legitimate rights, they publicly expressed few regrets about the outcome of the war. Few longed for the rebirth of the Confederate republic, and most insisted that the South remain solidly part of the economically growing nation. Some New South leaders speaking at Confederate Memorial Day ceremonies even suggested that the outcome of the Civil War helped the South by finally removing the curse of slavery.[44] In accepting reunion, however, Southerners had demanded autonomy over race relations and insisted they be allowed to celebrate the Confederate cause as an honorable one. But in many ways the crucial force behind reconciliation was northern Republicans. They not only abandoned African Americans but also joined Democrats in sponsoring a whole series of gestures granting legitimacy to the Confederate cause.

Northerners, especially Republicans, did not forget who had won the Civil War. As sentiment for reunion grew in the North, it spurred a wave of monument building. Many communities built monuments for the first time or commissioned additional ones. In the District of Columbia the federal government erected a series of monuments to leading Civil War generals, including, eventually, a supreme memorial to Abraham Lincoln. In 1889 Congress made Memorial Day a national holiday.[45]

In the 1890s and early 1900s there began a conscious effort to declare that the battles of the Civil War had finally ended. Memorial Day orators no longer stressed the need for vigilance against southern attempts to overturn the victory. Instead, they emphasized the importance of healing sectional divisions that had been intensified by the war. To underscore this theme of reconciliation, Southerners increasingly served as Memorial Day orators at Gettysburg and other major battlefield sites in the North. The GAR and other veterans' organizations often took part in joint reunions and encampments with their Confederate counterparts. In 1915, when a Long Beach, California, GAR post and a citizen's monument committee erected a memorial to Abraham Lincoln, it sought contributions from Confederate as well as Union veterans. The monument committee engraved an unfurled American flag on the pedestal bearing Ulysses S. Grant's memorable appeal: Let Us Have Peace. Although the GAR post conducted the dedication ceremony for the memorial, they selected a Long Beach clergyman who had been a native of the Confederate state of Tennessee to deliver the principal address.[46]

Beginning with President William McKinley in the late 1890s, successive Republican administrations made a number of gestures to honor the Confederate dead, in part as a way of gaining southern support for the GOP. Under McKinley, a former Union officer, a special Confederate burial area was created at Arlington National Cemetery. His successor, Theodore Roosevelt, signed legislation allowing the federal government to assume responsibility for the care of Confederate graves in the North. Roosevelt's successor, William Howard Taft, approved a bill allowing the United Daughters of the Confederacy to erect a Confederate memorial in Arlington National Cemetery. Union veterans buried in private cemeteries had been entitled since 1879 to a headstone issued from the War Department; just before leaving the presidency in 1929, Calvin Coolidge signed a bill that accorded the same right to Confederate veterans.[47]

In the 1890s Congress started acquiring Civil War battlefields as permanent war memorials to prevent commercial enterprises from intruding on them. Although purchased as national memorials, national military parks at Chickamauga and Chattanooga, Gettysburg, and Antietam commemorated a nationhood that recognized the strong ties of local community, statehood, and region. Congress allowed states and veterans' associations the right to build markers and monuments in these parks honoring their individual regiments. As a result, Civil War battlefields included monuments to Confederate as well as Union regiments.[48]

Those who favored purchasing the sites of major Civil War engagements insisted that they should be saved because of the epic nature of the battles fought there. In arguing for the purchase of the Chickamauga and Chattanooga battlefield, a House committee on military affairs report noted that the number killed on this field exceeded the death toll of many other famous European battles of the nineteenth century. And there was a pragmatic reason for authorizing this and other military parks: Congress mandated that they serve as a training field to study tactics and terrain for U.S. Army officers, placing them under the jurisdiction of the War Department.[49] In saving Civil War battlefields, the federal government granted equality of commemoration to both the North and South.

Even before the actions of Congress, Pennsylvania and other northern states in the 1880s appropriated public funds to purchase large sections of the Gettysburg battlefield and to erect monuments honoring state units. The Gettysburg Battlefield Memorial Association, a Pennsylvania chartered organization, supervised the preservation and marking of the battlefield but confined its activities to the battle lines and places associated with the Army of the Potomac.

When the federal government created a national military park at Gettysburg, it took control of the holdings of the Gettysburg Memorial Association and expanded them to include parts of the battlefield associated with the Confederate army. To a large degree, the federal government had little choice but to permit the continued marking of the battlefield with state-erected tablets and statues. By acquiring Gettysburg, the national government made it possible, both politically and culturally, for southern states and veterans' associations to place memorials at this northern battlefield. National military parks in the South made it easier for northern states and units to erect memorials there by creating landscapes controlled by the federal government.

Few places on earth possess as many monuments as the Civil War battlefields owned by the federal government. In the case of Gettysburg, state and veterans' organizations built nearly four hundred monuments. They range from the massive memorial building adorned with sculptured figures erected by Pennsylvania to statues representing soldiers in a range of battle actions. Equestrian statues dot the landscape and recall the role of generals from both sides. Hundreds of markers erected by the Gettysburg Battlefield Memorial Association, states, regimental associations, and the federal government also mark the battle lines.

The battlefield memorials erected by regimental associations and state governments at Gettysburg offered a vision of nationhood that recognized the primacy of local and state ties. Most Civil War regiments had been raised by individual communities, and the battlefield monuments that commemorated their service often reflected their unique ethnic and regional identity. Shamrocks adorn scores of memorials commemorating the service of New York regiments that compromised the Irish brigade. At the dedication of the monument to the Forty-fifth New York Regiment, Christian Boehm addressed his comrades and guests in German.[50]

Many southern states and Confederate military veterans' organizations built memorials on the Civil War battlefields preserved by the federal government, actions that gave rise to controversy and debate. For instance, Mississippi legislators who favored building a state memorial at Vicksburg had to overcome objections that such memorials tended to commemorate a northern victory. At Gettysburg, most Confederate veterans' organizations refused to erect monuments because of a federal policy that called for memorials to be erected in the "position occupied by the command in the main line of battle" and permitted only "subordinate tablets" to be placed at the advanced positions reached by military units. In the view of former Confederates, this rule unfairly discriminated against their units and ignored the fact that earlier northern monuments had not been subject to this rule.[51]

Although most memorials at Gettysburg and other military parks recalled the battlefield contributions of individual units, some monuments consciously evoked the theme of peace. For example, New York styled the monument it placed on the Chickamauga and Chattanooga battlefield as a peace monument. As a gesture of reconciliation, the federal government sponsored two Blue and Gray reunions at Gettysburg on the fiftieth and seventy-fifth anniversary of the battle. At the fiftieth anniversary gathering in 1913, aging veterans promised to sponsor a peace memorial to symbolize the reconciliation that had taken place between the North and South. Congress fulfilled this pledge, and the federal government built a peace tower in time for the final Blue and Gray reunion in 1938.[52]

Around the turn of the century, there remained dissenting voices who objected to a reconciliation that allowed for recognition of the Confederate cause as an honorable one. In 1910 the New York branch of the Loyal Legion of the U.S., a society of former Union officers, vigorously protested before Congress proposals that called for the erection of a national monument in Washington, D.C., to Robert E. Lee. They declared that it was bad enough that those who had committed treason and openly rebelled against the United States should be honored by the federal government with monuments or inscriptions in federal cemeteries, but the line must be drawn with regards to a memorial in the nation's capital.[53]

There were other voices objecting to the move toward reunion. Frederick Douglass and other African American leaders insisted that reconciliation came at too high a price. The South had been forgiven without repentance and without according African Americans full citizenship. To many African American leaders, the Civil War remained a war of liberation, and Abraham Lincoln was above all seen as the Great Emancipator. They feared that the drive for reunion would marginalize their group's place in the war and would encourage the spread of a series of racist-laden myths regarding African Americans and slavery in the North.[54]

Douglass's fears came to pass in the 1880s and 1890s. Only a handful of Civil War memorials commemorated the service of African American soldiers. Even when remembered in monuments, their role would often be marginalized, either given postures of deference and separation or placed in the background. In a monumental group completed by Frederick MacMonnies in 1900 for the Brooklyn Memorial Arch, a lone black sailor kneels while his white counterparts stand behind him. Even the monument built by the Boston Brahmins to the memory of Colonel Robert Gould Shaw and the fallen of the all-black volunteer regiment, the Fifty-forth Massachusetts Infantry, remained ambivalent about the question of race and the Civil War. The Shaw memorial, dedicated in 1897, was created by Augustus Saint-Gaudens and placed in the Boston Commons across from the Massachusetts statehouse. It featured a bas-relief that depicted the young colonel on horseback with his men marching in the background. On the back of the monument, inscribed on the stone pedestal, the Shaw Monument Committee listed the names of the officers, all white, killed in the assault on Fort Wagner in 1863, but included none of the names of the enlisted soldiers who died in the same attack. In his published memoirs, issued several years later, Saint-Gaudens displayed an attitude toward African Americans, particularly the models he hired for the Shaw monument, that was demeaning, patronizing, and racist.[55]

Many white Southerners insisted that chattel bondage be remembered as a benevolent institution that civilized savage Africans. In their view, paternalistic masters and mistresses presided over plantations filled with happy-go-lucky "darkies." White Southerners at Confederate reunions, Memorial Day ceremonies, and even in congressional speeches, recalled the slave, particularly the faithful "Mammy," who had remained loyal to the owner even as the Union armies approached. In 1937 the United Daughters of the Confederacy dedicated a stone at Harper's Ferry, West Virginia, to Heyward Shepherd, a former slave who had refused to join

Shaw Memorial dedication, Boston, 31 May 1897. Augustus Saint-Gaudens's monument to Colonel Robert Gould Shaw and the Fifty-forth Massachusetts Regiment is one of only a handful of monuments erected in the North that commemorates the Civil War service of African American soldiers. (Photograph by James H. Smith and William J. Miller; courtesy Massachusetts Historical Society)

John Brown's raid. An inscription on the memorial stone not only praised Shepherd's loyalty but also asserted that he was representative of thousands of faithful Negroes who resisted temptation and stayed with their masters during the Civil War.[56]

Many Union veterans approved of and supported the reunion movement. By the 1890s Blue and Gray reunions, often on the sites of former battlefields, were common. Union veterans, like northern business interests, had a price for reconciliation—generous pensions from the federal government. President Grover Cleveland's veto of liberalized pension bills for veterans laid the groundwork for the GAR's fiery opposition to his plan, during his first term in office, to return captured Confederate flags to the South. In 1905, after the eligibility requirements for a disability pension had been eased by congressional and executive action in the 1890s and 1900s, Congress returned the battle flags with hardly a murmur of protest.[57]

In the drive for reconciliation, Abraham Lincoln was remembered less as an opponent of slavery and more as someone who had wanted to heal the divisions caused by war. Southern Democrats joined Republicans in supporting a national memorial to him. In 1911, when a Democratic House had been elected for the first time since 1892, Congress established a special commission and appropriated money to build a suitable memorial. The commission settled on a Greek temple and a statue by Daniel Chester French of a somber Lincoln seated in an imposing chair. Above the statue the commission inscribed the words With Malice Toward None. In contrast to the Freedman's Memorial to Lincoln erected by African Americans in 1876, there were no images of African Americans on the new national memorial. Lincoln's tomb in Springfield, Illinois, featured images of Civil War soldiers whereas the new national memorial had none.[58]

Largely as a result of his nobility in defeat, Robert E. Lee emerged as a national hero. To many Northerners, Lee represented a noble aristocratic world doomed by the onslaught of industrial development. Although no memorial to Lee was ever built in Washington, D.C., Congress provided monetary compensation to his family for turning their plantation in northern Virginia into Arlington National Cemetery. To underscore reconciliation, the Arlington mansion, along with its original furnishings and reproductions, was declared a national historic site in 1925 and turned into a museum illustrating Lee's family life prior to the Civil War.[59]

During the 1890s and early 1900s, equestrian statues appeared in Washington, D.C., to Sherman, Sheridan, Logan, and other heroes of the war. The death of Ulysses S. Grant in 1885 led to an outpouring of interest in commemorating his military career. In 1897, when the general was entombed in a massive tomb built by a private association of New York business and civic leaders, more than a million New Yorkers attended the ceremonies. In Chicago, Philadelphia, St. Louis, and other major cities equestrian statues were built to his memory and dedicated with great fanfare.[60]

Equestrian statues in the early Republic had been controversial, associated as they were with monarchical Europe. Their use in commemorating Grant and other generals, North and South, reflected a shift in attitude toward war and toward the role of the military in society. In short, national and regional elites viewed war as a noble and heroic affair. In recounting his Civil War experiences in the early 1900s, Oliver Wendell Holmes remembered the "incommunicable experience of war" as a time of "glory" and "heroism."[61]

Sectional reconciliation that centered on the battlefield coincided with a vision that associated military achievement with nationalism. During the late nineteenth and early twentieth centuries, many national leaders, most notably Theodore Roosevelt, argued that the United States must maintain a large navy and adopt a system of universal military training. Before the First World War, the U.S. Military Academy at West Point actually used Civil War battlefields to instruct cadets on tactics.

National reconciliation thrived on remembering the Civil War with monuments, ceremonies, and organizations. By focusing on the battlefields, memorials to the common soldier and to generals permitted both the North and South to avoid or to minimize the political issues surrounding the conflict. In 1916, James M. Greer, a Confederate veteran and judge, greeted a delegation of Minnesota veterans who were taking part in the dedication ceremonies of a state monument in the national military cemetery in Memphis, and maintained that the experience of war had not aroused any "animosity" between "Johnny Rebs" and "Yanks." To his "one-time enemies," Greer insisted that "whatever bitterness came out of that struggle" developed only "after the Great Lincoln and Grant had lost their power and the small politicians succeeding them gave to this section of our common country the horrors of Reconstruction—when white men of your section sought to make of black men in our section a ruling class for which they were most unworthy."[62]

Although the mutual experience of war remained the central focus of the commemoration of the Civil War, few wanted to recall the brutal nature of combat. Generally, when veterans talked about war, they described it as an occasion of courage and honor. At reunions, particularly joint Blue and Gray ones, they dwelt at length on the comradeship among soldiers, even between former enemies.[63] The monuments built in town squares and on the battlefields echoed these themes. Death and destruction were not ignored; they retained a heroic quality and were represented as serving a transcendent purpose. Monuments depicted dying and wounded soldiers as remaining steadfast to the end. Fictional literature that tried to offer a realistic portrayal of combat fell far short in fully capturing the total horror of the war.[64] Not that the violence and bloodshed was ignored by the ablest writers of the post–Civil War years. The lost innocence of the raw recruits of 1861 as they confronted the carnage of the battlefield remains an important theme in a host of novels, most notably Stephen Crane's *The Red Badge of Courage*. Nonetheless, even the most realistic writers of the war, both participant and nonparticipant, despaired of ever communicating the

Secretary of War Harry H. Woodring stands between the commanders of the
United Confederate Veterans and the Grand Army of the Republic during the
federally sponsored seventy-fifth anniversary encampment at Gettysburg in 1938.
(Photograph courtesy National Archives, 111-SC–109184)

full extent of the filth, boredom, and fear that made up the experiences of
the average combatant.

Even the suffering that took place at Andersonville and other southern
prison camps was glossed over by many veterans and northern states. During the Reconstruction era, the memory of Andersonville aroused anger
among many veterans and it remained an important theme in the bloody-
shirt campaigns of the Republican Party. Despite reconciliation, however,
Andersonville was not completely forgotten. In the early 1900s, New York,
Minnesota, and several other northern states erected monuments at the
national cemetery there. Although these monuments mourned the dead,
they remained free of any symbolism that aroused sectional passions. At
dedication ceremonies, Northerners stressed the heroic qualities of the
Union soldiers imprisoned in Andersonville but also added: "The war is
over and with it ceased all anger and hate."[65]

Could sectional reconciliation have taken place without commemorating war as a courageous enterprise? A great many veterans failed to join veterans' organizations or talk about their wartime experiences until several decades after the conflict had passed. In 1876, the Pennsylvania Centennial Exposition banned works dealing with the war in its officially sponsored art exhibition.[66] Centering reunion on the shared experiences of the soldiers—as in the encampments—meant that much of the interest in commemoration would fade as Civil War veterans passed away. Succeeding generations had not participated in the war and, therefore, did not find its ceremonies or monuments as compelling. In the closing years of the nineteenth century, veterans bemoaned the commercialization of Memorial Day and the tendency of many Americans to enjoy picnics or other recreational activities on that solemn occasion. Sons of GAR and UCV members did not flock to join the auxiliary organizations attached to these two societies. Instead, the women's auxiliaries, composed mainly of widows, became one of the principal custodians and interpreters of the Civil War in both regions.[67]

The divisions spawned by the Civil War continued to be remembered, although in muted forms. Jefferson Davis remained a controversial figure in both the North and South, and in the North he never gained the same esteem as Robert E. Lee. Although a number of southern communities built monuments to honor the Confederate president in the 1880s and 1890s, many white Southerners remained divided over his role in the war. To a number of them, Davis should have shouldered much of blame for the collapse of the Confederacy. In much the same way, James Longstreet remained a scapegoat among Lee's generals for his supposed failures at Gettysburg.[68]

In the twentieth century, Confederate symbols, monuments, and organizations were used to differentiate the South from the rest of the country. For example, during the civil rights movement of the 1960s, white southern segregationists used the Confederate flag as a symbol of white supremacy and defiance against federal intervention. In the early 1990s, African American leaders began to call on states and the federal government to remove any official or semiofficial sanction of Confederate symbols.[69]

The rise of a new mass medium, the motion picture, offered a way of remembering and preserving the memory of the Civil War that encouraged white Americans to accept racism as the price of sectional reconciliation. On the fiftieth anniversary of the war, D. W. Griffith issued *Birth of a Nation*, which persuaded his audience to remember the tragic nature of this struggle and focused attention on the supposed evils of Reconstruction. The plot of this 1915 motion picture denigrated abolitionists, portrayed African Americans as either faithful Uncle Toms or corrupt sexual monsters threatening white womanhood, and depicted Reconstruction as an attempt to impose African American and carpetbag tyranny on virtuous white society. The film lauded the role of the Ku Klux Klan in saving the South from the evils of Reconstruction and in protecting the virtue of southern white women.[70] Lincoln remained a hero in the film, not for his championing of emancipation but for his intended policy of moderation toward the South.

The boycott and protests of the newly formed National Association for the Advancement of Colored People (NAACP) failed to dampen the box-office success of *Birth of a Nation,* but it encouraged Hollywood to mute or ignore the role of African Americans in the Civil War. As in the monuments and commemorative addresses delivered on Memorial Day, most features stressed telling the story of valor and heroism found on both the Union and Confederate sides. To further cloud or minimize the question of race, cinematic depictions of the war often focused on the war's western and frontier campaigns.[71]

Hollywood's use of the Western motif as a means of focusing attention away from the Civil War was not a unique tactic. Those who authored the movement for reunion through monuments and gestures of reconciliation sensed that the divisions engendered by the Civil War would linger. To minimize and counteract the divisions, they sought to remind Americans of earlier conflicts that came to be remembered as a time of national unity. During the late nineteenth and early twentieth centuries, national cultural, business, and political elites showed a renewed interest in building monuments, forming organizations, and creating holidays commemorating the American Revolution, the War of 1812, and the Mexican-American War, as well as the Civil War.

Beginning in the 1870s, a wave of activity began to commemorate the American Revolution. In 1876 millions of Americans flocked to Philadelphia to visit an international exhibition designed to celebrate the centennial of American independence. Congress appropriated the necessary funds to complete the unfinished giant obelisk monument to George Washington in the District of Columbia. At the same time, Congress proved more willing to provide matching grants to individual associations that wanted to mark revolutionary battlefields with memorials. Long-dormant chapters of the Society of Cincinnati experienced a revival as grandsons of the revolutionary generation flocked to join them. Descendants of the common soldiers who fought in the Revolution and were denied membership in the society formed their own societies, beginning with the Sons of the American Revolution (SAR) in 1877. By the close of the nineteenth century, a whole series of genealogically based societies had formed to preserve the memory of the Revolution and of other events associated with the nation's early history.[72] This interest in commemorating the Revolution crossed sectional lines. After Reconstruction, Southerners once again embraced the Fourth of July as their own holiday. Independence speakers and newspaper editorials in the South stressed Americans' common heritage, noting that it had only been interrupted by the Civil War.[73]

Even before the Reconstruction era had ended, state organizations of Mexican-American War veterans began appearing in the South. In 1876 former Confederate president Jefferson Davis addressed the Louisiana Associated Veterans of the Mexican-American War. In his address, Davis recounted the achievements and valor of Americans in this conflict and noted that they had come home from war

> with hands empty of plunder, they came with hearts free from the stain of injustice or cruelty to the helpless, they left behind them no widow of a non-combatant husband slain on the family hearth, they left no orphans destitute because of the destruction or appropriation of their property by the invading army. They came back poorer than they went, except in that which is the true soldier's treasure—*honor, Honor.*

Without even mentioning the Civil War in the speech, Davis had implied that the Union army had lacked the virtue of an earlier American army composed mainly of Southerners. He went on to declare that these noble men of the South, who had "brought to the altar of their country the priceless sacrificial offering of fame without spot or blemish,"[74] should be granted a pension by the federal government.

Over the course of the nineteenth century an increasing number of Union veterans and their families received pensions from the federal government. By the early 1900s at least one half of all elderly native-born American males in the North received a pension as a result of Civil War service. Although business interests often resisted the expansion of the federal pension, Republicans in Congress bowed to political pressure from the GAR in order to maintain the support of veterans.[75]

Although cut off from Civil War pensions, southerners who had served in the War of 1812 and the Mexican-American War claimed pensions by virtue of their service in these earlier conflicts. With little controversy, War of 1812 veterans managed to gain federal pensions in the early 1870s, but Republicans opposed granting them to their Mexican-American War counterparts because of the number of former Confederates who would benefit. Not until the Democrats regained control of the White House under Grover Cleveland in 1885 did these veterans finally gain a pension. By granting Mexican-American War veterans a monthly stipend, Democrats allowed the South, a vital region for them politically, to share in some of the federal largesse dispensed in the form of pensions.[76]

Veterans—both northern and southern—claimed that service to the nation granted them a special status that went beyond the right to pensions. Veterans also insisted that they serve as the prime custodians of the memory of the conflict in which they fought. Even when war memorials were built with public funds, former combatants wanted to oversee their design and construction. They hailed themselves as guardians of the national interest. To this end the GAR lobbied state legislatures to mandate the teaching of American history in the public schools, promoted military preparedness, and encouraged the display of the flag by citizens.[77]

During the late nineteenth century, many native-born whites, Anglo-Saxon Protestants of the middle and upper classes, who joined the burgeoning number of genealogical societies claimed that their ancestry made them the proper interpreters of the Revolution and of key events in American history. The Daughters of the American Revolution (DAR) and other societies worked to preserve historic sites, and to build monuments, and they took part in a whole array of additional holiday celebrations. Often they prodded local and state governments, and even the federal government, to do the same.

The cultural role of these societies and the renewed interest in the Revolution and other wars was complex. To a certain degree, native-born elites used ancestry to differentiate themselves from the new immigrants of the nineteenth century. Nonetheless, both the DAR and SAR represented a limited effort to democratize the memory of the Revolution by allowing the ancestors of the common soldiers a role in commemorating this struggle and by rejecting the claims of the revived Society of Cincinnati that only eldest male sons of officers should be the legitimate custodians of the Revolution.

The commemorative activity of the DAR and other societies served to give primacy to material objects over ideas in the depiction of the past. In a sense, the scores of statues and other artifacts and places served to draw attention away from the more radical aspects of the Revolution and other wars. Moreover, by saving the residences of generals and great statesmen and not those of urban workers or free African Americans allowed the role of the latter to be forgotten or obscured. The feverish attempt to acquire cannon, muskets, and other items associated with past wars represented an effort to portray historical memory as resting in material objects.[78]

The focus on material objects implied that their owners—governments, private genealogical societies, individuals—served as the principal custodians of the memory of war. But in other ways, the emphasis on material objects, as a means of remembering war, served to broaden the definition of what from the past remained important. This further increased the role accorded to women. The historic home was a central focus of many genealogical societies, particularly the DAR. Once saved and turned into museums or "restored," these homes often focused attention on daily life in the revolutionary era or in other periods in American history. The display of furnishings, kitchen implements, and other household items declared that the domestic sphere remained an important part of the memory of the past, particularly of the American Revolution.

In remembering the past, national political leaders at times wanted to define a less-inclusive vision of nationhood, one that remained wary of the new immigrants from southern and eastern Europe. Theodore Roosevelt and others advanced a new organic theory of nationalism that emphasized the need for unity among Americans and viewed participation in the military as one of the most important forms of service a loyal citizen could render to his country. This theory was challenged by an older humanistic and legalistic tradition of patriotism that insisted that the ideals of freedom, justice, and the promotion of peace could be the only true foundations of the American nation. Those who aspired to this vision of patriotism were more tolerant and frequently took issue with those who equated chauvinism, jingoism, and militarism with loyalty. At the same time, proponents of older definitions of nationalism remained far more comfortable with the influx of new immigrant groups to American shores.[79]

Ethnic groups challenged efforts to homogenize the past or to write them out of the American Revolution. During the late nineteenth century, immigrants in many communities sponsored monuments to their respective heroes of the War of Independence: the Poles honored Casimir Pulaski and Thaddeus Kosciusko; the Irish, John Barry; the Jews, Haym Salomon; and the Germans, Frederick Wilhelm von Steuben. In many places, the birth dates of these figures were commemorated with parades, dinners, and festivals. With increasing success, various ethnic organizations lobbied Congress for permission and financing to erect memorials to their revolutionary heroes in Washington, D.C. When Congress authorized a monument to an ethnic hero, it established a special commission to oversee its erection and invariably this body included representatives from the particular ethnic group. For instance, the president of the Pulasksi monument committee was designated by Congress to serve as a member of the federal government's Pulaski memorial commission. In addition, the specially appointed memorial commissions usually selected a sculptor with the same nationality of the hero honored.[80]

In many cases native-born Protestant elites endorsed projects to honor foreign-born heroes of the Revolution. For instance, both the Daughters and the Sons of the American Revolution supported the campaign by the National Commodore John Barry Statue Association to build a memorial in Washington, D.C. In 1910 the secretary general of the Society of Cincinnati welcomed an invitation to participate in dedication ceremonies for the Pulaski and Kosciusko monuments. But at the same time, this secretary reminded the statue commission that the proper protocol required the Society of Cincinnati to march ahead of all other private associations. In an eight-page letter, the secretary general described the society's participation in recent memorial dedications and anniversary celebrations designed to commemorate the Revolution.[81]

The sensitivity of the Society of Cincinnati to proper protocol highlighted the attitude of native-born Americans toward efforts to commemorate ethnic heroes. To a large degree, ethnic memorials were accepted as long as they offered a message supporting the established order. When President Woodrow Wilson spoke at the dedication of the Commodore Barry Memorial in 1914, he declared that the late naval hero "was an Irishman, but his heart crossed the Atlantic with him." In a time of concern about divided loyalties, Wilson deplored the hyphenated American who had not passed the "infallible test of a genuine American—that when he votes or when he acts or when he fights, his heart and his thought are nowhere but in the center of the emotions and the purposes and the policies of the United States."[82]

No doubt Wilson aimed his remark at many in the Irish American community who wanted the United States to take a strong stand against British imperialism, particularly in Ireland. In a 1904 speech urging a Barry Memorial, Representative Michael Driscoll recited the accomplishments of the man he called the father of the American navy. At the same time, this New York congressman reminded his colleagues that unlike such heroes as Rochambeau, Steuben, and Pulaski, Barry could not return to his native land because he had fought against the British. By honoring Barry, the nation remembered a great man who was born in "poverty, adversity, and circumscribed environments" and who had been forced to flee "an oppressive and shortsighted government." To Driscoll, a memorial to Barry served as a reminder of British tyranny and of the wars waged by that imperial power against the United States.[83]

In 1910 the District of Columbia's chapter of the SAR protested against the inclusion of the European battle of Reclawice in Poland, a battle in which Kosciusko also fought, on the pedestal of the Kosciusko memorial. In the view of the association, reference to this event on a U.S. memorial was "not in keeping with the History of the American Revolution." They also felt that such a reference might offend Russia, a nation with whom the United States had "ever been friendly." The SAR thought that such a inscription created a bad precedent for future memorials.[84]

Perhaps the most intense opposition of native-born elites to an "inappropriate" ethnic memorial occurred in Boston. When the state legislature in 1887 proposed building a monument to the victims of the Boston Massacre, a number of good brahmins of the Massachusetts Historical Society howled in protest. In their view, those "hoodlums, rioters, and ruffians" remained unworthy figures and should not be associated with the struggle for independence. Despite this outcry, Boston city officials went ahead with the memorial and commissioned a monument that featured several common people, including Crispus Attucks, a West Indian–born former slave killed by British troops. The Boston Massacre Memorial remained one of only a handful built during the nineteenth century that commemorated African American participation in any war.[85]

Professional artists, sculptors, and architects, and even some commercial monument makers, also criticized memorials built by ethnic groups, but they did so on aesthetic grounds. They rebuked ethnic groups for their propensity to erect "cheap" and "garish" monuments. To stop this trend, the art community called for the establishment of public art commissions at all levels of government to rule on the suitability of public art and architecture. In praising the idea of a municipal art commission, *Monumental News*, a trade journal for commercial monument makers, praised the disinterested art commission for ending the prevailing custom of "allowing anything in the form of a monument to be erected in public places." It commended the Chicago Art Commission for turning down an equestrian statue of Kosciusko proposed for a city park. In the view of *Monumental News,* Poles would eventually be grateful for being forced to chose a new sculptor who would produce a "meritorious work of art."[86]

At first glance, the rise of municipal art commissions appears motivated by a desire on the part of native-born white Protestant elites to create another "disinterested," nonelected, "professional" commission to assert control over ethnically controlled city governments. The American Federation of Arts, the National Sculpture Society, and the Municipal Art Society of New York lobbied state and local governments to establish art commissions to pass judgment on public art and architecture. In 1890, beginning with Boston, and soon followed by New York, Chicago, and Philadelphia, several cities established such commissions.[87]

The effort by professional art organizations and art commissions to control the design of public monuments built by ethnic organizations represented more than simply a chauvinistic effort on the part of native-born Americans to impose their parochial view of culture. To begin with, many of the leading "American" professional sculptors and artists of the period were foreign born, most notably Augustus Saint-Gaudens. Moreover, many native-born artists received their training and took up residence in Europe, often in Paris and Rome. For many professional American artists, the beaux-art school of Paris was the model to emulate.[88]

Immigrants from southern and eastern Europe were not the only targets of public art commissions. Veterans received some of the harshest criticism for their repeated "defacement" of American battlefields and town squares with cheap, mass-produced, commercial monuments. Isabel McDougall, writing in a *Chicago Evening Post* article reprinted by *Brush and Pencil,* lambasted the monument proposed by the state of Illinois for the Civil War battlefield on Missionary Ridge. Selected by a committee of GAR members, the memorial consisted of what McDougall called a "silly stiff, thick-jointed, graceless" goddess of victory surrounded by four bronze soldiers who had "arms and legs like sausages, clad in misfit uniforms." For this "travesty" of art, Illinois contemplated spending eighteen thousand dollars. McDougall maintained that the Missionary Ridge fiasco was not an isolated case; more than 75 percent of Civil War memorials depicted the "everlasting infantryman at parade rest," and "50 percent of these were made from the same model."[89]

Artists and their allies formed professional associations such as the National Sculpture Society and publicized the need for art commissions. They

*No More of Those Hideous Monuments!* This cartoon reflects the sentiments of professional artists and sculptors in the late nineteenth and early twentieth centuries against mass-produced soldier monuments. (Photograph by Gordon Miller; reprinted from *Puck*, 19 August 1885)

wanted to replace mass-produced commercial monuments with memorial art completed by specially trained artists who had the proper credentials. Stylistically, fine memorial art from the past could not be reproduced, but it drew on the classical Greek, Roman, and Renaissance styles for inspiration and for allegorical symbols. Even realistic statues, sculptors said, should conform to the ancient Greek principles of beauty and form. In short, good "modern" memorial art remained a synthesis of both the new and the timeless.[90]

Professional artists and sculptors, as well as their political supporters, maintained that good memorial art should encourage Americans to emulate the heroic deeds portrayed and to support a strong military establishment. In their view, the obelisks and bronze-soldier monuments that had typified American monumental art had failed on these accounts. The American sculptor Frederic Wellington Ruckstull observed that these memorials offered "consolation" but failed to offer inspiration to the next generation. In a 1902 address at the Boston Public Library, Ruckstull maintained that a good monument should not only inspire the next generation but also stimulate fathers to "resolve to push his boy as far as he can on to a finer manhood, and to make him his votive offering to his country and thus enrich mankind with the most royal gift a father can offer."[91]

Although public art commissions increased in number and influence, their success in stopping "bad" monumental art remained spotty. In a 1910 article in *Art and Progress,* James Barnes concluded that countless battlefields had been disfigured more "than they ever were by shot or shell" with bad monumental art and that most local and national cemeteries were similarly spoiled. He expressed hope regarding recent trends in memorial building in large urban centers but feared that "smaller towns may still continue, in all ignorance, their work of self-disfiguration."[92]

At times veterans and other locals openly resisted the judgment of professional artists, sculptors, and architects, but not always with the loftiest of motives. In 1898, the GAR post in Jersey City sued to prevent the Soldiers' and Sailors' Monument Committee from erecting a memorial selected by a professional jury composed of three sculptors from the National Sculpture Society. In the GAR's view, the choice of a female Victory lacked the proper "martial character," and they questioned the use of Greek mythological symbols to represent a period in the history of New Jersey. The Hudson County Granite and Marble Dealers' Association joined the GAR post in opposing Philip Martiny's *Victory.* The commercial monument makers protested awarding an outside commission to a New York sculptor and insisted that a local monument firm could provide a better monument at a lower price. However, the New Jersey Chancery Court refused to issue an injunction halting construction of the memorial. The judge declared that the monument committee had made the monument appropriately commemorative for the state by listing the names of Jersey City soldiers and sailors who had died in the war. The court also claimed that time would show the superiority of the design:

It is exceedingly difficult to get at the average taste of the individual in this matter . . . The scholars of an academy would have one opinion, the children of a lower school another opinion, while barroom habitues would advance still another. According to the popular mind, when the educated taste of the individual is perhaps better developed, the design accepted by the committee represents war. The leaves, the sword and the inverted torches are to the educated mind symbolic. The world is advancing to a higher degree of knowledge and this monument is to stand for ages.[93]

Professional sculptors and artists considered the conflict over the Jersey City monument to stem from both the public's lack of understanding of the nature of good memorial art and the crass self-interest of commercial monument makers. As far as some veterans were concerned, however, the symbols and allegorical figures professional sculptors used were inappropriate for the purposes of monumental art. In their view, they should be the ultimate interpreters of the war, and they therefore were reluctant to cede authority to groups who claimed superior credentials. Commercial monument makers saw the problem from another perspective. Often these firms used the rhetoric of professional sculptors and stressed the need for better designed memorials. *Monumental News* urged monument makers to work together through associations in order to upgrade design standards and applauded the growth of public art commissions.[94]

Some commercial monument makers, nevertheless, viewed professional sculptors as a threat, or at least feigned this position. The *Monument Retailer*, a short-lived trade publication, complained that sculptors with their professional associations and competitions sought to shut out the high-quality monument maker even if he submitted a worthy design. In a November 1916 editorial, the *Retailer* attacked the two artists of the Civil War Army and Navy Monument Committee in Scituate, Massachusetts, for resigning after the three GAR members voted in favor of a design submitted by local monument makers instead of supporting one by a prominent sculptor, Augustus Lukeman. The editorial conceded that the monument selected by the committee reflected "no credit upon the craft" and that in the past monument makers had "sacrificed art to the unshapely masses that bulk the quarry." Nonetheless, the Scituate incident suggested that art associations wanted to build an impassable barrier between artist and the monument houses. In short, by forming associations, professional sculptors practically guaranteed their success in competition. The lesson for commercial firms was to establish and join associations.[95]

Many of the issues surrounding the role of the artist in creating public memorials came to a head in the congressional debate over the creation of the Commission of Fine Arts. The establishment of this body in 1910 marks the first time that the federal government created a permanent agency charged to provide expert advise on the aesthetic merits of public art and architecture in the District of Columbia. Although it had little legal power, it played a central role in shaping the development of Washington, D.C., and the national memorials built there in the twentieth century. When Representative Samuel W. McCall of Massachusetts and Senator Elihu Root of New York proposed legislation to establish the commission, several members of Congress raised strenuous objections. They protested the continued delegation of political power to unelected commissions in the executive branch staffed by professionals with what they considered dubious credentials. The dissidents felt that the "professionals" had erred too often in the past. Many obliquely criticized the master plan developed for the District of Columbia by Daniel Burnham, Charles McKim, Frederick Law Olmsted, Jr., and Augustus Saint-Gaudens when they served in 1901 as members of the Senate Park Commission, better known as the MacMillan Commission after its chairman, Senator James MacMillan of Michigan. Many blamed the recommendations of this body for placing the Agriculture Department building on an unsuitable site. Several hinted that the assistance of Daniel Chester French and other professional sculptors had led the Ulysses S. Grant Memorial Commission to place the Grant monument in a location that only served to deface Washington's botanical gardens.[96]

Representative Michael Driscoll of New York, the leading proponent of the Commodore Barry Memorial, argued that a presidentially created Council of Fine Arts, founded by President Theodore Roosevelt shortly before leaving office in 1909, favored a design for the Barry monument that remained "pedestrian" and that portrayed this distinguished naval officer as a "swaggering Bowery tough on a rolling deck." Driscoll thought the monument should commemorate a heroic American of Irish descent, but this body favored a statue that, in Driscoll's words,

represented a fountain with a pool of water around it, with a long frieze of bold-relief figures, starting in with the history of Ireland when the people were naked or clothed in skins. It undertook to represent various events and misfortunes in the history of the Irish people, from the baptism of the King of Tara by St. Patrick down to the present time. . . . the driving of the native people toward the west, their misfortunes and their miseries; and finally it represented various Irish immigrants, men and women, landing at Castle Garden absolutely nude.[97]

Despite the objections of critics such as Driscoll, Congress overwhelmingly voted in favor of creating a national Commission of Fine Arts. The fear expressed by critics that the commission would be dominated by one school of style proved correct. From 1910 until 1945, the sculptor members of this body remained committed to the French-inspired beaux-arts style and envisioned good monumental art as adhering to the classical and Renaissance principles of beauty. Although the commission wanted monumental art to avoid too slavish an adherence to classicism, it remained cool toward modernistic designs. The members favored memorials that made extensive use of allegorical designs drawn from ancient Greece and Rome, and they remained a strong proponent of the MacMillan master plan. The Commission of Fine Arts argued that the founders of Washington, D.C., had conceived of it as a classical city and that it should, therefore, continue to be developed along such lines. As a result, most national memorials constructed after both world wars remained firmly in the classical tradition.[98]

The widespread use of classicism contributed to the movement to gloss over the brutality of the Civil War and the world wars. It reflected an effort to minimize and rationalize the tremendous suffering these conflicts caused. To a large degree, it encouraged those who wanted to make modern warfare acceptable as it emphasized the heroic nature of battle and of dying for one's country.

In remembering the nation's wars, the nation's elites in the late nineteenth and early twentieth centuries not only wanted to confirm the validity of that struggle but also to encourage harmony and peace within American society. By commemorating the Civil War, they sought to heal the divisions it caused. By remembering the Revolution and the postrevolutionary wars, they attempted to further instill a vision of nationhood that viewed sectional and other divisions in American society as transitory. But focusing on the military aspects of past struggles, and viewing war as central to the national identity, had a price.

In the late nineteenth and early twentieth centuries, many intellectuals portrayed war as an aberration of an earlier "less-civilized" age. It was argued by positivists like Auguste Comte that industrialization and the growing importance of international commerce served to make war increasingly obsolete. This confident view had great currency, not only in the United States but also in Europe. Organized peace movements grew in strength, although they remained for the most part an affair of the genteel middle and upper classes. On the world stage some nations appeared to be moving in the direction of the peaceful settlement of disputes through arbitration. International conferences at The Hague and elsewhere during this period led to a series of treaties that "humanized" warfare and protected prisoners of war.[99]

Not everyone welcomed the prospect of peace fostered and ensured by interdependency in a new age of ever-expanding markets and the globalization of culture. Some, like Theodore Roosevelt, feared that unchecked industrialization threatened to commercialize all aspects of human life and would serve to undermine the masculinity of men. Some who supported public art commissions insisted that these bodies served to limit the worst excesses of capitalism by promoting the beautiful and the enduring, values that seemed threatened by the tyranny of profit. Although a terrible affair, war was viewed as a time of individual courage, comradeship, and noble sacrifice.[100]

Although efforts to commemorate the Civil War and other conflicts stressed the terrible costs and the blessings of peace, war came to be seen as an acceptable option when the national interest was at stake. Some advocates of a strong national military establishment, such as naval strategist Alfred T. Mahan, argued that a strong navy was vital to a country's security and position in the world.

To a certain extent, many Americans were looking for a war in the late 1890s. In 1898 Spain provided the United States with an easy adversary and the necessary pretext for armed conflict. In the eyes of many Americans, the United States needed to go to war with Spain in order to liberate Cuba. The competing Hearst and Pulitzer newspapers published scores of lurid stories of Spanish tyranny and cruelty. But jingoists were not the only ones to deplore Spain; William Jennings Bryan and many other midwestern agrarians expressed sympathy for the plight of Cuba.[101]

The destruction of the *Maine* in Havana Harbor served as the spark that led to America's first foreign war since 1849. Although little evidence linked Spain to the explosion that sank the *Maine,* it made little difference to the press, to much of the public, and to many within the McKinley administration, who were stirred by the slogan, "Remember the *Maine.*" Only sabotage, many thought, could explain the loss of the *Maine,* and those who died aboard her must be remembered and their deaths avenged. Within days of the sinking, the Hearst newspapers in New York City began a campaign to raise a memorial to the martyrs of the *Maine* and to wage war with Spain. In the end, William McKinley reluctantly bowed to pressure and led the United States into war against a nation that had wanted to avoid one.[102]

At the beginning of the war, scores had flocked to join state-raised volunteer regiments, but only one such unit, the Rough Riders, ever left Florida. The regular army did most of the fighting, and in many ways the Spanish were the least formidable obstacle facing American forces. Insufficient planning on the part of the War Department resulted in ill-equipped and poorly supplied troops who failed to observe the most elementary standards of sanitation. As a result, although little more than one hundred soldiers died at the hands of the Spanish, more than one thousand succumbed to disease. The Spanish-American War became a "splendid little war" for the United States, both at sea and on land. American fleets annihilated Spanish naval forces in Manila Bay and Santiago Bay. Admiral George Dewey's triumph in the Philippines catapulted him into national prominence and made him a likely presidential nominee. To greet Dewey's stunning victory and return, New York City staged an elaborate welcoming ceremony and parade. The National Sculpture Society volunteered its services to the city and built a huge temporary victory arch adorned with statues.[103]

Despite the fact that professionals had won the war, most Americans associated the conflict with the dashing image of Colonel Theodore Roosevelt and the Rough Riders. According to Roosevelt, the Spanish-American War had allowed his generation the chance to distinguish themselves on the battlefield. And as he noted in his 1907 address dedicating a memorial to the dead of his regiment in Arlington National Cemetery, a few had the "supreme good fortune of dying honorably on a well-fought field for their country's flag." During the early 1900s the former lieutenant colonel portrayed his volunteer regiment as a model for dealing with the sectional, economic, and ethnic tensions inherent in American society. At one reunion of the Rough Riders in 1905, Roosevelt spoke of the wide variety of men brought together in the pursuit of glory—Harvard and Yale men, the wealthy and the cowboys, new immigrants and men who traced their ancestry back to the Mayflower.[104]

Roosevelt praised the Rough Riders and minimized the role of regular units, particularly of an African American regiment, in achieving victory against Spanish forces on San Juan Hill in 1898. Nonetheless, President Roosevelt worked to professionalize the American military and to institute universal military training. When war broke out in Europe in 1914, Roosevelt added his voice to the chorus urging that the United States prepare for war. For the rest of his life, Roosevelt argued that the Spanish-American War had been a necessary conflict that had strengthened the nation. But other Americans remained less sure of what this conflict had accomplished and raised doubts about the way the United States had entered it. Moreover, the decision of the McKinley administration to retain the Philippines and turn it into an American colony provoked fierce debate at home. Many Filipinos demanded immediate independence and waged war on the United States.

The Philippines Insurrection proved to be everything the Spanish-American War had not been. It lasted more than three years and ended with more than four thousand Americans and one hundred thousand Filipinos dead. To suppress the guerrilla campaign, the United States resorted to torture and to a scorched-earth policy to starve out the rebels. In the United States, opponents of intervention denounced as immoral the tactics used to suppress the insurrection and urged withdrawal.[105] Unlike the Spanish-American War, the Philippines Insurrection became twentieth-century America's forgotten war. No national monuments were built by the federal government, and public discussion of the war diminished soon after it ended. Until 1922 the federal government denied veteran's status to U.S. soldiers involved in the conflict.

The Philippines Insurrection influenced the way many Americans viewed the Spanish-American War. It helped diminish Dewey's reputation, for example, and discouraged efforts to venerate his victory. In 1899 a number of cities organized celebrations on the anniversary of his victory at Manila Bay, but in the early 1900s, these celebrations ceased as Dewey's conduct in negotiations with Filipino leaders during the Spanish-American War were questioned. The Dewey Arch in New York City never became a permanent memorial and was eventually torn down.[106] Although Americans distanced themselves from Dewey, they still remembered the *Maine*. Throughout the early 1900s, the annual anniversary of the sinking, on 16 February, sparked memorial services in New York and elsewhere. Veterans and others urged Congress to discover the actual causes of its sinking in 1898 and to retrieve the *Maine* from Havana Harbor in order to recover the bodies of those who had died.[107]

In 1910 Congress appropriated the funds necessary to salvage the *Maine*, but it took two years before the Army Corp of Engineers accomplished its mission. The bodies of those who had died were recovered from the sunken ship and returned to the United States for burial in Arlington National Cemetery. President William Howard Taft, members of Congress, military attachés from the diplomatic community, military units, and a host of others attended a memorial service. Rev. Father John P. Chidwick, a Roman Catholic Priest who had served on the *Maine* as chaplain, delivered the principal oration, in which he dwelt on the tragic character of the events of 1898.[108] Although Chidwick affirmed that the United States had fought in Cuba for a noble cause, he offered a pluralistic vision of nationalism that urged Americans to work for peace:

About the graves of our dead we shall lift our hearts to God in thanksgiving for all that God has done for our country, but let no bitter or resentful feeling dwell within them. Let us renew our patriotism in peace as we excite it to sacrifice in war. Would

The salvaging of the USS *Maine* in Havana Harbor. The hull was raised from the bottom, towed out to sea, and sunk with honors. The mast of this ship became part of a memorial in Arlington National Cemetery; some other parts of the ship were incorporated into monuments throughout the United States. (Photograph courtesy National Archives, 111-SC–84882)

that we have loved her with the same pure, disinterested love when God blesses us with tranquillity and prosperity as we do when He tries us in danger and war. . . . Over the graves, let us recall and pledge ourselves to our ideals—brotherhood in the citizenship of a land which recognizes, encourages, and develops the rights and gifts of every one of her children, whosoever he may be, and . . . that we may be gathered as brothers about the throne in the land beyond the blue.[109]

As for the ship itself, sections were removed and turned into relics. For instance, the main mast became part of the funerary memorial at Arlington to those who had lost their lives on the ship. The foremast went to the Naval Academy and was displayed at Farragut Field. Communities across the nation received smaller parts of the ship. For example, Columbia, South Carolina, acquired a small cannon; a shell was placed in a monument in Queens, New York; and Woburn, Massachusetts, gained a ventilator cowl. The anchor went to the U.S. Spanish War Veterans, one of the veterans organizations that emerged from the conflict, which melted it down to make membership insignias for its members. The parts that did not become relics were buried at sea. The U.S. Navy towed the hulk of the *Maine* out to sea off the coast of Cuba and then sank her as part of an elaborate ceremony.[110] What remains most striking about the continued interest in remembering the *Maine* was the growing acknowledgment by the navy and by many others that the Spanish government might not have been responsible for sinking the ship. During the early 1900s some, in the navy and elsewhere, had argued that the *Maine* sank because of an internal explosion, not as a result of an external one.[111]

Time served to transform the *Maine* from a crass jingoistic symbol into a more ambiguous and tragic one. To a great many Americans it stood in sharp contrast to the bellicose image of Teddy Roosevelt and the Rough Riders, who not only viewed war as acceptable but also welcomed it. Divisions that developed over how the Spanish-American War should be remembered influenced the ways in which Americans viewed the onset of war in Europe in 1914. To some, like Roosevelt and Mahan, the Spanish-American War confirmed the need for preparedness and supported the notion that war was a noble and heroic enterprise. But to others, such as William Jennings Bryan, Andrew Carnegie, William James, and other anti-imperialists, war, including the Spanish-American War and the Philippines Insurrection, remained an evil the United States should avoid at all cost.

Burial services of sailors recovered from the USS *Maine,* held at the south end of the old State, War, and Navy Department building, Washington, D.C., 23 March 1912. These ceremonies helped transform the ship, sunk in 1898, from a jingoist symbol to a more melancholy one. (Reprinted from J. Heller, *War and Conflict,* National Archives, 1990, 89; original source, Office of Building and Grounds)

# 3

# REMEMBERING
# THE WAR TO
# END ALL WARS

Woodrow Wilson displayed little of Abraham Lincoln's reserve as he took the United States into its first European war. When Lincoln led the North into the Civil War, he insisted initially that the war was to save the Union, not to abolish slavery. He waited for more than a year before turning the conflict into a war of liberation fought on ideological grounds. In 1917, however, Wilson portrayed World War I as a Manichaean struggle between good and evil. It had to be won not to advance narrow self-interest or to protect American commerce, but to build a new democratic world order. Idealism played a major part in moving the country toward war.

Soon after America entered the conflict, the Wilson administration organized a massive public relations campaign to win support for the war. The Committee of Public Information blanketed the country with posters, speakers, and tracts that depicted a united nation ready to sacrifice for the good of all mankind. According to the committee, America fought a foe who committed the most vile atrocities. By defeating the Hun in a "war to end wars," the United States would create a "world safe for democracy." Despite the fervid pitch of American propaganda, the United States was reluctant to enter the conflict and did so only after a long, torturous debate.

Rural isolationists and a number of ethnic groups, particularly Irish and German Americans, staunchly opposed America's entrance into the conflict. Wilson himself was reelected president in 1916, in part, as a result of the slogan, "He Kept Us Out of War." Even after German attacks on American merchant ships in early 1917, a majority of Americans were ambiguous about entering the war. Americans had not rushed off to fight; for the first time the nation raised a wartime army largely through conscription. Many on the political Left refused to support the war, insisting that it was fought to protect capitalist interests. Labor unrest afflicted many key industries. The loyalty of many newly arrived ethnic Americans, particularly German Americans, remained suspect, as the war exacerbated the divisions already present in society.

In order to quell dissent, all levels of government supplemented propaganda with coercion. The Wilson administration jailed antiwar activists under the Espionage Act and considered drafting striking workers. It stood aside in the face of an unprecedented wave of vigilante activity aimed at suspected radicals, German sympathizers, and "slackers." Despite the divisions, however, the United States triumphed, and in contrast to other combatants, it emerged from the war with increased prestige, wealth, and power. But victory did not ensure domestic tranquility. Many Americans feared that the revolutionary climate gripping Russia and much of Europe could easily cross the Atlantic. In 1919 millions of American workers went on strike, race riots engulfed several northern cities, and a number of national leaders became the target of terrorist bomb attacks. Southern and eastern European immigrants received much of the blame for these upheavals. Under the direction of Wilson's attorney general, A. Mitchell Palmer, the federal government summarily deported hundreds of suspected foreign-born radicals.

Although Germany had been crushed, many Americans remained uncertain over what the war had accomplished. Wilson called on the country to embrace the League of Nations in order to guarantee a lasting peace. But the league treaty foundered in the Senate as critics charged that it would abridge national sovereignty and had the potential to draw the United States into another European conflict. In 1920 Wilson called on Americans to make the election of his successor a referendum on the league. Instead, they elected a president who promised to return the country to "normalcy."[1]

After the Armistice, national leaders rushed to build monuments and create rituals honoring America's victory. Through these monuments and rituals, they hoped to camouflage the divisions caused by the war. They wanted Americans to expiate their doubts, and sometimes their guilt, about this ambiguous conflict. National leaders wanted desperately to define an American identity that supplanted class, ethnic, and sectional loyalties. As portrayed in stone and in ceremony, America's first European land war remained an idealistic struggle for liberty and democracy waged by a united people. A new association, the American Legion, the largest organization of First World War veterans, viewed itself as champion and protector of the war's heritage. Founded in Paris in 1919, the legion proclaimed that its mission, along with preserving the comradeship of the battlefield, was to inculcate and disseminate the principals of "Americanism" as a bulwark against the threat of radicalism.

To the dismay of national leaders, however, rancor engulfed efforts to commemorate the First World War. Heated controversies developed over what types of monuments should be built at home. Many progressive reformers wanted to replace traditional memorials of stone with utilitarian structures. Art organizations heaped scorn on the living-memorial movement and insisted that a worthy monument must be devoid of self-interest. A fierce debate even emerged over the question of whether the fallen of the war should be buried at home or remain abroad.

Soon after the United States entered World War I, the War Department began to consider where the dead from this conflict would be buried. Following the Spanish-American War and the Philippines Insurrection, the federal government had repatriated the bodies of the several thousand soldiers who had died in these two conflicts. Most families, therefore, assumed that if their son had died in France, his body eventually would be returned to them.

Volunteers stepped forward to aid the army in discharging its responsibilities to the war dead. The Purple Cross, a newly created funeral organization, offered to send a legion of embalmers to France to ensure that those who died in battle received adequate care. According to the organization, "Each American Hero" who died in battle could be returned to the states in "a sanitary and recognizable condition a number of years after death" if they had been dealt with using the latest advances in mortuary sciences.[2] A skeptical War Department rejected the services of the Purple Cross and instead planned initially to entrust the burial of the dead to the newly created Graves Registration Service of the army. The slow pace of mobilization and the lack of adequate shipping forced the American

Expeditionary Force commander in France, General John J. Pershing, to limit the role of the service in December 1917. As in earlier conflicts, Pershing ruled that individual units must assume prime responsibility for the burial of their battle dead. The Graves Registration Service would be responsible for registering all graves, and for concentrating on hasty or scattered burials. Scarce cargo space certainly could not be used for burial supplies or equipment and, moreover, repatriation of the dead would certainly have to wait until the end of hostilities.[3]

When the war was over, many within the army, in Congress, and in other positions of leadership argued that the war dead should remain interred overseas as a symbol of U.S. commitment to Europe. Former president William Taft, American Federation of Labor president Samuel Gompers, American Expeditionary Force chaplain Charles H. Brent, and other supporters of overseas burial formed the American Field of Honor organization in January 1920 to work for the establishment of overseas cemeteries. This society insisted that the "sacred dust" of American soldiers had made the soil of cemeteries in France forever American, a place where the Stars and Stripes would always fly.[4]

The army, particularly the Quartermaster Corps, objected to the repatriation of the war dead for more practical reasons. They noted many of the logistical problems in removing thousands of decomposing bodies from France. Despite their misgivings, Secretary of War Newton D. Baker, insisted in 1919 that his department would honor its commitment to bring fallen soldiers home. Baker allowed family members to make the final decision on whether they wanted their next of kin to remain in France, to be brought home for internment in a national cemetery, or to be returned to them for burial in a family plot.

Supporters of the overseas cemeteries waged a vigorous campaign in 1919 and 1920 to convince widows and parents not to bring their husbands and sons home. They pointed out many of the obvious problems in disinterring bodies that had been buried from one to three years. For example, war-devastated France raised serious objections to using scarce railroad stock for the return of war dead. Although never fully comfortable with publicly bringing up the subject, proponents of overseas burial did from time to time note the tremendous financial cost of the undertaking. Many privately hoped, therefore, that the French would forbid the removal, thus taking the decision out of the hands of the federal government.[5]

Instead of dwelling on the financial and logistical problems of repatriation, supporters of military cemeteries in France emphasized the continued service the war dead could perform for their country and for Western civilization. Each individual soldier's grave would serve as an enduring monument to the cause of freedom for which they bled and died. By not scattering the war dead across the United States, by leaving them massed together in France, their valiant role in history would not be forgotten or obscured. Moreover, the presence of fallen American soldiers in France served to heighten the bonds of friendship between the two countries. Already, it was claimed, the French people treated American graves with reverence and considered them "sacred."[6]

By leaving their loved ones in Europe, family members, especially mothers, were asked to make one final sacrifice for their country. Parents were urged by the opponents of repatriation to follow the example of former president Theodore Roosevelt, who after learning of the death of his son Quentin, insisted that he be buried on the spot where he fell. Roosevelt declared that the proper resting place for a warrior was on the battlefield.[7]

Most families, however, refused to join Roosevelt in making an additional offering to the nation. Nearly 70 percent of them opted for repatriation. At the same time, many feared that the federal government would use French objections to the repatriation as a pretext for maintaining cemeteries in Europe. In 1919 some formed the Bring Home the Soldier Dead League to ensure "an American tomb in America for every American hero who died on foreign soil." Often inspired by league efforts, letters poured into Washington, reminding the Wilson administration and Congress of their commitments. As one mother bluntly told Secretary of State Lansing, "You took my son from me and sent him to war . . . my son sacrificed his life to America's call, and now you *must* as a duty of yours bring my son back to me."[8]

The fight over what to do with the war dead became a bitter one. Supporters of repatriation insisted that France wanted to benefit by the maintenance of overseas cemeteries. One congressman suggested that France hoped to gouge thousands of sorrowing Americans who would have to journey across the ocean in order to see their loved ones' graves. Another feared that France planned to keep American soldiers buried in France as "hostages" in order to compel the United States to defend their graves if German aggression should reappear.[9] Those who wanted American cemeteries in Europe attempted to portray unscrupulous funeral directors as the driving force behind the movement for repatriation. In fact, some funeral-industry trade publications and organizations had bluntly talked about the financial gain to be made from bringing home fifty thousand bodies. Although their connection remains nebulous, the funeral industry had played a major role in organizing the campaign for repatriation. Nevertheless, the movement would not have succeeded without the strong desire of most parents and widows for their sons and husbands to be brought back to the United States.[10]

In the end, the War Department heeded the wishes of the parents and widows. More than 70 percent of those killed in the First World War came back to the United States, after France dropped its objections to removal in March 1920. For the remaining war dead, the United States established permanent cemeteries in France, Belgium, and England. What is striking is where the United States opted *not* to maintain some of its cemeteries. In 1919 the War Department decreed that the American dead would be removed from Russia, Germany, and the former Austro-Hungarian Empire. This decision highlighted the degree to which the American cemeteries on the Continent were designed to serve as reminders of the ties that existed between the United States and her former allies, particularly England and France. The *New York Times* applauded the decision to bring home the dead from "desolate" Russia, insisting that this land had offered no "associations for them or for us to make it a suitable resting place." In sharp contrast, the fallen soldier could sleep in France as if he were in "another home." It urged survivors to allow the war dead to remain in France so that their "fame can best be preserved through the centuries."[11]

When the War Department and the U.S. Commission of Fine Arts began to design the overseas cemeteries and monuments, they wanted them to symbolize a vision of uniform nationalism. Citing British practice, both insisted that there should be no distinction in the care accorded to officers or enlisted personnel. According to British custom, United States' officers were buried next to their men and commemorated with identical headstones.[12] Equality of commemoration represented an effort by the commission and others to foster a vision of American nationalism that stressed the voluntary and willing sacrifice of the individual to the nation as a whole. The uniform gravestones that varied slightly in their inscriptions symbolized the submergence of individual identity to the nation's cause. They also reflected Theodore Roosevelt's belief that military service should minimize class and regional differences. As a result, an army general from a patrician background rested next to newly arrived immigrant from eastern Europe.

Military service entitled each man to be treated equally. This symbolic egalitarianism was no small right in a society in which poverty was so widespread that many Americans were buried in potter's fields.

Although the War Department and Commission of Fine Arts adopted several British practices concerning war cemeteries, they nevertheless wanted to make the cemeteries distinctly American. Britain lost more than a million men in the war and maintained hundreds of cemeteries on the Continent. Out of necessity, the British left little space between graves and marked them with large individual headstones. Because the United States had suffered far smaller losses, about fifty-five thousand men, both the War Department and the commission decided to concentrate burials into eight large cemeteries in Europe in order to ensure cemeteries large enough to serve as sufficient symbols of American participation in the conflict. A concurrent desire was to recreate the parklike setting that characterized the soldiers section of Arlington National Cemetery by planting an abundance of trees and a thick carpet of grass. In contrast to British cemeteries, they allowed more space between graves and planned to identify each with a smaller headstone.[13]

The War Department and Commission of Fine Arts hoped, for both symbolic and aesthetic reasons, to prevent the profusion of monuments that had engulfed Civil War battlefields. They believed that any memorials built in France must commemorate the entire nation; they sought to avoid scores of artistically flawed state and private monuments. To ensure that American battlefields were properly marked and to thwart private efforts, the War Department established the Battle Monuments Board in order to mark important battlefield sites in Europe with bronze plaques offering historically correct information. In 1923, Congress, at the urging of the Commission of Fine Arts and the War Department, vested oversight responsibility for the construction of all overseas memorials and cemeteries in a newly created independent agency, the American Battle Monuments Commission. Those who lobbied for this commission wanted it to regulate with the utmost care the private and the state monuments planned for Europe. The War Department insisted also that this new, presidentially appointed commission carry out the plans of the Battle Monument Board to mark the overseas cemeteries.[14]

The American Battle Monuments Commission, chaired by General John J. Pershing, consisted of Senator David Reed of Pennsylvania, a member of the House of Representatives, members of three veterans' organizations, and a mother who had lost her son in France. Soon after the

Sunset at an American cemetery in France, taken sometime during the late 1920s and 1930s. (Photograph courtesy National Archives, 66-G-7A-12)

commission opened for business, it worked to have France and Belgium prohibit all American war memorials not approved by the commission. Following French precedents, in contrast to practice during the Civil War, it declared that no regimental monuments would be allowed in Europe, only branches of the service, divisions, or other larger units could be honored. Although the commission approved some monuments proposed by Pennsylvania and other states, it frowned on monuments that honored troops "from a particular locality."[15]

In 1926 the commission required that all monuments proposed by state governments or private groups have a utilitarian, not just a commemorative, function. In announcing this policy, it declared that the official memorials contemplated by the commission were adequate for commemorating U.S. participation in the First World War. It noted that European nations contemplated few memorials and that a proliferation of American monuments of dubious merit would be in poor taste. Even if built by private groups or state governments, these monuments would be viewed by Europeans as American memorials. Given the fewer casualties suffered by the United States, even a modest number of nonfederal monuments would be "conspicuous" and "create an entirely erroneous impression of the American object in erecting them."[16]

By banning all but utilitarian monuments, the commission wanted to ensure the primacy of its own memorials. In 1925 it had abandoned earlier proposals to mark American battlefields with relief maps because they would be located in a region of France and Belgium few Americans ever visited. The commission determined that Americans and others would be drawn to the battlefields only if they contained impressive monuments and cemeteries. As a result, the commission decided to build several large monuments to mark the most important American engagements of the war. To commemorate several other noteworthy, but lesser, actions, it planned a second tier of less-expensive monuments and commemorative tablets. For each cemetery it planned a nondenominational chapel.[17]

The American Battle Monuments Commission wanted its monuments to represent continuity between the past and present. Architecturally, most memorials drew on classical or medieval designs. Invariably then, when the Commission of Fine Arts reviewed submitted designs, it placed them in the context of the Western architectural tradition. One member of the Commission of Fine Arts applauded a design for the Montfaucon monument that called for a large ceremonial column to be erected, because the column represented the "highest form of architecture" and had been the "product of an intellectual age." He cited "famous monuments of the world" that incorporated columns, beginning with the Trajan Column and ending with "our First Division Memorial, A.E.F."[18]

No one would mistake the chapels planned for the overseas cemeteries as anything other than Christian places. In another attempt to forge national unity, the American Battle Monuments Commission and the Commission of Fine Arts wanted to identify American nationalism with Christianity. When the president of the Jewish Welfare Board, Cyrus Adler, criticized the use of the cross in the design of the Suresnes Chapel, its architect, Charles A. Platt, wrote that he had been led to believe that although the chapels should be nonsectarian, "they were Christian." Platt announced his willingness to remove the cross if ordered to by the American Battle Monuments Commission, observing caustically that "if the Jews are strong enough to prevent us from using any insignia of the Christian religion, I suppose I shall have to comply with their desire." The Commission of Fine Arts refused to order the cross's removal, insisting that the board's authority extended only to aesthetic questions. As for the American Battle Monuments Commission, it refused to remove the cross from Suresnes and took full responsibility for the use of Christian symbolism. In fact, when the architect of the Somme Chapel, George Howe, refused to use such symbolism, the commission became disturbed. Howe submitted a design for the Somme Chapel that served as an "adaptation of a Roman tomb," but the commission rejected this stark, windowless block initially because its exterior was not based on "Christian ritual." In order to appease his patron, Howe added both "Romanesque" windows and a crystal cross to light the altar.[19]

The cross developed into a central symbol of the American overseas cemetery. During and immediately after the war, the army marked soldiers' graves with temporary wooden crosses or Stars of David, but the War Department planned to replace each of them with a single permanent headstone of uniform size that contained the appropriate religious symbol engraved near the top. In the view of the War Department and the Commission of Fine Arts, such headstones served to minimize "individual character" and promoted harmony of design. Despite these plans, however, the American Battle Monuments Commission decided in 1924 to adopt the marble cross, and where appropriate a marble Star of David, as the permanent headstone for the overseas cemeteries. In reversing their earlier policy, the commission responded to pressure from a number of religious and veterans groups that insisted that the public associated the cross with the American cemeteries.[20]

The use of the cross indicates the degree to which many Americans, particularly many national elites, considered the United States a Christian nation. In addition, it suggests a great deal about how they viewed the war. Although the cross signified the promise of resurrection in the Christian tradition, it also stood for suffering and sacrifice; by adopting it, Americans declared symbolically that the war dead had offered their lives in order to redeem the nation. Their loss remained extraordinary and far removed from the profane. But it also showed a lack of sensitivity to non-Christian Americans who also had made the highest sacrifice.

The war dead were not the only ones being honored for their sacrifice; Americans also focused their attention on the contribution made by mothers who had lost their sons in the war. Known as Gold Star Mothers because of the star they were urged to display in their homes during the war, these women won praise for sacrificing their sons to the nation. The

Gold Star Mothers served as the theme of many speeches and poems commemorating the First World War, and monuments were erected in their
honor. Gold Star Mothers formed their own organizations, which sought
to preserve the memory of the First World War and to emphasize their role
in nurturing those who had fought in it.[21]

During the 1920s, Gold Star Mothers' societies lobbied vigorously for
a federally sponsored pilgrimage to Europe for mothers with sons buried
overseas. They insisted that the federal government owed every mother
who had sacrificed her son to the nation at least one visit to his grave. Gold
Star Mothers and their supporters in Congress dwelt on the inseparable
bond between mother and child. As one Gold Star Mother declared, they
had given their sons freely to the nation, and their hearts were "just breaking for the sight of the grave of their boy."[22]

A Gold Star pilgrimage to France proved impossible to resist politically,
and throughout the 1920s scores of congressmen sponsored legislation to
authorize funds for such a trip. Although few publicly questioned the wisdom of the idea, some in Congress and the War Department grumbled
about the cost. When the subject emerged, however, authors of pilgrimage
bills noted that the mothers who had not brought their sons back to the
United States had saved the federal government more than $23 million.
Given these figures, they insisted the cost of such a pilgrimage was irrel-
evant.[23]

In 1929 Congress passed legislation authorizing the secretary of war to
allow Gold Star Mothers and widows with next of kin buried overseas to
travel to Europe as guests of the nation. The notoriously frugal Calvin
Coolidge signed this legislation shortly before he left office in March 1929.
The administrations of Herbert Hoover and later Franklin D. Roosevelt
authorized these pilgrimages from 1931 to 1933, even as the Depression
raged and federal government reduced expenditures in the face of deficits.

The Gold Star pilgrimages provide a remarkable insight into the way
many mothers and the larger society attempted to portray and define the
relationship that existed between mother and son and the war dead of the
nation. The Gold Star pilgrimages declared that a woman's greatest role in
life remained that of mother and nurturer. It maintained, moreover, that
the maternal bond surpassed the paternal one. Although there had been
some talk of including fathers in the pilgrimage, in the end Congress decided that only women could take part. Interestingly, widows received invi-
tations almost as an afterthought. The sponsor of one unsuccessful 1924

A group of African American Gold Star Mothers preparing to leave for Europe in
the early 1930s. (Photograph courtesy National Archives, RG 92, Office of the
Quartermaster General Miscellaneous File, 1922–1935, 004.511)

pilgrimage bill excluded them because he believed that their relationship
with their husbands paled to that of mothers and their sons.[24]

The Gold Star pilgrimage served to affirm that those who had died for
their country in Europe had fought for a noble cause. In a sense the lavish
care extended to the mothers and widows during their journey sought to
highlight how exceptional their contribution had been. From the moment
a mother or widow stepped aboard a train to leave her hometown, the
federal government paid all reasonable expenses. Before their European
departure, Gold Star pilgrims assembled in New York and attended a
reception in city hall, where they were greeted by local civic officials. As
specified by Congress, women taking part in the pilgrimage traveled cabin
class, stayed at first-class hotels, and had an army officer, physician, and
nurse accompany them abroad. Not only were pilgrims taken to the graves
of their sons and husbands, but each party spent a week in either Paris or
London and were honored by the French or British government with receptions.[25]

A delegation of American Gold Star Mothers laying a wreath at the Tomb of the Unknown Soldier in France. (Photograph courtesy National Archives, RG 92, Office of the Quartermaster General Miscellaneous File, 1922–1935, 004.511)

The War Department and press accounts of the pilgrimage stressed how each woman who participated received the same treatment. War had united women from all walks of life and regions of the country by creating a common bond. Socialites and farm women; Catholics, Protestants, and Jews; native born and foreign born had all sacrificed their sons to the nation and now shared the same feeling of loss.[26]

Yet not all women received the same treatment. The Gold Star pilgrimage offered a vision of nationhood that placed African Americans in a subordinate position. The War Department segregated black pilgrims from their white counterparts, going so far as to place them on separate ships. Whereas the white pilgrims traveled aboard luxury liners, the African Americans crossed in commercial steamers. Neither the protest of African American organizations nor the refusal of some African American Gold Star Mothers to take part in the pilgrimage convinced the War Department to alter its policy.[27]

Accordingly, Jim Crow accommodation for African American Gold Star Mothers and widows reflected the unequal status granted their sons and husbands. African American soldiers had fought in segregated units and were disproportionately assigned to service in subservient and menial support positions, usually with the Quartermaster Corps. The unpleasant task of disinterring, removing, and reinterring the scattered graves of the war dead had usually fallen to African American units. Even in death they were separated from the white soldiers. The army and the wider public ignored or trivialized their achievements, and no African American regiment marched in the great victory parade held in Paris on Armistice Day in 1919. Efforts by Hamilton Fish, a Republican congressman from New York, to build a monument in France to the U.S. 369th regiment, a highly decorated African American unit attached to the French army, faced the opposition of the American Battle Monuments Commission. The overwhelming majority of war monuments built abroad and at home depicted soldiers as white.[28]

The treatment accorded to the African American soldier remains one of the most glaring contradictions in efforts to portray the First World War as a struggle for democratic principles. But this was by no means the only paradox in efforts to commemorate America's first European war. For example, although the overseas monuments and cemeteries proclaimed America's strong ties to Europe, the U.S. Senate refused to ratify American participation in the League of Nations. The monuments offered a picture of a united people who had willingly submerged their separate identities to the nation, but the majority of parents and widows asked that their next of kin be returned to their hometowns. A pluralistic vision of nationhood competed with one that defined America as a nation of white Christians.

Like those abroad, the monuments built at home sought to celebrate and define the nation. And similarly, sharp differences emerged over what type of memorial would best promote this end, each side in the debate insisting that it sought to serve the greater good of society while the other merely wanted to further narrow self-interest. The bitter divisions that emerged over the commemoration of the First World War at home reflected the important role national and community leaders wanted monuments and rituals to play. They were seen as a means to help produce consensus in a fragmented society.

Many progressive reformers insisted that efforts to remember the Civil War had left a dubious legacy in the form of useless and horrendous stat-

An American Gold Star Mother signing the Memorial Book during ceremonies in the early 1930s at the Tomb of the Unknown Soldier in France. (Photograph courtesy National Archives, RG 92, Office of the Quartermaster General Miscellaneous File, 1922–1935, 004.511)

Reaching the ultimate goal of the Gold Star pilgrimage, an American mother stands beside the grave of her fallen son at an American military cemetery in Europe. (Photograph courtesy National Archives, RG 92, Office of the Quartermaster General Miscellaneous File, 1922–1935, 004.511)

ues. Urging Americans not to repeat this mistake in commemorating the First World War, they recommended living memorials, instead, including bridges, parks, libraries, playgrounds, and community centers. War memorials, they maintained, should contribute to the reconstruction of American society and meet the needs of communities. To many, community centers and auditoriums, nicknamed "Liberty Buildings" or "Memorial Buildings," could best accomplish this task and also capture and inculcate the democratic spirit of the war.[29]

Professional recreation workers supported the memorial buildings, believing they would serve as bases of operations for their efforts to mobilize communities. In 1919 a grant from the Laura Spelman Rockefeller Memorial Fund enabled Community Service, Inc., an organization affiliated with the national Playground and Recreation Association, to start a public campaign on behalf of memorial buildings. The *American City* called on municipal managers to embrace liberty and memorial buildings as a means of promoting community harmony and as a scheme of municipal improvement. Not only did the magazine devote large amounts of editorial space to publicizing the need for these structures, it even organized a coordinating committee to promote their adoption.[30]

In describing the goals and purposes of the memorial building, the *American City* waxed eloquent about what they could accomplish. Memorial buildings would serve to unite the communities by meeting a wide variety of needs. In addition to auditoriums, they could contain pools, gymnasiums, classrooms for adult education, and office space for community organizations. Going beyond the settlement house, these buildings would serve all the people, not merely a section or class. To ensure this, they must be kept free of "party, class, or sectarian aims" and within them, "employer and employed, Republican and Democrat, Catholic and Protestant, Jew and Gentile, man and woman, must stand on an equal footing."[31]

Supporters of memorial buildings insisted that such structures be funded through voluntary contributions, not through taxes. And to be effective, they must reflect and meet the needs of each individual town or city. The desire to seek widespread "popular" support for memorial buildings and to avoid government funds stemmed from a wish on the part of the living-memorial advocates to limit the amount of coercion needed to achieve reform in society. They stressed that America's success in the First World War stemmed from an effective mobilization of the home front through publicity and public education.

Memorial-building advocates' aim to promote civic unity and the public good had, however, a more ominous side. Like other progressive reforms, the vision of community remained one that was wary, even hostile, toward immigrants and organized labor. By claiming that memorial buildings united all citizens, those not included could be considered beyond the pale. As one proponent of memorial buildings put it, there "are only two classes of citizens—those who are Americans and those who should be interned."[32]

Although many communities adopted memorial buildings and other utilitarian monuments, there remained many who vigorously opposed them. Artists, commercial monument makers, professional art organizations, and public-art commissions castigated them for their crass materialism. They insisted that only sculpture, painting, and other forms of artistic expression could commemorate appropriately the First World War. Supporters of traditional monuments also believed that war memorials should contribute to the stability of society, but they maintained that these functions could only be performed if they were places for contemplation and nourishment of the soul. Beauty, not utility, must be the standard by which war memorials are judged. To a large degree, they saw war memorials as antidotes to the tension inherent in the modern capitalist society. As one writer put it: "Let our materialists also remember that every step in advance towards civilization that the race has made was in answer to the call of [the] ideal, the spiritual, the poetic; and every fall backwards was, through the worship of the crassly material."[33]

In a society marked by change, they insisted that statues served as enduring symbols of stability:

The monument in our park or square is PERMANENT! Neither fire nor the progress of science will destroy it! Commerce dares not hope to banish it! . . . It may be a poor piece of art, but on Memorial day we gather there with bared heads and pay tribute to the glorious men of another day! We cannot gather about some pile of money which is left as a Memorial fund . . . Our old Memorial Hall will not accommodate us! But here beneath the shadow of this sacred monument we collect as a congregation about its altar, and we pay sincere and inspiring tribute to the memory of the thousands who gave up life forever that we might enjoy liberty and freedom.[34]

Supporters of ideal monuments stressed the need for delay and caution before building monuments to the First World War. They conceded that scores of "atrocious" Civil War monuments only served to bolster the living-memorial cause. As one writer observed in a magazine of the American

*If the "Useful Memorial" Cranks Had Built Them.* One of the many satirical attacks on living memorials made by professional sculptors and commercial monument makers. (Photograph courtesy National Archives, 66–G–12B–18; reprinted from *Monumental News*, February 1919)

Federation of Arts, the bronze monuments of the Civil War had an ugliness that typified their age:

It was an era packed with blunders in art (if art was present at all), and of bad taste. . . . The stamp of the period is unmistakable, on everything . . . including taste. The statues are ugly with the ugliness of the great President's frock coat, his boots, the marble-topped table by which he sits; the ugliness of the spotted brussels carpet, the cast-iron inkstand, and the spittoon.[35]

Monuments to the First World War must be different. By their uniqueness and beauty, they would show that America had entered a new era.[36]

Supporters of traditional memorials represented another branch of the progressive reform movement. Like other progressives, they stressed the need to educate the public through publicity regarding the value of traditional monuments. They wanted "disinterested" professional experts to have the power to pass judgment on public monuments in order to eliminate bad ones. Many professional art associations, most notably the American Federation of Arts, the National Sculpture Society, the Municipal Arts Society in New York City, and the U.S. Commission of Fine Arts, wanted all states and large communities to establish public-art commissions, composed of artists, architects, and sculptors, to have the final say before any monument could be built.[37]

Of course, many who advocated "ideal" monuments benefited from their adoption. For instance, the monument makers' rhetoric aimed at the selfishness of the living-memorial movement served to deflect attention from their industry's self-interest. Like many other special interest groups in this era, the monument industry insisted that their goals served the greater common good. Monuments should be built not to provide a lucrative source of revenue for commercial firms, but because they provided the only fitting physical remembrance to those who had served their country.

Although decried by professional artists, most communities selected mass-produced memorials representing and commemorating the average soldier. The average soldier was usually a doughboy dressed in full battle gear, charging into battle or standing at attention. Frequently, a tablet at the base of the monument recorded the names of the community's war dead and veterans. Nearby there often stood part of the booty of war— captured German artillery pieces that had been distributed by the federal government.[38] The popularity of the doughboy statue suggests the eagerness among many community leaders and veterans to remember the First World War as a national cause. In many cases doughboy statues stood alongside Civil War monuments honoring either Johnny Reb or Billy Yank. At dedication ceremonies for these statues, speakers reminded Americans how the First World War had continued the long process of reconciliation between North and South.

The American Legion, the largest veterans' organization to emerge following the First World War, echoed this theme of national unity. Founded in 1919 in Paris by a group of politically and socially prominent officers and enlisted personnel, the legion insisted that the World War veteran had saved American society and Western civilization from the threat of German tyranny. Veterans, the legion maintained, must take it upon themselves to ensure that their achievements were remembered. The legion claimed,

Colonel Donovan and staff of the 165th Infantry passing under the Victory Arch, New York City, in 1919. Built by members of the city's professional art community to commemorate victory in World War I, this monument never became permanent. (Photograph by Paul Thompson; reprinted from J. Heller, *War and Conflict*, National Archives, 1990, 173; original source, War Department)

moreover, that veterans had an ongoing responsibility to preserve the peace. Although the threat from German autocracy had been met, the specter of the radical subversion of American society remained an ever-present danger.

During the Red scare of 1919 and 1920, the American Legion actively gave its support to efforts to crush radicalism. It applauded the federal government's deportation of foreign radicals and harassment of the International Workers of the World. Although it insisted on obeying the law, the legion condoned the use of extralegal means to combat crippling strikes. In a number of communities, groups of legionnaires harassed suspected radical agitators and worked as strikebreakers.

Even after the imminent threat of international revolution had passed, antiradicalism remained central to the legion's definition of Americanism. America, it insisted, must be kept free from the tyranny of the Right and the Left, emanating, they believed, from foreign shores. Often a nebulous ideology, "Americanism" remained heavily influenced by the ideas of Theodore Roosevelt. It rejected internationalism and insisted that the nation-state remained the highest form of human civilization. Because the citizen must always be ready to serve his country as a soldier, the legion stressed the need for universal military service.[39]

The legion insisted that the First World War had united a diverse nation and made those who participated in it Americans. Although it campaigned vigorously for restrictions on foreign immigration, it admitted foreign-born soldiers as members. It hailed itself as a heterogeneous organization that united veterans from different religions, classes, ethnic groups, and races (but it placed African Americans in segregated posts and in many states excluded them). During the 1920s, the legion elected several Catholic priests and a Jewish rabbi to serve one-year terms as national chaplains. Articles within the American Legion magazine frequently dwelt on the need for religious and ethnic tolerance. After the Red scare had ended, the legion declared a policy of neutrality toward strikes and affirmed the right of labor to organize, particularly when workers joined the mainstream American Federation of Labor.[40]

The legion maintained that it transcended sectional divisions and loyalties. To this end it sought and gained the endorsement of both the Grand Army of the Republic and the United Confederate Veterans. On Memorial Day, the legion joined Civil War and Spanish-American War veterans in ceremonies and rituals honoring the war dead, thus helping to make this holiday one in which the dead of all conflicts were honored. Legion posts placed flags and flowers on the graves of departed world war soldiers. To make certain that each overseas grave would be suitably marked on this day, the legion's national headquarters established a special endowment fund.[41]

Although the legion embraced Memorial Day, it also promoted the observance of Armistice Day as a national holiday devoted exclusively to the commemoration of U.S. participation in the First World War. To the legion, Armistice Day was a watershed in American and world history, heralding a new era of peace. It offered assurance to the public and to veterans themselves that the United States had wisely "rescued" Europe from itself. Armistice Day ceremonies sponsored by the legion struck a responsive chord within American society because they emphasized the terrible cost of war and offered a message of peace. They usually included hymns and prayers in memory of those who had not come home, and occasionally the names of a community's war dead were read aloud. Orators dwelt on the need to work for a new, more harmonious world order to ensure that the war dead had not died in vain. At the eleventh hour of 11 November, citizens joined legion members in observing two minutes of silence, to both honor the fallen and promote the cause of peace.[42]

During the interwar period, newspaper editorials, cartoons, and news stories on Armistice Day echoed this theme of peace. The "greatest" of all wars had been "dreadful," and to commemorate it would serve to prevent another. One *Chicago Daily Tribune* cartoon declared in 1925 that "if the world would always remember how thankful it once was for peace: There would never be another war." Editorials described the progress, or lack thereof, in efforts to promote a new and better world. In the 1920s the conclusion of several disarmament treaties, the restructuring of European debts under the U.S.-sponsored Dawes Plan, and the reintegration of Germany into the international order following the Treaty of Locarno all fostered a sense of optimism. One year, the *Christian Science Monitor* reported that "editorials everywhere" proclaimed that "friendliness has routed hate."[43]

Americans wanted peace, but there was no consensus over how to preserve it. Despite the First World War's terrible destructiveness, the legion maintained that America had wisely entered the conflict. It further declared that military preparedness provided the best assurance that the United States would never again enter into war. Legion parades, especially in larger cities, included units from various branches of the armed forces, and they usually featured rifle or artillery salutes in memory of the dead.

Legion orators often not only spoke on peace but also denounced pacifism and radicalism.[44]

According to internationalists, a lasting peace could only be achieved if the United States embraced collective security. On the eve of Armistice Day 1923, Wilson declared in a radio address to the nation that the memory of the First World War had been forever scarred by the selfish decision of the United States not to join the League of Nations. After Wilson's death in 1924, supporters of the league organized an annual memorial ceremony on Armistice Day at the National Cathedral in Washington.[45]

Many in the peace movement insisted that war could be stopped only through disarmament and pacifism. They wanted to strip Armistice Day of its militaristic character and emphasize that war is a tragedy that can be avoided. To this end, the National Council for the Prevention of War proposed and sponsored alternative Armistice Day ceremonies that most often took the form of a religious service. In 1925 the Federation of Greater Boston Churches even organized a "parade for peace" that included disabled veterans, but did not include units of the American military. Several years later, college pacifists decided to march without an invitation in several American Legion parades held in Massachusetts.[46]

In 1929, the *Chicago Daily Tribune* ran a cartoon that reminded its readers that Armistice Day represented not simply peace, but victory. In an editorial it noted why it had been in the national interest to enter the First World War. The editorial and cartoon indicate how ambivalent Americans remained regarding the First World War. During the interwar period, some of the most widely read fiction and poetry about the war, by authors such as Erich Maria Remarque, Ernest Hemingway, Robert Graves, and John Dos Passos, dwelt on the alienation, senselessness, and brutality of the First World War. Films based on Remarque's *All Quiet on the Western Front* and Hemingway's *A Farewell to Arms* attracted large audiences. Partly as a result of the Great Depression and the rise of militaristic regimes in Germany, Italy, and Japan, many liberal intellectuals who had supported America's entrance into the First World War in 1917 reexamined their position. Historians such as Charles Beard argued that the United States had entered the war because we had allowed ourselves to become attached economically to the Allied cause. In the mid-1930s a congressional panel, the Nye committee, held public hearings that documented the strong ties munitions makers and major financial institutions had had with England and France before America's entrance into the war.[47]

As the threat of war arose in the 1930s, most Americans wanted to guarantee that the United States avoided another conflict. At the urging of many peace groups and isolationists, Congress enacted stringent neutrality laws that limited the economic and travel ties that the United States could have with a belligerent power. The worsening international climate served to heighten the association made between peace and Armistice Day. Newspaper editorials emphasized the need to avoid entanglement in another European conflict. In 1936 one paper observed that Armistice Day should symbolize the reconsecration of the "nation to the cause of peace and the undying hatred of war, the greatest evil that can come to any people."[48]

Cynicism regarding the First World War and the custodians of its memory also increased during the 1930s. Across the nation college students flocked to join the Veterans of Future Wars in 1936. Founded by Lewis J. Gorin and several other Princeton undergraduates, this organization satirized the efforts of veterans to use their war-time service as a reason for federal cash benefits. Gorin and his organization called on the government to pay an early war bonus to every male citizen between the ages of eighteen and thirty-six. They also wanted the future wives and mothers of America to be given the opportunity to participate in a "holy pilgrimage" to Europe in order to "view the future battlefields." In his book *Patriotism Prepaid*, Gorin called on the future veterans to imitate the example of veterans' organizations in gaining favor by adopting programs with "parades—conventions—uniforms—pretty women—drum and bugle corps—and all the other gay embellishments of peace." As for an official salute, Gorin called on his colleagues to use an outstretched hand with an open palm.[49]

The Veterans of Future Wars survived only a year, but it offered a revealing glimpse of how disenchanted some Americans had become with the First World War. To many college students, the rituals and monuments to the war proclaiming sacrifice, victory, unity, and peace were being used to justify veterans' raid on the federal treasury. More important, Gorin and other members of the Veterans of Future Wars sensed that their generation would not be spared another European War.[50]

Many efforts to commemorate the First World War had earlier precedents, but there remained one that did not. On Armistice Day 1920 England and France each honored one unidentified soldier among the millions killed with an elaborate state funeral and burial in a national shrine. A tomb beneath the Arc de Triomphe in Paris served as the final resting place for France's Unknown Soldier. By his burial in Westminster Abbey, England's Unknown Warrior gained a place near the tombs of illustrious poets, generals, and statesmen. Exactly one year later, the United States honored one of its own anonymous dead with burial in a special tomb in the Memorial Amphitheater of the Arlington National Cemetery.[51]

England and France hoped that an unknown soldier would be a symbol of national unity transcending regional, class, and political loyalties. Lacking a name or identity, this anonymous figure acquired all the virtues of the model soldier and citizen. To highlight his bravery and selfless sacrifice, this symbolic citizen-soldier received the highest military decorations. National political and military leaders paid homage to him to recognize the importance of his accomplishments, to acknowledge the debt owed to him by his country, and to emphasize implicitly the duty citizen-soldiers owed their country.[52]

In both Europe and the United States, the Unknown Soldier remained the culmination of a concerted effort to democratize the memory of modern war. Those who created the idea wanted this figure to commemorate all the soldiers who fought for the nation and to make the enormous loss of life in the war comprehensible. Symbolically, the Unknown Soldier raised the status of the common soldier to that of a general or head of state. It also reflected the loss of individual identity that soldiers experienced in the armies of the First World War.

In 1920 Congressman Hamilton Fish, Jr., introduced legislation that called on the secretary of war to provide an unidentified soldier with a hero's burial in Arlington National Cemetery. Fish's proposal gained bipartisan support in Congress as well as the endorsements of General Pershing; Major General John A. LeJeune, the Marine Corp commander in France; and the leaders of the American Legion. As in Europe, those who wanted to honor an anonymous hero wanted him to embody the "national spirit" and the "imperishable" sacrifice of all those who had served.[53]

Soon after Fish made his proposal, disagreements developed over where the Unknown Soldier should be buried. Some in Congress suggested that it might be better to select several unknown soldiers to represent each state or each branch of the armed services. A group of New York civic leaders asked Secretary of War Newton D. Baker in November 1920 for permission to entomb an unidentified soldier in the city's proposed Victory Hall, a planned civic center and auditorium to be located in the heart of Manhattan. Fearful that other communities would make similar requests, Baker refused to consider returning the bodies of any unidentified soldiers except for the one chosen for burial at Arlington.[54]

Some Americans voiced concern about the suitability of Arlington National Cemetery as the burial site of the Unknown Soldier. Noting the relatively isolated location of Arlington and its association in the public mind with the Civil War, a *New York Times* editorial wondered if the rotunda of the Capitol might not be better. The American Legion privately expressed a similar wish and hoped to convince the incoming Harding administration to change the burial place to the Capitol. Fish himself had originally wanted the Unknown Soldier placed beneath the rotunda of the Capitol. He was later convinced by architect Thomas Hasting that his recently completed Arlington Memorial Amphitheater offered a better location. In the end, the Harding administration in early 1921 decided to designate Arlington as the site for the tomb as specified in the congressional resolution.[55]

Congress vested the secretary of war with the responsibility for selecting the Unknown Soldier and deciding on the ceremonies that would take place prior to his burial. In a letter to John Weeks, secretary of war under Warren G. Harding, Fish urged that the Unknown Soldier be buried on Memorial Day 1921 in order to promote reconciliation between the North and South. By conducting ceremonies on Memorial Day it was hoped that this holiday would lose much of its regional flavor and become a celebration for the entire nation. It was hoped that impressive ceremonies would encourage world war veterans to take a greater interest in the holiday and make it their own, thus wresting control of it from the Grand Army of the Republic. To incorporate further the World War I veteran, Fish wanted the War Department to invite a member of each American Legion post to the ceremonies. To Fish's dismay, however, the Harding administration reaffirmed Secretary Baker's earlier decision to bury the Unknown Soldier on 11 November 1921, the third anniversary of the Armistice. This significantly bolstered efforts by the American Legion to make Armistice Day into a separate national holiday.[56]

The ceremony honoring the Unknown Soldier rivalled any funeral for a president or general. The Unknown Soldier was selected in France at the end of October 1921 and placed aboard Admiral Dewey's Spanish-American War flagship, the *Olympia,* for the trip across the Atlantic. Despite pleas from Philadelphia and New York, the War Department brought the Unknown Soldier directly to Washington and on 9 November placed

President Warren G. Harding placing a wreath of flowers on the casket of the Unknown Soldier in the Capitol rotunda prior to its internment at Arlington National Cemetery. 9 November 1921. (Reprinted from J. Heller, *War and Conflict*, National Archives, 1990, 170; original source, U.S. Army)

the body in the rotunda of the Capitol. Resting on the Lincoln catafalque, the president, vice president, Speaker of the House, chief justice of the Supreme Court, secretaries of war and of navy, and General Pershing all placed wreaths before his casket. The following day the diplomatic corp and scores of veterans and fraternal and service organizations presented their wreaths. More than ninety thousand private citizens filed past the Unknown Soldier's casket, and officials kept the rotunda of the Capitol open until midnight in order to accommodate the crowds.[57]

On 11 November a long procession, accompanied part of the way by a military honor guard, formed to escort the Unknown Soldier to the Arlington amphitheater. The president, all members of Congress, the Supreme Court, cabinet members, state governors, and high-ranking foreign representatives were joined by a long list of official mourners who had been

invited by the War Department. Woodrow Wilson briefly joined the procession in a horse-drawn carriage; members of his wartime cabinet were
also in the line of march. Each branch and service of the army was represented by an enlisted man and officer. All holders of the Congressional
Medal of Honor had been asked to attend the ceremonies, and many were
present. American Legion representatives from most states and territories
in the Union joined the procession.[58]

The selection of the official mourners by the War Department was intended to symbolize the heterogenous, but unified, nature of the nation.
More than a dozen organizations representing veterans from the Civil War,
the Spanish-American War, and World War I took part in the march. Service and professional organizations closely connected with the war efforts,
such as the Red Cross, the American Library Association, and the YMCA,
provided representatives. The Daughters of the American Revolution, the
Society of Cincinnati, and other hereditary societies offered contingents.
The Jewish Welfare Board, the Jewish Veterans of the World War, the
Knights of Columbus, the National Catholic War Council, and a committee of prominent African American leaders from the Washington area all
paid tribute to the Unknown Soldier.[59]

The amphitheater ceremonies further highlighted a vision of national
unity. A rabbi read from the Twenty-third Psalm, and the presiding chaplain had tried to secure a Roman Catholic priest to participate in the services. When addressing the assembled mourners, President Harding
declared that it mattered little whether this Unknown Soldier was a "native
or an adopted son," because both "sacrificed alike." Because those from
"mansion or cottage" offered their sons in order to preserve the Nation
and civilization, there would be no way of knowing his "station in life."
Chief Plenty Coups of the Crow nation further underscored this theme of
national reconciliation by offering a prayer to the Great Spirit and placing
his war headdress and crop on the casket.[60]

All across America millions heeded President Harding's call to observe
two minutes of silence. Large and small communities organized public ceremonies to pay tribute to the Unknown Soldier. World war veterans
paraded, and the American Legion organized commemorative events.
Newspaper stories and editorials described the unprecedented honors bestowed on this "nameless soldier" whose "sacrifice and loyalty" embodied
the American spirit. For instance, a headline reporting the event in the
*Washington Post* declared: "All America, Rich and Poor, Aged and Young,
President and Commoner, Solemnly Bares Head to Unknown Hero."[61]

In his novel *Nineteen Nineteen,* John Dos Passos later satirized the hypocrisy of national leaders regarding the Unknown Soldier, maintaining that they worked to "Make sure he ain't a dinge, boys. / make sure he ain't a guinea or a kike."[62] Dos Passos was not completely wrong. Many of the rituals and symbols associated with the Unknown Soldier defined the ideal American as a white, most likely Protestant, Christian. The Cavalry Band played "Onward Christian Soldier" as the Unknown Soldier was escorted from the Washington Navy Yard to the Capitol on 9 November. Protestant hymns dominated the amphitheater service, and when the former chaplain of the American Expeditionary Force, Episcopal bishop Charles Brent, read the committal service, he prayed that this fallen hero would be resurrected in the name of "Jesus Christ our Lord." Few white southerners or northerners, certainly few surviving Confederate soldiers, conceived of the Unknown Soldier as being nonwhite. When imaging the Unknown Soldier's origins, no speech suggested that he might have come from a black sharecropper's cabin or from Harlem. Several years later, when the Jewish Welfare Board learned that a proposed monument for the Unknown Soldier's tomb contained a cross, they had to remind the Commission of Fine Arts that this anonymous individual may well have been a Jew.[63]

During the amphitheater ceremonies, medals of heroism were bestowed on the Unknown Soldier by President Harding and representatives of foreign governments. This anonymous hero garnered the Congressional Medal of Honor, the Distinguished Service Cross, the Victoria Cross, France's croix de guerre, Italy's Gold Medal for Bravery, Poland's Virtuti Militari, and several other awards. Harding praised the willingness of the Unknown Soldier to withstand the trials of modern warfare for the good of the Republic and wider humanity.[64]

But peace remained the central theme of the ceremonies. Both American church leaders and Harding wanted the memorial to represent a transcendent purpose and to go beyond the commemoration of a particular battle or war. Several months earlier the Federal Council of Churches had called on churches to hold services on 11 November that centered on the cause of peace. Harding devoted the bulk of his address at the tomb to how a just and peaceful world would be the "loftiest tribute" the nation could bestow on the Unknown Soldier. Moreover, there remained a practical side to this talk of peace. The entombment of the Unknown Soldier coincided with a major international conference on disarmament in Washington presided over by Secretary of State Charles Evans Hughes.[65]

Few Americans wanted war, but the rituals of that November day could not fully obscure the conflict among Americans over how to prevent another one. Although Wilson and Harding had saluted each other on the eleventh, they offered alternative visions of how best to create a stable and peaceful world. Until his death Wilson remained a committed internationalist, heartbroken both literally and figuratively that the United States had failed to join the League of Nations. Harding rejected league membership as an infringement on American sovereignty, but pursued an activist foreign policy that in the case of the Washington disarmament conference led to a major reduction in naval armaments.

Over the course of the interwar period, tension developed as to whether the tomb was a symbol of war or a symbol of peace. Peace activists saw the Unknown Soldier as a tragic figure who served as a grim reminder of the terrible cost of war. During the interwar years one national church organization circulated a play that had the Unknown Soldier coming back to life and embracing the cause of pacifism and disarmament. Organizers of a peace parade in New York in 1934 suggested to participants that one float could show that the struggle for which the Unknown Soldier had died "has yet to be won; that militarism is his continual crucifixion."[66] Both the War Department and the American Legion believed that the message of the tomb was misunderstood. One Military Intelligence officer, W. K. Naylor, feared in 1923 that the tomb had come to "personify a policy of disarmament." Somber wreath-laying ceremonies on Armistice Day, Military Intelligence feared, "conveyed the idea of mourning rather than patriotism." Clergymen misread the message of the tomb, using it as a "text for idealistic peace sermons or as the basis for advocating some form of internationalism."[67]

In the 1920s the American Legion called on the army to place a sentry at the tomb to increase its dignity and to encourage the proper reverence. They complained that many visitors had failed to show proper respect at the grave, and in some cases they dishonored it by using it as a bench or picnic table. The army, which was short of funds, resisted the idea, insisting that visitors had not dishonored the Unknown Soldier. But under pressure from the White House and Congress, the army relented in 1926 and detailed soldiers from nearby Fort Meyers to guard the tomb daily.[68]

Both the American Legion and the War Department wanted a suitable monument erected over the tomb in order to ensure that its symbolic meaning was correctly interpreted. But there were sharp divisions among congressional leaders, the Commission of Fine Arts, and the War Department over what type of memorial should be built. The Commission of

Thomas Hasting's design and model for the American Tomb of the Unknown Soldier was temporarily installed but failed to secure the necessary approval from the Arlington Memorial Amphitheater Commission. (Photograph courtesy National Archives, RG 66, Project Files)

The winning design by the sculptor Thomas Hudson Jones and the architect Lormier Rich for the Tomb of the Unknown Soldier necessitated substantial changes to the Arlington Memorial Amphitheater. (Photograph courtesy National Archives, 66-G-4-88)

Fine Arts wanted the amphitheater architect to design a monumental shaft to be placed over the tomb. Many in Congress and in the War Department considered this design inappropriate, and the secretary of war refused approval. The War Department in turn proposed a low marble sarcophagus, which the Commission of Fine Arts rejected. And to the dismay of the commission, Congress mandated that a competition open to architects and sculptors be held to find a suitable design.[69]

In 1928 the sculptor Thomas Hudson Jones and the architect Lormier Rich won the competition by offering designs heavily influenced by the classical tradition. Rich called for the creation of a long stairwell leading up to the tomb and for the removal of nearby roadways. Jones offered a marble sarcophagus sparsely ornamented on three sides. On the final side facing away from the amphitheater, Jones designed three allegorical figures that could have graced any monument in ancient Greece or Rome. Jones wanted these figures to collectively represent the "spirit of the Allies in the War." He showed Victory spreading her wings, with a male figure, Valor, on the right and a female figure, Peace, on the left. Peace stood ready "to crown the devotion and sac courage to make the cause of righteousness triumph

The victory and peace commemorated by the t Soldier would prove fleeting, for the United States would, by drawn into another world war. Once again, Americans would have to demonstrate their valor. Americans had to assimilate the experience of the second global war within less than a generation, and the very experience of that second war led them to reexamine the way they viewed the struggle of 1917. Nevertheless, after 1945 the rituals, organizations, and monuments commemorating the First World War survived and continued to contribute to the definition of the national identity. Armistice Day took on a new name and new emphasis, but it remained a national holiday. The American Legion opened its membership to veterans of the Second World War. The Tomb of the Unknown Soldier remained a national shrine.

# 4

# THE "GOOD WAR" AND MODERN MEMORY

Most Americans did not want to fight another war in Europe. From the beginnings of World War II in 1939 until the sudden fall of France in the spring of 1940, isolationist sentiment dominated public and congressional opinion. Even many who believed that Nazi Germany posed a threat to United States interests hoped that America could avoid actual entry into the war by simply providing economic and military aid to Britain.

With Japan's attack on Pearl Harbor on 7 December 1941 and Germany's declaration of war on the United States a few days later, public opinion shifted. In many ways this explains the more muted tone of American propaganda during World War II in contrast to that of World War I. The moralistic and messianic themes so prevalent in 1917–18 were largely absent in 1941–45. Most people considered World War II a war of self-defense and, particularly in the Pacific, of revenge for a surprise attack on America. Only relatively late and reluctantly did President Franklin D. Roosevelt establish an Office of War Information. In his view, Wilson's Committee on Public Information had fueled much of the hysteria that had swept the country during the First World War, and Roosevelt wanted to avoid a recurrence. He also believed that public expectations concerning the results of the Second World War should not be raised unrealistically, as they had in 1917.

Like many of his contemporaries, Roosevelt believed that much of the popular disillusionment with the Versailles Treaty and the League of Nations had stemmed from overinflated wartime promises by the Wilson administration.

Idealism, however, was not entirely absent from World War II propaganda. The government and the mass media often stressed that the United States was fighting against the morally repugnant ideologies of Nazism, fascism, and militarism and in defense of what Roosevelt called the Four Freedoms—freedom of religion and speech, and freedom from fear and want. The government's wartime message emphasized that the United States had joined forces in a Grand Alliance with Britain, and also with Nationalist China and Stalin's Russia. By 1944 American war publicity predicted that out of this wartime union would grow a permanent international organization—a United Nations—designed to ensure a more stable and peaceful world.[1]

American propaganda inflamed emotions—particularly against the Japanese, who were portrayed as an evil, inferior, and barbaric race lacking all sense of decency. These Asians had not only bombed Pearl Harbor without warning but also committed scores of atrocities against American prisoners of war during the Bataan Death March. Hatred of the stereotyped "Jap" quickly reached such a state that the federal government interned American citizens of Japanese descent living near the Pacific Coast in special camps.[2]

Because of the Pearl Harbor attack and as a result of earlier isolationism, public support for the war against Japan proved much stronger than support for the war against Germany. Initially, the president feared that the United States might be forced to reverse its goal of defeating Germany before dealing fully with Japan. American propaganda, as well as public attitude, remained restrained regarding Germany, failing to match the anger expressed against Japan, or even the level of emotion raised against the "Hun" in 1917. Before the public discovered the concentration camps at the end of the war, the atrocity story failed to become a staple of wartime publicity against the Germans. Perhaps this was partly due to the large number of German Americans living in the United States. It also may have stemmed from the fact that the German army and its soldiers were generally granted more respect than Japanese troops.[3]

Discovery of the Nazi concentration camps ended any remaining doubt of America's need to crush Germany. In contrast to the aftermath of the First World War, no significant revisionist school emerged questioning the wisdom of America's entering the war in Europe. Revisionism was only a minor undercurrent—a few old isolationists and, later, neo-isolationists. Most Americans remembered the struggle against Germany as a conflict between good and monstrous evil. In fact, criticism later emerged over the failure of the United States to grasp fully and quickly enough the true nature of Nazism. By the 1970s and 1980s, many were faulting the United States for not doing more to halt the Holocaust.[4]

The First World War, to a large degree, established the organizations and the rituals that the United States used in remembering the Second World War. Once again the U.S. government created a series of overseas cemeteries and monuments. At home, government authorities brought back another unknown soldier, who received a hero's burial at Arlington National Cemetery. The American Legion remained the principal veterans' organization.

In the eyes of many Americans, the Second World War vindicated the first one. The decision to halt German aggression in 1917 was thought correct; the mistake was in not preventing the rise of Hitler. To many internationalists, the great lesson to be learned was that the United States must abandon isolationism. They insisted that America use its economic and military power to shape the international order. Some, especially those on the Left, felt this should be done with the cooperation and help of the Soviet Union. In the late 1940s, however, many liberals and conservatives considered communist Russia the greatest threat to world peace.

Ironically, far more ambiguity surrounded the war in Asia. The Far East conflict had ended in a controversial and sobering manner with the destruction of two Japanese cities by American atomic bombs. A debate subsequently developed over the wisdom and necessity of using weapons of such unprecedented power. Some feared that the atomic bomb might, if not properly regulated, eventually lead to the destruction of humanity. As early as the 1950s historians started to question U.S. policy toward Japan in 1940–41. Charles Beard and, more recently, John Toland argued that Roosevelt's policies had provoked the Japanese attack, in part to foster America's entrance into the war in Europe, a point disputed by most historians and by general public opinion.[5]

American involvement in the Second World War dwarfed that of the First World War. The United States mobilized more than fifteen million servicemen and fought a two-front war in Asia and Europe. During that conflict American industrial production soared and the nation not only equipped its own forces but also met many of the needs of England and the Soviet Union. The United States built the largest navy and air force in the world. Although American casualties never approached those of Japan, Germany, or the Soviet Union, they remained substantial and far greater than the losses sustained in World War I. The navy, for instance, lost more men during the single day's attack on Pearl Harbor than it had during the entire course of World War I. All told, almost three hundred thousand American soldiers, sailors, and marines died in World War II, compared with slightly more than fifty thousand in World War I.[6]

Despite the unprecedented magnitude of the U.S. effort in the Second World War, Americans did not create a distinct national holiday to commemorate it. Although there were attempts to create specific organizations representing only World War II veterans, those efforts ultimately were aborted. In contrast to the immediate aftermath of the First World War, there was little interest in 1945–47 in building innovative war monuments in the United States.

In 1945, as in 1919, Americans pondered the wisdom of maintaining military cemeteries overseas. Both the army and the American Battle Monuments Commission believed they would serve as useful symbols of national unity, as permanent reminders to other nations of the sacrifices made by the United States, and as symbols of an ongoing friendship between the countries. Because the next of kin had been allowed in the 1920s to determine whether a particular soldier would be buried at home or abroad, it proved virtually impossible to deny this option in 1945. Few wanted to reopen the "unpleasant debate" that took place in the 1920s, but many in the military and the American Battle Monuments Commission hoped that by quickly restoring the World War I cemeteries to their pre-1940 beauty, they could prepare the American public for a "free and cheerful acceptance" of overseas burial of the World War II dead.[7]

This idea won considerable support in the media. Articles appearing in *Reader's Digest*, the *Saturday Evening Post*, and other popular periodicals offered reasons for not returning the war dead, particularly from Europe. It was again argued that those who died in battle would have wanted to remain buried near their comrades. Invariably the views of living soldiers were cited to reinforce this sentiment. Burial on the battlefield forever associated the fallen with a victory considered "one of the great achievements of history." On a more practical level, internment in an overseas cemetery would ensure that sons and husbands would rest in a beautiful parklike cemetery.[8]

With far less furor than in the aftermath of the First World War, Congress decided in 1946 that widows, children, parents, and siblings, in that order, could make the final determination regarding the burial place of their loved ones. Despite the government's pleas against removal, the majority of widows and parents once again wanted the bodies of their next of kin brought back to the United States.[9]

For those who remained buried overseas, the United States again decided to abandon isolated or less-accessible locations and concentrate all overseas burials into several large military cemeteries. It declared that permanent cemeteries would not be established in either Germany or Japan, because these nations had been former enemies, although Italy was deemed a suitable site because it had joined the Allies during the war. The U.S. Army and the American Battle Monuments Commission concluded that most temporary sites in Africa and Asia were unacceptable because they were difficult to reach. The majority of U.S. burial grounds (ten out of fourteen) were based in Europe. Of the permanent cemeteries established, only one was in North Africa, in Tunisia, which was at the time a French colony, only three in the Pacific, one each in the U.S. territories of Hawaii and Alaska, and one in the former colony of the Philippines. Despite the epic nature of the fighting on Iwo Jima, Okinawa, Tawara, and other such islands, no burial grounds were established on any of them. Both the army and the American Battle Monuments Commission stated that parents and widows would be reluctant to allow their next of kin to remain buried on these remote islands. The American Legion echoed these sentiments, insisting that these "desolate" islands experienced "volcanic action, earthquakes, typhoons and other extremely hazardous forces of nature" and that their distance from "civilization" ruled them out as the final resting places for fallen American servicemen.[10]

Both the army and the American Battle Monuments Commission wanted to symbolize the bond between the United States and Europe by locating most U.S. military cemeteries on the Continent. Although there were logistical problems in the Philippines, the army and the commission decided that the importance of political ties with the former U.S. colony outweighed such inconveniences. Thus, authorities established a military cemetery in Manila. In one meeting of the American Battle Monuments Commission, General George Marshall, former army chief of staff, stressed the important "psychological effect" a cemetery in the Philippines would have on the Filipino people, serving as "permanent evidence of American sacrifice." Some in the commission wanted to retain a cemetery in India, but the army ruled against it. In the view of the commander of the army's Memorial Division, the effect of an American cemetery would be lost on the people of India, because of what he called the Indians' "lack of respect" accorded to their own dead.[11]

In designing the overseas cemeteries and monuments, the American Battle Monuments Commission and the U.S. Commission of Fine Arts again adhered to many of the policies that had been established after World War I. The graves of World War II veterans were to be marked by uniform gravestones, and grass and trees were to dominate the cemeteries. A marble cross or Star of David would be placed on each gravestone, and each cemetery would contain a permanent, nondenominational chapel.[12]

Like their First World War counterparts, Second World War chapels defined the United States as a predominately Christian nation. Although Jewish symbolism was incorporated in some chapels, the American Battle Monuments Commission again showed considerable insensitivity. In considering what it called the "Jewish question," the commission in 1949 refused to heed the calls of many American Jews to abstain from using the cross in chapel designs or to establish an advisory committee to provide advice on religious symbolism. There was even retrogression in this area, as the commission had randomly marked unknown soldiers' graves during the interwar period with either a cross or a Star of David in relation to the "proportion of known Jewish dead to known Christian dead." In 1948 it decided that all unidentified graves would be marked with a cross in order to avoid having a Star of David mark the grave of what the commission suggested might be "an unknown Christian."[13]

In selecting architects and sculptors to design the World War II overseas monuments, both the Commission of Fine Arts and the American Battle Monuments Commission again preferred those who worked in traditional styles. Consequently, most chapels and overseas monuments were built along classical lines. Idealized figures clothed in the garb of Greek citizens, Roman soldiers, or medieval saints served as focal points for several monuments. As they had during the interwar period, the two commissions viewed American overseas memorials as part of a long, European-based cultural tradition dating back to ancient Greece and Rome.[14]

To highlight the continuity between the two world wars, the American Battle Monuments Commission made the World War I cemetery at Suresnes, on the outskirts of Paris, a burial ground and memorial to the dead of both conflicts. The remains of twenty-four unidentified soldiers from the Second World War were placed in the cemetery. At the same time, the commission added two loggias to the original chapel in order to commemorate the unknown dead from both wars. The northern loggia was dedicated to the dead of the First World War, the southern to those of the Second World War.[15]

The history of Quentin Roosevelt's burial site provides yet another illustration of how the First World War came to be viewed as but a prelude to the second. After the First World War, former President Theodore Roosevelt had insisted that his son, Quentin, be buried on the spot where he had fallen. The government had granted his request and had allowed the Roosevelt family to erect a special memorial over Quentin's isolated grave in France. During the Second World War, Theodore Jr., another of Roosevelt's sons, died of a heart attack during the Normandy invasion. His wife and his brother, Archibald, insisted that he be buried in the permanent U.S. military cemetery near Normandy. Shortly after the Second World War ended, the Roosevelt family requested that Quentin's body be removed from its isolated location and buried next to that of his brother. After some hesitation, the army and the American Battle Monument Commission granted the Roosevelt family's request, and these two sons of Theodore Roosevelt lie today near each other at the Normandy cemetery.[16]

The overseas cemeteries served to symbolize U.S. global military commitments undertaken after 1945. The army, by placing most of the cemeteries in Europe, indicated that it wished to have even greater ties with the Continent. In 1948 the United States began providing economic aid to European countries under the Marshall Plan, and a year later, it joined the North Atlantic Treaty Organization, thereby forming a permanent military alliance with most of western Europe.

There is no solid evidence to suggest that the decision not to maintain permanent cemeteries in Asia or other regions of the Third World was motivated by racism. The correspondence and minutes of the American Battle Monuments Commission emphasize only that non-European regions were excluded because of their geographic inaccessibility. Nonetheless, government reluctance to place permanent burial grounds in the Third World, particularly in Asia, mirrored the ambivalence many Americans felt toward these regions. Most felt the United States had little in common, culturally or politically, with most African or Asian peoples and nations. Although during the late 1940s, U.S. foreign policy emphasized the need to bolster Western Europe economically and militarily, the United States fought its next two wars not in Europe, but in Asia.

In the late 1940s there were a few efforts to establish the anniversary of V-J Day as a national holiday. On the first anniversary of that day, President Harry S. Truman issued a proclamation urging Americans to observe 14 August 1946, as "Victory Day" by publicly displaying the American flag and by remembering those who had sacrificed their lives for the cause of "justice, freedom, peace and international good-will." Many communities held church services or other public ceremonies to mark the anniversary. Every year from 1946 to 1949, New York's governor Thomas E. Dewey issued a proclamation calling on citizens of the Empire State to remember 14 August as V-J Day. In addition, during the late 1940s, Arkansas and Rhode Island made the day into a legal state holiday.[17]

V-J Day never became a national holiday. Instead, Armistice Day, 11 November, was redefined to include the commemoration of both world wars and, eventually, all American wars. Armistice Day was chosen, in part, because the Second World War had really ended on two different dates: V-E Day in Europe was 8 May 1945, and V-J Day in Asia was 14 August 1945. In addition to that confusion, by making V-J Day into a national holiday, the majority of attention would have been focused on the war in the Pacific. Armistice Day still held a special significance for many Second World War veterans. Many of the senior officers of the 1941–45 war had served in the 1917 conflict. Also, many of the citizen-soldiers of World War II had come of age during the interwar period and had never known a time when Armistice Day was not observed.[18]

The development of a separate holiday commemorating the Second World War was impeded most by the cold war and the threat of hostilities with the Soviet Union. It became clear following the Korean War (1950–53) that Armistice Day must be formally redefined, because, in the words of one congressman, it was "simply not feasible to establish a national holiday to commemorate the closing of each war." In 1954 Congress renamed Armistice Day, Veterans Day, proclaiming it as a day to honor the participants of all American wars. A House committee supporting this change declared that the veterans of Korea and World War II had, like their World War I comrades, fought for the same noble objective: the advance of a "permanent peace by halting aggression of those who would destroy our democratic ideals."[19]

The monuments built within the United States to commemorate the fallen of the world wars served to highlight the continuity between the two conflicts. Many in 1945, like their predecessors, hoped to use the commonality, sacrifice, and victory to encourage domestic reform and the reconstruction of American society. Advocates of "living memorials" once again repeated their calls for the construction of playgrounds, parks, highways, bridges, and other useful structures promoting the well-being of communities. Monuments that had a "truly social purpose" would honor the memory of the fallen far better than what one critic called the "mediocre or even tawdry 'monumental' monstrosities that have been left in the wake of all our earlier wars."[20]

In defence of living memorials, Archibald MacLeish, poet and librarian of Congress, accepted the fact that a great monument could be inspirational, but noted that the supply of great sculptors was limited and their cost beyond the reach of most communities. At best, he claimed, most towns could afford a "mediocre piece," and such works quickly become invisible. A properly selected living memorial had a far better chance of entering the "life" and "consciousness" of a community. MacLeish insisted that every community was different, and what worked in one community might fail in another. Thus, in some areas a park would be a meaningful monument, whereas in others a school would be preferable.[21]

Those who favored living memorials were more reserved about what they would accomplish than they had been after World War I. *American City* once again supported living memorials for their ability to promote community and "practical democracy," but in contrast to the rhetoric it used in 1919 and 1920, the magazine did not justify them as providing a bulwark against possible class and ethnic upheavals. Instead, living memorials, such as community houses, swimming pools, parks, or other civic improvements were seen as enhancing an already stable society.[22] Supporters of traditional monuments, such as the Commission of Fine Arts and the National Sculpture Society, used the same arguments they had in 1919 and 1920 to criticize living memorials. The traditionalists insisted that a "true" war memorial must be imbued with beauty and spirituality, something, they claimed, a utilitarian structure could never do. Moreover, they said it was easier to forget the purpose of a living memorial than of a traditional sculptured figure.[23]

To the relief of the National Sculpture Society, there were no stock figures of "G.I. Joe" erected in town squares alongside doughboys from World War I and the solemn stone sentinels of the Civil War. But to their dismay, many large and small communities opted to build stadiums, parks, recreation centers, auditoriums, libraries, and other structures rather than statues. In many communities, the monument to World War II was a bronze table or single granite marker containing the names of those who had fought and died, added to or alongside the marker commemorating the fallen of World War I.[24]

To a large degree, it was not traditional monuments that preserved and commemorated World War II, but newspaper photographs, newsreels, motion pictures, and, eventually, television. A dramatic picture by press photographer Joseph Rosenthal, which showed five marines and a navy medic raising an American flag on Mount Suribachi during the battle for Iwo Jima, quickly became one of the most popular symbols of the Second World War. Soon after its publication in February 1945, editorial writers and members of Congress called it a "work of art" representing one of the great historical events in American history. Its imagery of heroism, bravery, and courage was frequently compared with that of Emanuel Leutze's painting of "Washington Crossing the Delaware." The Treasury Department used a representation of the Iwo Jima flag raising as the basis for its seventh loan drive poster. The Post Office also broke all sales records with a stamp depicting the flag raising.[25]

Congress quickly introduced legislation to build a permanent monument to the flag raising at Iwo Jima. Within days of the event, Felix DeWeldon, an Austrian-born sculptor serving in the U.S. Navy, at the behest of his superiors, created a sculptured work depicting the heroic scene. Hastily completed in August 1945, the work was temporarily erected on Constitution Avenue in Washington, D.C.[26] The Marine Corps League and the Navy Department viewed DeWeldon's figure as a superb representation of the event and of the "fighting spirit" of the Marine Corps. The Marine Corps League lobbied Congress for permission to erect a permanent monument based on Rosenthal's picture and DeWeldon's sculpture as a memorial to the Marine Corps' dead from all of America's wars. The Commission of Fine Arts, the National Sculpture Society, and the Artist's Guild of Washington considered this an appalling idea. DeWeldon's professional credentials remained suspect, and they believed his temporary monument was artistically horrendous. One former naval officer and sculptor accused DeWeldon of having falsified his artistic accomplishments and education. In addition, a report asserted that DeWeldon had entered the United States illegally in the 1930s and had attempted to commit insurance fraud. The Commission of Fine Arts insisted that a competition be held in order to ensure that only the best design and sculptor were selected to complete this or any major memorial to the Second World War. Moreover, the commission opposed the strict use of Rosenthal's picture as the model for any

Flag raising on Iwo Jima, 23 February 1945. This widely reproduced image, by Joe Rosenthal of the Associated Press, quickly inspired a monument and host of other commemorative activities. (Reprinted from J. Heller, *War and Conflict*, National Archives, 1990, 276; original source U.S. Navy)

memorial. The commission thought that the winning design should strive for an ideal representation of the event in the classical tradition.[27]

In the end the commission and the professional art organizations lost their battle against the DeWeldon monument. The photographic image was simply too popular. Congress mandated the use of Rosenthal's photographic image and did not require the Marine Corps League to hold a competition. Although the Commission of Fine Arts had to approve the final design, Congress limited its power on this issue. DeWeldon's design won the favor of the navy, the Marine Corps, and of many veterans. Although the commissioners won some modifications of DeWeldon's work and influenced its final location, they could not prevent its completion. The commission was forced to welcome DeWeldon as a colleague when President Harry S. Truman appointed him a member in 1950.[28]

The inability of the Commission of Fine Arts and the National Sculpture Society to prevent the construction of DeWeldon's Iwo Jima monument illustrates their weak positions in determining how the Second World War would be commemorated. The conservative, classically oriented approach of the commission and sculpture society to public art had increasingly fallen out of favor, both in artistic circles and among various elites in American society. As one member of the National Sculpture Society reported gloomily in 1951:

Circumstances and conditions during the past 25 years have not been kind to sculpture. It is today almost completely overlooked as decoration for homes, for gardens, and for public architecture. Its use for commemorative monuments has of recent years faced much opposition. If ever sculpture was in the dark shadows of near oblivion it is now.[29]

Many art critics questioned whether classically inspired monuments adequately captured the terrible destructiveness and horrible violence of the Second World War. They insisted that memorial art aim for greater simplic-

Felix DeWeldon's first statue commemorating the flag raising on Iwo Jima originally stood on Constitution Avenue in Washington, D.C. Both the artist and statue he created received searing criticism from the professional art community. (Photograph courtesy National Archives, 80-G–386592)

ity and starkness in design and form. Modern art and sculpture were far more appropriate for modern wars. To many critics the cemeteries and monuments built by the American Battle Monuments Commission symbolized all that should be avoided in memorial art. In their view, the massiveness, uniformity, and stiffness seemed too much like the commemorative structures of fascist Germany and Italy. One critic considered the stiff and lifeless statues authorized by the commission as the "world's worst sculpture."[30]

The lack of interest in building traditional monuments to the Second World War also suggests that government leaders and much of the public were content with the way First World War memorials and rituals defined the American identity. After 1945 both were even more comfortable than in the interwar period with an ethnically heterogeneous vision of nationhood. In 1954, the first year Armistice Day was formally commemorated as Veterans Day, the federal government organized an unprecedented series of mass naturalization ceremonies. These symbolized the connection of military service to citizenship and declared that the United States had been created from many diverse peoples. In part, the dramatic appeal of the Iwo Jima flag raising image stemmed from the fact that the individuals who had taken part in that event were perceived as "average" Americans drawn together from disparate backgrounds. As was widely publicized, the participants included an American Indian, a Texan, a Kentucky mountaineer, a French Canadian from Vermont, and a Czech-American from central Pennsylvania.[31]

During the interwar years, anticommunism and opposition to what was perceived as foreign-inspired radical subversion had been a core tenet of the American Legion. In 1933 the organization had actively opposed diplomatic recognition of the Soviet Union. Although the legion supported military preparedness in the 1930s, it believed that the United States should intervene militarily only in the Western Hemisphere. The legion insisted that the U.S. alliance with the Soviet Union during World War II had been strictly a matter of necessity.[32]

To many other Americans, however, and to President Franklin D. Roosevelt, the Soviet-American alliance represented the beginning of a new era of cooperation between the two countries. Many American soldiers who had met the Red Army at the Elbe on 25 April 1945 insisted that they would keep alive the spirit of goodwill once they returned to America. One veteran, Chicago cab driver Joseph Polowsky, dedicated much of his life to fostering reunions between Soviet and American troops who had met at the close of the war. In the 1940s and 1950s, Polowsky worked to have the United Nations and the United States declare 25 April a day dedicated to the pursuit of peace. Before his death in 1983, Polowsky directed that his body be buried at the Elbe meeting site as a symbol of goodwill and understanding between the United States and the Soviet Union.[33]

The American Veterans Committee (AVC), started by World War II veterans, hailed the spirit of Yalta and insisted that Soviet-American cooperation was still possible. They offered a liberal vision of the 1941 conflict and insisted that the United States continue to promote Roosevelt's Four Freedoms domestically and internationally. In contrast to the American Legion, the AVC argued that veterans should not simply lobby for benefits for themselves but also seek to promote a reordering of American society that would benefit all. As cold war tensions worsened, the American Veterans Committee faltered, suffering from internal strife as competing groups from the Left struggled to control it. Labeled a communist front organization by the American Legion and others, the AVC sought to combat this charge by expelling all communists from its ranks. Nonetheless, the accusations proved effective, and by 1950 the AVC had shrunk to insignificance.[34]

The failure of the AVC to supplant the American Legion remained part of a wider movement toward making anticommunism central to the definition of the American identity. To the legion, and to President Truman and his successors, the great lesson of the Second World War had been the need to contain early on totalitarian aggression. In contrast to earlier eras in American history, the boundary between peace and war seemed thin during the cold war. The United States spent large sums on the military and in foreign assistance to those who resisted the actions of the Soviet Union and of Third World guerrilla movements.

The cold war grew increasingly strained, casting a long shadow over efforts to commemorate the Grand Alliance of the Second World War. In the late 1940s and the 1950s, Veterans Day ceremonies emphasized the need to meet the threat posed by the Communist bloc. In 1950, after protests from Admiral William H. Standley, a former ambassador to the Soviet Union under the Roosevelt administration, that two of the Four Freedoms (from want and from fear) were inspired by communism, the San Diego City Council decided not to sponsor a World War II monument in which the four freedoms were listed next to the names of those killed from that city.

In many ways the fate of the tomb of the Unknown Soldier provides a microcosm for understanding how the cold war shaped the remembrance of World War II.[35] In 1946 the federal government decided to honor an Unknown Soldier from World War II with a burial in the Arlington National Cemetery amphitheater. Like his counterpart from World War I, this anonymous hero was the embodiment of the unity and diversity of the American character. Authorities also wanted him to symbolize the sacrifice of all World War II servicemen who had fought on behalf of the nation and in the cause of peace. By burying another unknown soldier, Congress and the newly created Defense Department wanted to affirm both world wars as conflicts fought in defense of U.S. interests against outside aggression.

In considering where to bury the second unknown soldier, both the Defense Department and the Commission of Fine Arts pondered the soldier's relationship with the unknown soldier from the First World War. Should he be buried next to his predecessor? Would it be better to destroy the first monument and build another one honoring both? Should space be created for unknown soldiers of future wars?

In 1949 the Defense Department favored a radical overhaul of the tomb and amphitheater. In one plan the department proposed to place the latest unknown soldier in the amphitheater proper. To accomplish this, it wanted grass to replace the marble floor and seats in the amphitheater. To relate the existing tomb to the newer one, the Defense Department called for the destruction of the current museum building. As alternatives, the Defense Department offered more modest plans. One called for merely building a flat tomb at the base of the existing monument, and another, favored by the Commission of Fine Arts, called for the construction of a monument of equal size and shape next to the First World War tomb.[36]

The Defense Department abandoned plans for radical alterations to the amphitheater. As the Commission of Fine Arts had pointed out, the amphitheater was originally created as a monument to Civil War veterans, and destruction of the building on the East Side could provoke controversy. The department also had misgivings about creating two separate tombs, even if they were near one another. As one department official noted, two tombs would create logistical difficulties when the president and other officials sought to honor the Unknown Soldiers.[37]

With the blessings of the Commission of Fine Arts, the Defense Department decided in February 1950 to bury the Unknown Soldier from World War II next to his First World War counterpart. The current sarcophagus would be retained, but the inscription on the tomb would be modified to show that it honored both Unknown Soldiers. At the same time, the Defense Department anticipated the need to bury additional unknown soldiers from future wars. As one general noted, plans for the new tomb included a "preparatory base at least for the burial of a world war III veteran."[38]

In the end the Defense Department's plans to bury additional unknown soldiers proved to be far-sighted. The Korean War led to a cancellation of plans to entomb an unknown soldier on Memorial Day 1951. After the war ended, Congress decided that an additional unknown soldier should be selected. On Memorial Day 1958, the Defense Department simultaneously honored these two anonymous soldiers in an observance reminiscent of that conducted in 1921 for the Unknown Soldier of World War I. President Dwight D. Eisenhower and a host of other mourners paid their respects as the soldiers lay in state in the Capitol rotunda. A military procession escorted them to the Arlington amphitheater for a funeral service that included the bestowing of military honors, speeches praising their sacrifice, and hymns mourning their passing. To emphasize the heterogeneous character of the nation, a Catholic priest, a Protestant minister, and a Jewish rabbi took part in the ceremonies.[39]

It had been intended that the Unknown Soldier from World War I serve as a symbol of peace, and, as has been noted, the ceremonies in his honor coincided with a major international disarmament conference. The peace theme was not entirely absent in 1958, but it seemed more ephemeral. For instance, Eisenhower, in a reception for all the living Medal of Honor recipients, dwelt on the need for military unification in order to assure a strong national defense. By burying the Unknown Soldier from Korea next to his comrades from 1917 and 1941, this Arlington memorial became the link between the world wars and the cold war.[40]

The cold war also had a profound impact on how the federal government sought to preserve the memory of the dropping of the atomic bomb, which marked the end of World War II but also heralded the opening of the nuclear age. Within days after the surrender of Japan, Secretary of Interior Harold L. Ickes directed the Park Service to start planning the incorporation and preservation of the site of the first atomic bomb test site in Alamogordo, New Mexico, as part of the national monument system. In response to this directive, the Park Service formulated plans that called for a museum on site that illustrated the workings and nature of the atomic bomb. In addition, it wanted to obtain and put on display two B–29 aircraft that had dropped the bombs on Hiroshima and Nagasaki. In the view of Interior Department and Park Service officials, the "use of atomic energy [was] so revolutionary" that Alamogordo was of unprecedented and immediate interest to both the nation and the international community.[41]

The residents of Alamogordo, state officials, and the congressional delegation from New Mexico all desired to make the Alamogordo test site into a national monument. John J. Dempsey, governor of New Mexico, encouraged Park Service efforts to preserve the site because it offered a vital argument for "maintaining the peace of the world." He suggested establishing a museum at the proposed national monument and suggested it include a mural of pictures portraying the destruction at Hiroshima and Nagasaki and a display of "relics" from these two cities that underscored the tremendous power of the bomb.[42]

Some parties calling for the preservation of the atomic bomb site did not grasp the full meaning of the weapon. Many local officials and residents of New Mexico quickly realized the potential of Alamogordo as a Mecca for tourists. And there were those who wanted to trivialize the power of the bomb by suggesting that the fused sand found near ground zero be sold as souvenirs. One resident of Albuquerque, New Mexico, applied to open a souvenir and curio shop near Alamogordo that would have an exclusive right to sell "limited quantities of the fused soil of the Monument site."[43] The federal government's attitude toward the site and the bomb itself was less benign. Initially, the army sought to discredit so-called Jap propaganda claiming that the radiation from the atomic bomb explosions lingered in the environment. The military insisted that the bombs dropped on Japan had exploded at a high enough altitude to prevent contamination of the soil. In order to bolster their case, the army invited a team of journalists and photographers to inspect the Alamogordo site two months after the atomic explosion.[44]

In the end, conflict with the Soviet Union derailed efforts to create the Atomic Bomb National Monument. Most of the rickety structures at the site were dismantled by the army for safety reasons and because of indifference regarding their historic nature. Additionally, the passage of time and the forces of nature lessened the effect of many of the site's dramatic features. In the words of one Park Service regional director, the "Atomsite is breaking up badly and is becoming quite dull and drab-looking." Perhaps equally important, as the Los Alamos site continued to produce nuclear technology, the Alamogordo site could not be spared. The War Department turned over the site to the newly established Atomic Energy Commission in 1946 and the laboratory at Los Alamos continued to work on weapons of mass destruction. The Park Service shelved plans to create a national monument at Alamogordo.[45]

The weapons technology used in the Second World War fascinated both federal officials and much of the wider public and remains a reason for the interest in commemorating the creation of the atomic bomb. This interest in modern warfare helps explain why a year before Congress authorized a monument to the marine's flag raising on Iwo Jima, lawmakers passed legislation creating a National Air Museum. Designed in 1946 to document the history of American military and civil aviation, the Air Museum, a part of the Smithsonian Institution, began to acquire a wide array of famous aircraft used in both World Wars—most notably the *Enola Gay*, the plane that dropped the atomic bomb on Hiroshima. Until a permanent museum was completed in 1976, the National Air Museum, renamed the National Air and Space Museum in 1966, mounted exhibitions in temporary quarters at the Smithsonian.[46]

Many states, local communities, and private organizations from the mid-1950s to the 1980s shared a fascination with the technological artifacts of the Second World War and clamored for a chance to turn deactivated U.S. naval vessels from that war into floating museums. Several states, such as North Carolina and Alabama, for example, created special committees to maintain decommissioned battleships bearing their states' names as memorials. Other states and private groups wanted to save particular ships because of their "uniqueness" or illustrious records. For instance, a nonprofit organization was formed in 1978 in California to preserve the last remaining Oakland-built liberty ship of the war, the USS *Jeremiah O'Brien*.[47]

Most states and private groups declared that the ships they saved from the scrap heap would serve as war memorials. Alabama decided that the battleship bearing its name should serve as a "state shrine to the sacrifice and courage of Alabamians who served in World War II and Korea." When the Chicago Museum of Science and Industry placed a captured German submarine on display in 1954, it formally dedicated the craft to the "memory of the American seamen who went down to unmarked ocean graves helping to win victory at sea."[48] Although World War II museum ships were called memorials, they were advertised and valued as tourist attractions. During the early 1980s, the Alabama Battleship Commission put out a pamphlet that assured visitors that they would "enjoy every minute aboard" the vessel. Each year the commission held a pageant to select several young women to serve as "crewmates" and to publicize the battleship memorial and other tourist sites in Alabama. The Massachusetts Memorial Committee invited Boy Scouts and other youth groups to "bunk down" aboard the USS *Massachusetts* in Fall River and experience "24 memorable hours." It also advertised the former warship as an ideal site for business meetings, luncheons, and other special events.[49]

The transformation of a war memorial into tourist attraction was not unique to the warships or to the period after the Second World War. In the late nineteenth and early twentieth centuries, many communities valued their revolutionary and Civil War battlefields for their ability to draw visitors, although many political leaders and veterans expressed misgivings about the commercialization of sacred sites and holidays. As the nineteenth century drew to a close, many Civil War veterans expressed displeasure that Memorial Day had become a day for picnics and shopping. During the early 1920s, a congressional opponent of transferring the care of Civil War battlefields from the War Department to the National Park Service denounced such a plan for fear the battlefields would fill with hot dog and souvenir stands.[50]

Nor did all weapons of war stand idle and passive after 1945. In 1951, a group of retired military pilots formed the anachronistically titled Confederate Air Force (CAF) and started rehabilitating and flying vintage aircraft from the Second World War. During the 1960s and 1970s, this southwestern-based organization acquired a national and even international membership. The United States Air Force granted the CAF an aura of legitimacy by inviting the organization to perform aerial demonstrations and programs at air force bases around the country.[51]

The reenactments sponsored by the CAF attempted to convey an aura of realism and included a narration that highlighted the central political and military events of the Second World War. Airplanes simulated bombing runs, ground controls set off explosives buried in the airfield, and aircraft "hit" in mock combat turned on smoke generators. The recreated "battles" focused not only on American triumphs but also on catastrophes such as Pearl Harbor. Until 1976, CAF air shows even recreated the atomic bombing of Hiroshima by featuring a lone B–29 flying over the airfield.[52]

Battle reenactment as a form of commemoration has a long history. During the antebellum period, elite militia companies from Philadelphia often journeyed to revolutionary battlefields to restage American triumphs as part of Independence Day celebrations. In 1913 at the Gettysburg Blue and Gray reunion, reenactors took part in one last "Pickett's charge" and its defeat by Union forces. Beginning in the 1950s, scores of amateur military companies attracted members interested in restaging Civil War battles. At the one-hundredth anniversary of Gettysburg, a thousand members of the North-South Skirmishers Association joined the Sons of Union Veterans in another Pickett's charge. After the First World War, veterans and organizers of community pageants depicted the trench warfare of that conflict. Several Kansas American Legion posts in October 1920 raised money to assist twenty-six comrades who had been wounded in the war by organizing an event that featured "sham battles, the thrills of No Man's Land and miniature naval engagements."[53]

In one symbolic manner, the CAF served to link the Lost Cause with the triumph of the Second World War. Once again, this melding and reworking of the past had ample precedents. After the Spanish-American War and the First World War, national leaders and many veterans, particularly from the South, linked these two conflicts with the Civil War. As a result of criticism from civil rights groups in the 1970s, the leadership of the CAF started to minimize the overt link between the organization and the Confederacy. Members were urged to stop wearing Confederate flags and to cease displaying them on their airplanes. At air shows, narrators no longer offered long homages to the virtues of the Old South and the fighting spirit of the Confederacy. Despite these changes, gray remained the color of the "official" uniform that in most other respects was a copy of that worn by army–air force officers in the Second World War. Pilots of the CAF still bore the title colonel, and many wanted to retain the Confederate flavor of the organization.[54]

In the 1970s, critics insisted that the historical reenactments performed by the CAF trivialized the death and destruction of the Second World War. Protests from the Japanese government and pressure from the federal government forced the CAF to end their depictions of the Hiroshima attack. Despite this concession, the CAF defended their aerial combat demonstrations and maintained that these mock battles neither minimized the tragic qualities of war nor sowed the seeds for future ones. To the CAF, their reenactments served to remind Americans of the need to support a strong military in order to deter future aggression.[55]

Controversy failed to dampen public attendance at public air shows sponsored by the CAF. No doubt their continued popularity stemmed from the relatively limited destruction the United States experienced during the Second World War. Because the mainland United States never suffered the terror bombings of European and other civilian centers,

Americans could cling more easily to a depiction of aerial combat as a glorious affair that served to test the strength and skill of individual aviators and American technology. In a sense, many Americans did not want their memories of the Second World War as the "good war" dimmed by reflecting on the terrible nature of modern warfare. Furthermore, the cold war led policy makers to temper or obscure the destruction caused by the Second World War, especially by the atomic bombs that ended it.

The American peace movement challenged efforts to legitimize the atomic bomb and the use of air power against civilian targets. As early as the late 1940s, peace groups commemorated the anniversary of the bombing of Hiroshima with religious services and other ceremonies. By the early 1960s, a number of scholars and activists within the peace movement were insisting that the United States could have ended the Second World War without using nuclear weapons. A revisionist historian, Gar Alperovitz, even suggested that the United States had dropped the atomic bomb on Japan primarily in order to intimidate the Soviet Union into becoming more compliant in the race for postwar power.[56]

The atomic bomb served as one of the dominant symbols of the Second World War and the cold war. After 1945, politicians, diplomats, intellectuals, writers, and the general public struggled to cope with the implications of this weapon. Certainly, the atomic bomb ensured that even at the height of the cold war, ceremonies honoring the Second World War stressed the theme of peace. Speakers and newspaper editorials on Veterans Day spoke of the need to avoid war.

Escalating tensions with the Soviet Union served to hasten reconciliation between the United States and its former enemies. In an effort to combat communism and possible Soviet expansion, the United States allied itself with West Germany and Japan. For the same reason, the United States also permitted a number of former Nazis and Japanese militarists to hold important positions in government and in the economy. Animosity toward the former Axis nations did not disappear completely, but it did diminish—even among many United States war veterans. By the 1970s joint reunions between American troops and their former adversaries, particularly the Germans, became common.[57]

Although many Americans by the mid-1950s viewed Germany and Japan as friends of the United States, the memory of the Second World War loomed large in the public imagination. This war, particularly with regard to the conflict with Germany, was the "good war." In motion pictures such as the *Longest Day*, *Midway*, and *Patton* World War II remained an epic struggle of national and moral triumph. Although many movies offered an empathetic portrait of the "good" German and Japanese during the war, the Nazis were depicted as the ultimate incarnation of evil because of their extermination of millions of Jews and other civilians.

Even with the pressures of the cold war, reconciliation with Japan and Germany was not free of controversy and tension. Some veterans of the Pacific Theater harbored deep resentment toward Japan and wanted strict limits placed on how far the United States should promote reconciliation between the two nations. And on the fortieth anniversary of the Second World War, differences developed over how the United States should remember the Holocaust and the German role in this crime.

The horror of the Holocaust gradually became part of the memory of the Second World War in the United States. The late 1970s and 1980s witnessed a growing interest in the commemoration of the Holocaust. In 1978 Congress designated 28 and 29 April 1979 as days dedicated to the remembrance of the victims of the Holocaust. To recommend appropriate observances and to examine the entire question of how the Holocaust should be remembered, President Jimmy Carter established a special commission headed by death-camp survivor and author Elie Wiesel.[58]

The Wiesel Commission urged the establishment of a museum and memorial in Washington, D.C., dedicated to the memory of the Holocaust. The commission also called for the nation to observe an annual week of remembrance for the victims of the Nazi death camps—an observance, which the commission recommended be timed to coincide with the day established by Israel for commemorating this tragic event, that would attempt to establish an "internationally recognized Holocaust Commemoration Day." To ensure that the United States would never again sit idly by while genocide was repeated, it called for the creation of a national committee of conscience, which would bring cases of genocide to the attention of the American government and public.[59]

In 1980 Congress voted unanimously to create a permanent United States Holocaust Commission vested with the responsibility of building a museum on the mall in Washington, D.C. Although a committee of conscience was not established, Congress gave the Holocaust Commission the responsibility for planning annual observances of the Holocaust. During the 1980s these observances generally followed the pattern established in 1979, featuring a national memorial ceremony held in the rotunda or another site in Washington. Often the president or a high official in the administration spoke, and the ceremony featured a recitation of the Kaddish and other prayers, the lighting of a menorah composed of six candles in memory of the six million dead, and mournful hymns. It also promoted local observances in communities throughout the nation and urged governors as well as mayors to issue proclamations marking Holocaust Remembrance Week.[60]

Widespread efforts to commemorate the Holocaust on the national and local level were an attempt, in one sense, to recognize Jews and Judaism as part of a pluralistic American national identity. At the same time, those who promoted rituals and monuments to mark the Holocaust, particularly Jewish groups, wanted them to underscore the ties that existed between the United States and the state of Israel. For instance, President Jimmy Carter announced the establishment of a Holocaust commission at ceremonies marking the thirtieth anniversary of Israel's independence. During this 1978 celebration, which was held in Washington, D.C., and attended by Israeli prime minister Menachem Begin, Carter affirmed America's continued support for Israel and stressed that the United States viewed that nation as having been founded originally as a refuge for Jews persecuted by Nazi Germany.[61]

In a sense the memorializing of the Holocaust helped affirm America's moral virtue. Americans had fought the good fight against Nazi Germany, and the Second World War could be remembered as one of liberation. During the 1980s many national observances sponsored by the United States Holocaust Commission included a military honor guard, which displayed the battle flags of those army divisions that had liberated the death camps. In 1985 the commission sponsored a separate memorial service at Arlington National Cemetery in memory of those who had liberated the concentration camps. And in 1989, the State of New Jersey dedicated a Holocaust memorial, in Liberty State Park across from New York City, a statue entitled *Liberation,* which portrayed an American soldier carrying out a death camp victim.[62]

In promoting observances of the Holocaust, Jewish leaders and organizations wanted to redefine the memory of the Second World War and offer a more somber interpretation of the conflict. They maintained that the Holocaust remained a singularly unique event in human history and must be remembered in order to ensure that neither the Jews nor any other people would ever again become the victims of genocide. Although Holocaust observances would commemorate liberation, Jewish leaders and organizations also wanted them to remind the American public how little the

*Liberation* by Nathan Rapoport, 1984. This statue in Liberty State Park, Jersey City, New Jersey, in remembrance of the Holocaust represents the increasing American commemoration in the 1970s and 1980s of both the Second World War and the Holocaust. (Photograph courtesy Gordon Miller)

United States had done to avert the tragedy before it happened or to aid Jewish refugees.

Except for neo-Nazis, a small fringe group, most Americans viewed the Holocaust as one of the darkest chapters in human history. But Americans were divided over the lessons to be learned from this event and how to commemorate it. For example, some conservatives vehemently opposed the ratification of an international convention outlawing genocide for fear it would set a precedent abridging national sovereignty. Others maintained that the Holocaust should be remembered as an event that afflicted not only the Jews but also non-Jews, including Russians, Poles, Gypsies, homosexuals, and the mentally retarded. Others believed that efforts to remember the Holocaust should not stand in the way of a German-American reconciliation.[63]

In early 1985 President Ronald Reagan announced plans to visit West Germany on the eve of the fortieth anniversary of the Second World War. As part of that trip, the White House announced that the president would visit the German military cemetery at Bitburg in order to join West German chancellor Helmut Kohl in a wreath-laying ceremony for German soldiers killed in the Second World War. Reagan hoped the Bitburg visit would serve to highlight the ties of friendship that had emerged between the United States and West Germany. Even after Reagan learned that Bitburg cemetery contained the graves of more than twenty soldiers of the SS, he still defended his plans to go there. At a press conference prior to his trip, Reagan asserted that German soldiers who lay buried at Bitburg were just as much the victims of the Nazi regime as the inmates of the concentration camps. Although Reagan eventually added a visit to the Bergen-Belsen concentration camp in an attempt to assuage public protest, he maintained that there was little reason to remind Germans of the Holocaust

since the German people—and very few alive that remember even the war, and certainly none of them who were adults and participating in any way—and they have a feeling, and a guilt feeling that's been imposed upon them, and I just think it's unnecessary.[64]

Many Jewish, Christian, and veterans' groups expressed outrage that the president wanted to go through with the visit. In their view, Reagan's actions served to obscure the horrific crimes committed by the Nazis. Moreover, most found that Reagan's belated acknowledgment of the Holocaust only compounded the problem. According to Elie Wiesel and other Jewish leaders, combining a visit to a death camp with that to a cemetery containing the graves of SS soldiers only served to dishonor the memory of those who had been victims of the Nazis. Not all Americans condemned Reagan's decision to travel to Bitburg. Some former policy makers and press commentators thought the president should go through with the visit in order to maintain a good relationship with the West German government. Shortly after Reagan's trip, half of all Americans, according to one public opinion poll, approved of the trip as an appropriate gesture of reconciliation.[65]

To many Jewish Americans, however, Bitburg aroused fears that the memory of the Holocaust would be forgotten with the passing of time. Before the controversy many sponsors and creators of Holocaust memorials were anxious to find ways to ensure that future generations remembered the tragedy. During the 1970s and 1980s Holocaust memorials built or proposed tended to be stark and modern in their design. Art and architectural critics called them part of a new wave of "anti-monuments" because of their rejection of classically inspired designs and their bleak efforts to evoke a sense of tragedy. One memorial in San Francisco contained an actual barbed-wire fence, behind which stood a lone figure and, farther away, a sculptural group of dead bodies. The design of the National Holocaust Museum incorporated architectural elements used in the death camps.[66]

The movement to commemorate the Holocaust in memorials and ceremonies represented an attempt to alter the way the Second World War was commemorated. It served, in a sense, to focus attention on one of the most sobering aspects of this conflict. To a large degree this represented a departure from the traditional pattern of remembering war. The passage of time has usually led to conscious efforts to emphasize the heroic qualities inherent in particular conflicts. Only the passage of time will tell whether the movement to commemorate the Holocaust will convey to succeeding generations the terrible nature of the Second World War. Surprisingly, German reunification and the collapse of the Soviet Union in the late 1980s failed to reignite a significant debate within the United States over how the Second World War should be remembered. Rather, the end of the cold war and the fiftieth anniversary of Pearl Harbor exacerbated relations with Japan and rekindled the debate over how the war in the Pacific, particularly Pearl Harbor, should be remembered.

During the Second World War, the Pearl Harbor attack symbolized both Japanese treachery and American unpreparedness. In the postwar period's interest in reconciliation, presidents and military leaders glossed over this earlier view of Japan's motives, even as they reminded the public of the "lessons" taught by Pearl Harbor. In later years, national leaders expressed regret at the hysteria and racism that had led to the internment of Japanese Americans in "resettlement" after Pearl Harbor. In the 1980s, the United States Congress issued a formal apology to those who had been interned and offered them limited compensation. On the fiftieth anniversary of Pearl Harbor, President George Bush echoed these sentiments and declared flatly that the internments had been wrong. In the bulk of his address, Bush urged fellow veterans of this conflict to join him and free themselves of any bitterness or hatred toward their one-time foe.[67] Like his predecessors, Bush stressed that Pearl Harbor must continue to symbolize the dangers of unpreparedness. During the cold war, this theme took on added immediacy as result of the prevalence of nuclear weapons. The fear of another "surprise attack" remained a central problem for those Americans who planned responses to possible Soviet attacks.[68]

Yet despite the symbolic importance of Pearl Harbor, two decades elapsed before a national memorial was built commemorating the attack. Although the federal government had established an elaborate network of cemeteries for the war dead of the Second World War, not until 1962 did any permanent monuments mark the underwater graves of those entombed aboard the USS *Arizona,* which remained sunk in the waters of Pearl Harbor.[69] Even before the end of the Second World War, the unsalvaged *Arizona* had served the navy as an object of veneration. Warships entering and leaving Pearl Harbor often "saluted" the sunken vessel. In 1950, the navy formally recommissioned the *Arizona,* attached a flagpole to a sunken mast of the vessel, and hoisted the national colors over it. The navy, veterans' groups, and local leaders in Hawaii wanted a permanent memorial for the *Arizona.* In 1946, the government of Hawaii created the Pacific War Memorial Commission to develop memorials commemorating the territories' role in the Second World War. With the consent of the U.S. Navy, the commission gained permission from Congress in 1958 to conduct a national fund-raising campaign to build a memorial to the *Arizona.*[70]

The memorial, finally completed in 1958 with a combination of private and public funds, left the *Arizona* on the harbor floor. Despite the calls from some to salvage and rebury the ship and crew on land, the vessel was left undisturbed. Instead, a memorial building was built in the harbor and near the vessel in order to permit relatives and other visitors to view the ship's remains. In a shrine room, a marble wall contains an alphabetical list of all those killed aboard the *Arizona.*[71]

Like most American memorials, the USS *Arizona* Memorial focused on the tremendous cost of war and offered no overt message of hostility toward Japan. On the other hand, the Pacific War Memorial Commission had rejected proposals calling for incorporating the USS *Arizona* Memorial into a memorial emphasizing Japanese-American reconciliation. Moreover, efforts by the Park Service to display Japanese artifacts—a midget submarine, for example—at the memorial's visitors center met with vehement opposition from some veterans.[72]

On the fiftieth anniversary of Pearl Harbor, some Americans argued that the United States must again guard against a threat from Japan. Although few feared the resurgence of that country's military power, Japan was labeled a potent economic rival that has not "played by the rules." Automobile executives and other manufacturers urged the United States government to pry open closed Japanese markets and to place restrictions on access to American markets in order to meet the economic threat.[73] Fears of "Japan bashing" worried political and economic elites who benefited from the strong ties that had developed between the United States and Japan. In the 1980s, a number of American states and cities courted Japanese investments and wanted to avoid gestures that served to antagonize them. For example, in 1988 Rhode Island considered ending the celebration of V-J Day as a state holiday in order to make it easier for the state to lure Japanese business. In 1992, the Hawaiian tourist industry feared bellicose commemorations of the anniversary of Pearl Harbor could deal a crippling blow to the state by discouraging Japanese visitors.[74]

Will Pearl Harbor be used as a symbol to rekindle emotions of fear, betrayal, and treachery in the coming years? It could, if the economic position of the United States were to decline relative to that of Japan. At the same time, the memory of Pearl Harbor might with the passing of the World War II generation fade into the recesses of the nation's memory. Although the USS *Maine* memorial at Arlington continues to endure, the memory of this vessel and the Spanish-American War no longer arouses intense emotions among Americans. It would be unfortunate if Americans completely forgot the loss and destruction caused by the Japanese attack on Pearl Harbor; nonetheless, it would be tragic if the events of the Second World War inflamed a new generation of Americans and ended the reconciliation that has developed between Japan and the United States.

# 5

# FROM THE KOREAN WAR
# TO THE VIETNAM
# VETERANS MEMORIAL

The cold war radically altered America's relationship with the rest of the world. The United States proclaimed itself leader of the Free World and moved to counter the perceived threat of communist aggression with massive amounts of economic and military assistance to friendly governments. As part of this effort, the United States signed multilateral and bilateral defense agreements with dozens of European, Latin American, and Asian nations. This large overseas role was all the more remarkable when compared with the previous tradition of isolationism.[1] Americans' acceptance of these vast overseas responsibilities did not come without controversy. A minority rejected the idea that anticommunism should be the cornerstone of U.S. foreign policy. Still, until the 1960s most Americans were willing to support a foreign policy that stressed the need to counter communism and that took U.S. military forces all over the world.

Before the cold war it had been argued that there existed a distinctively American way of war. Often the United States had entered conflicts divided, unprepared, and unable to avoid an initial series of defeats. But these setbacks only served to spur the United States to mobilize fully its resources and to seek a climactic victory over the enemy. Except for the South during the Civil War, America had never lost a war. Even the nearly disastrous War of 1812 could be portrayed as a triumph after Andrew Jackson's success at New Orleans.[2]

Initially, the Korean War seemed destined to follow the pattern established by earlier conflicts. An imminent defeat at the beginning of the war in August 1950 seemed destined to become a stunning victory by the end of the year. In the fall of 1950, the commander of the United Nations, U.S. general Douglas MacArthur, promised that the boys would be home by Christmas and the Korean peninsula unified under a noncommunist government. But the entrance of the People's Republic of China into the conflict at the end of November dashed that hope. Although Douglas MacArthur wanted to widen the war to include military targets in China, the Truman administration placed clear limits on American involvement and abandoned plans to reunify Korea. In July 1951 the United States began truce talks with the Chinese and North Korean representatives that dragged on until 1953. When Eisenhower assumed the presidency in 1953 he continued Truman's policies aimed at preventing an escalation of the conflict and signed an armistice that recognized the de facto existence of a divided Korea.[3]

Americans were ambivalent about the indecisiveness of the Korean conflict and of the cold war in general. The emergence of McCarthyism stemmed, in part, from an effort to silence the voices of those who opposed making anticommunism a central aim of American foreign policy. But at the same time, it expressed the deep frustrations within American society over the inability to win a decisive victory and thus return to "normalcy." Although most Americans, especially conservatives, wanted to triumph over communism, they also longed for peace. These often conflicting goals and desires would be reflected in the way the Korean War and the cold war would be commemorated.[4]

Even before the Korean War had ended, an important decision had been made regarding how this conflict would be commemorated. In March 1951 the Defense Department decided that the bodies of all American service people who died in Korea would be returned to the United States for burial. In contrast to the overseas internments after the two world wars, there would be no overseas cemeteries in Korea to mark American combat there. This decision reflected the ambivalence of the U.S. government and of the American public about the war's outcome and the uncertainty of the Truman administration and the Department of Defense over whether future access to a U.S. military cemetery in the Republic of Korea could be guaranteed.[5]

Marines of the First Marine Division pay their respects to fallen comrades during memorial services at the division's cemetery at Hamhung, Korea, only a few weeks after the break-out from Chosin Reservoir. 13 December 1950. In contrast to the foreign U.S. military cemeteries created after the world wars, the United States decided not to maintain any permanent military cemeteries in Korea. (Photograph by Corporal Uthe; reprinted from J. Heller, *War and Conflict*, National Archives, 1990; original source, U.S. Marine Corps)

No dissenting voices were raised in public questioning the wisdom of bringing back all the American war dead. No one suggested that the proper place for a fallen soldier remained the battlefield. A *New York Times* editorial in 1951 welcomed the return of the first group of American war dead and praised the sacrifice of those who had given their lives for the cause of freedom. For the most part the tone of the editorial remained somber, and it expressed uncertainty over the outcome of the Korean War. It asked, without providing a definitive answer, "What place will this peninsula, remote from us and from our normal interests, have in the history of our time?"[6]

Would the Korean conflict be remembered as a "war"? In 1951 the army decided that because the Korean conflict had not been declared a war but instead was officially described as a "police action," the headstones used in national cemeteries in the United States would not bear the inscription "Korean War," only the name, rank, and dates of the deceased. After congressional protests and unfavorable publicity, the secretary of the army decided that the word "Korea" would be added to headstones, but not the word "War." This action failed to mollify conservative critics on the Right who insisted that it remained representative of the political "chicanery" practiced by an administration that had also steadfastly refused to acknowledge that this "police action" was actually a war that America had entered into without the consent of Congress.[7]

A military armistice in 1953 ended the fighting in Korea. That year returning veterans received a heroes' welcome with elaborate ceremonies. The American Legion and other established veterans' organizations courted them in hopes they would join their ranks. But because of its ambiguous outcome, the Korean War soon became another one of America's "forgotten" wars. The United States had not been defeated, but neither had it triumphed. Moreover, the cold war with the Soviet Union and China continued unabated and throughout the 1950s and early 1960s threatened to draw America into other regional conflicts. As a result, Korea remained to the public, and even to many national leaders, an unpleasant and costly military action that they wanted to forget.[8]

Until the late 1980s, the federal government showed little interest in a national memorial devoted exclusively to commemorating the Korean War. In 1954 Congress expanded the authority of the American Battle Monuments Commission and authorized it to construct memorials in Korea. Beginning in the late 1950s the commission tried to convince Congress to appropriate the funds needed to build a memorial in South Korea, but it failed. As a substitute, the commission decided to expand the World War II memorial planned for Hawaii's Punch Bowl Military Cemetery in Hawaii, to include the commemoration of the Korean War. In the memorial's "museum" a written narrative etched in bronze and a series of mosaic maps documenting the Korean War joined similar ones recording the Asian and Pacific campaigns of the Second World War. One long wall outside of the memorial building recorded the names of the missing from the Second World War's Pacific campaign, and another bore the names of their counterparts in the Korean War.[9]

Expanding the Punch Bowl memorial into a memorial to both the Second World War and the Korean War solved the problem of where to build a new memorial. It also represented another effort to link symbolically these two conflicts. As pointed out earlier, the Korean War had served as a catalyst in the early 1950s for turning Armistice Day into Veterans Day. In 1958 the remains of an unidentified combatant killed in Korea and one from the Second World War were honored with a state funeral and burial at the Tomb of the Unknown Soldier in Arlington.

The decision to emphasize the continuity between World War II and Korea ensured, of course, that the latter would be overshadowed. The Second World War had been a global conflict of unprecedented magnitude and had ended in triumph. In sharp contrast, Korea had been a "police action" confined to a narrow peninsula in an "out of the way" part of the world, and it had concluded in a stalemate.

In the 1950s and 1970s, the South Korean government, not the United States government, dedicated several memorials heralding American participation in the Korean War. In 1957 a memorial statue to General Douglas MacArthur was built in Inchon to commemorate the most successful campaign of the war. In 1975 South Korea dedicated a memorial in front of its Ministry of Defense at Paju. Fifty flagpoles, one for each state in the Union, encircles four black marble triangles resting on their tips and supporting a square plate with a circular opening. On each of the four triangles, representing the four services of the American military, a bronze relief depicts a battle scene. Three years later South Korea honored American involvement in the United Nations Memorial Cemetery at Pusan. On three concave walls shaped to form a triangle, there rests at each point a statue of two seated individuals linked together. In each sculptural grouping, one of the figures holds up a hand in order to symbolize the unity among the nations who fought in defense of freedom. Two of the memorial facades contain twenty-two bronze plaques with individual inscriptions that describe the participation of the United States and the other countries that fought on behalf of the United Nations. To symbolize peace, the memorial facade depicts two doves holding a branch.[10]

Although the American Battle Monuments Commission never formally abandoned efforts to build a memorial in Korea, in the wake of the agreement to memorialize the Vietnam War, it sought in the 1980s congressional permission to erect one in Washington, D.C. In 1986 Congress finally authorized the commission to build a national Korean War memorial, but it required that the funds needed to complete it be raised from private contributions.

To many Americans in the 1950s and 1960s, the Korean War remained only one episode in the cold war, and not a successful one at that. In a sense, Korea became a forgotten war because of its inconclusive outcome. The struggle against the forces of communism continued, and the time had not come to build memorials to such a limited war.

The cold war between the United States and the Soviet Union was a conflict, yet not a war. As in earlier conflicts, national leaders during the cold war promoted the remembrance of earlier wars as a way of inspiring the American people. During the Korean War the American Battle Monuments Commission successfully urged the Truman administration to continue construction of Second World War memorials in order to boost American morale. Speakers on Memorial Day, the Fourth of July, and Veterans Day implored Americans to continue the struggle for freedom begun by their forefathers.[11]

During the 1950s and 1960s there were several efforts to build what might be termed national cold war memorials. One initiative passed by Congress in 1953 called for the creation of a memorial dedicated to and perpetuating the principle of freedom. The National Memorial Commission planned a massive freedom shrine on a tract of land near the Iwo Jima Memorial in Arlington, Virginia. Supporters of this memorial wanted to build a copy of a massive classical Greek temple and fill it with a series of bas-reliefs depicting the history of the United States. Local opposition by county officials and residents together with the National Freedom Memorials Commission's inability to convince Congress to support the proposal doomed the project.[12]

At the urging of a former army commander, General Kenyon Joyce, President Dwight Eisenhower revived the idea of building a national military museum, an idea first proposed during the Second World War. In 1956 the president appointed a committee chaired by Nelson Rockefeller, then governor of New York, to examine the need for such an institution. The Rockefeller Committee called for the creation of the National Museum of Peace and War under the auspices of the Smithsonian Institution. It would document the history of the armed forces in order to promote "sound patriotism." The proposal included a "Hall of Today," which served to educate the public on the need for a continued strong national defense. Through technologically innovative exhibitions, Hall of Today visitors would learn first hand of the important part NATO played in preserving peace, of the economic value of earth satellites, and of the usefulness of atomic-bomb shelters as a deterrent against nuclear attacks.[13]

After receiving the report of the Rockefeller Committee, Eisenhower appointed another committee in 1958, chaired by Earl Warren, chief justice of the Supreme Court, to formulate more definitive plans regarding the governance, site, and operation of a military museum. Although that committee agreed with Eisenhower's charge to design a "dynamic" museum, members differed over how best to accomplish this. General Kenyon envisioned a huge monumental structure patterned after the architecture of classical Greece and Rome. For instance, he wanted the pediments of the museum topped with war chariots modelled after the ones found on the colossal Victor Emanuelle memorial in Rome. Rockefeller wanted to ensure that the museum did not become merely a collection of "artifacts"; he wanted it to emphasize the need for public education regarding issues of national security. John Nicholas Brown, a Smithsonian Institution regent from Rhode Island, favored a theme park. He called for the historical reconstruction of a colonial fort, a revolutionary encampment, a segment of a Civil War battlefield, a World War I trench, and an amphibious landing site from World War II.[14]

The Warren Museum Committee never fully resolved the divisions that existed between its members, and the final report to the president gave few specifics regarding the proposed museum. After receiving the report, Eisenhower called on Congress to create yet a third committee, this time under the authority of the Smithsonian Institution, to study the issue. In 1962 Congress accepted these recommendations, and a new committee was formed under the continued leadership of Earl Warren. Although officially chaired by Warren, the panel was guided by John Nicholas Brown and by its staff director, Colonel John Magruder III, a marine officer detailed to the project.[15]

Interagency disputes within the federal government, ineffective leadership on the part of Colonel Magruder, and lack of support by Smithsonian officials conspired to doom the project. The design for the museum envisioned by Brown and Magruder proved far too costly and controversial. In 1966, in the midst of the Vietnam War, Magruder publicly unveiled plans that called for a $40 million museum located on the Potomac River that would include a military airfield, several ships, the reconstruction of several battlefields, and an underground ballistic-missile silo. Critics labelled it a "Disneyland of destruction" and denounced it as an effort to glorify war. Never enthusiastic about the museum, Smithsonian officials

After a B–29 Superfortress dropped an atomic bomb on Nagasaki, a dense column of smoke rose more than sixty thousand feet into the air. American ambivalence about the atomic bomb has frustrated efforts to commemorate its use. (Reprinted from J. Heller, *War and Conflict,* National Archives, 1990; original source, Office of War Information)

A preliminary sketch for a missile silo that would make up part of the National
Military Museum proposed in the 1960s. Critics maintained that this park
amounted to a "Disneyland of destruction." (Reprinted from *Preliminary
Development Plan: National Armed Forces Museum;* courtesy Smithsonian
Institution Archives)

further distanced themselves from the project and gave it a low priority.
The National Park Service even refused to give up the ground necessary to
build the museum.[16]

In an attempt to save the military museum, the advisory committee in
1969 offered a new plan that tried to avoid controversy. Instead of documenting the entire scope of American military history with an emphasis
on the twentieth century, the committee proposed building an outdoor
bicentennial park featuring living exhibits documenting camp and community life during the age of the American Revolution. Although the new
project managed to gain the endorsement of the Nixon administration,
the advisory board failed to convince Congress to appropriate the necessary funds. In the end the board decided to abandon the project and turn
over the collection of artifacts it had gathered to the Smithsonian Institution.[17]

Opposition to the Vietnam War helped prevent the completion of a national military museum, but the antiwar movement alone cannot explain
why the museum was not built. Opposition to the museum merely served
to confirm misgivings that Smithsonian officials had always had toward the
project. In 1966, for instance, one assistant secretary of the Smithsonian

expressed sympathy with opponents of the Armed Forces Museum. In a memorandum to the Smithsonian secretary, he wondered whether his earlier proposal, made in jest, to vest management of the Armed Forces Museum in the hands of the Disarmament Agency might not really be such a bad idea.[18]

The fate of the national military museum suggests the misgivings many public officials and much of the public had toward the large military establishment that had to be maintained during the cold war: Americans did not want to see themselves as a militaristic people. Even those who proposed the military museum in the late 1950s continually stressed that the United States maintained a strong military, for defense and to ensure a peaceful world, not for conquest.

Although plans to build cold war memorials faltered, government spending on public art and culture soared. Although proposals for a national military museum foundered, the Smithsonian Institution carried out an ambitious expansion program that included the opening of a series of new art museums, most notably the Hirshhorn Collection and the National Portrait Gallery. In 1965 Washington, D.C., acquired a national cultural center dedicated to the memory of John F. Kennedy. Eisenhower and

The proposed National Military Museum included plans to recreate a World War I battlefield with barbed wire made out of plastic to ensure children did not injure themselves. (Reprinted from *Preliminary Development Plan: National Armed Forces Museum;* courtesy Smithsonian Institution Archives)

Kennedy proposed, and Lyndon Johnson finally succeeded in convincing Congress to provide, direct federal support of the arts through the National Endowment for the Arts (NEA). During the 1960s and 1970s, the NEA provided funds to communities to purchase, among other things, the latest modern sculpture.

Although not in a crude sense, proponents of an expanded federal role in the arts, most notably President Kennedy, viewed culture as a weapon to be used in the struggle against communism. Art and culture, Kennedy insisted, had a larger and transcendent purpose. Artistic achievement offered a means by which to measure the success of a civilization. To Kennedy, the artist, scholar, and writer could best serve their nation by creating lasting works of culture that would inspire the present and endure for the ages. In order for the arts to flourish and to ensure that they reflected the diversity inherent in American culture, the artist must have total freedom to create. As a result, professional artists, not the government, must have sole power to set aesthetic standards.

By allowing the professional artist to determine the criteria for the selection of public art, the National Endowment for the Arts helped further the ascendancy of modern sculpture and art within the United States. The government's support of modernism stood in sharp contrast to the Soviet Union's efforts to force artists and sculptors to conform to the demands of socialist realism. In contrast to the United States, the Soviet Union embarked on a wave of monument building in the 1950s and 1960s to commemorate the Second World War and forced their creators to conform to a rigid and somber style of sculpture and architecture. Although Presidents John F. Kennedy and Lyndon B. Johnson proclaimed the blessings of artistic freedom as representative of the larger freedoms inherent in American society, their Soviet counterparts condemned modernism as reflective of bourgeois decadence.[19]

Modern art, architecture, and sculpture gained increasing acceptance within the United States in the 1950s and 1960s, but there remained substantial opposition to it. Until the 1970s the national Commission of Fine Arts proved reluctant to embrace memorials too heavily influenced by modernism. In the most famous case, the commission in 1962 rejected an innovative monument proposed by the Franklin D. Roosevelt Memorial Commission.

Although most policymakers and Americans longed for peace in the 1950s and 1960s, they also wanted to contain communism. The Korean War was an example of increasing U.S. intervention in the Third World. As a result of Korea, the Truman administration resumed aid to the nationalist government on Taiwan and shelved indefinitely any plans to recognize the communist government on the mainland. The Eisenhower administration under Secretary of State John Foster Dulles signed a series of mutual-defense treaties with a host of Asian and Middle Eastern nations in order to clearly delineate where the Free World began. Military and economic assistance to "friendly" governments in the Third World was increased, and in the interests of halting communism, the United States often aligned itself with repressive, undemocratic regimes. The Central Intelligence Agency orchestrated the overthrow of governments in Guatemala and Iran that threatened American economic interests and that appeared too radical in their political orientation.

Most Americans were willing to rely on proxies to meet the communist threat and frequently showed little enthusiasm for direct U.S. involvement. In the case of Vietnam, the United States went to great lengths to minimize American involvement and fully entered the war only when it appeared that South Vietnam would fall. In 1965 the deteriorating situation of the South Vietnamese government forced President Lyndon Johnson to commit substantial American ground and air forces to the conflict or else face the probable victory of the Vietcong. In many ways his decision to escalate the war had been preordained by twenty years of cold war ideology. Johnson, like most U.S. policy makers, saw the world in stark bipolar terms and thought that a communist victory, even in distant Vietnam, would threaten American national security. If Vietnam fell to communism, Johnson argued, other nations of Southeast Asia would topple like dominoes. In justifying U.S. involvement, Johnson stressed the need to halt acts of aggression before it was too late and made repeated analogies to World War II. As a statesmen, Johnson remained haunted by the memories of Munich; as a politician, he wanted to avoid spawning another wave of McCarthyism.[20]

A vigorous antiwar movement developed soon after the Johnson administration committed substantial ground troops to the conflict. Many in the peace movement protested that American involvement in Vietnam was immoral and illegal. Through protests, teach-ins, and publicity the antiwar activists sought to educate the wider public. They also sought to subvert the traditional symbols associated with the war. To the dismay of "hawks," the names of Americans killed in Vietnam were read aloud at peace rallies. One organization, Another Mother Against the War, urged mothers to oppose the war and not freely sacrifice their sons to the nation. A small minority of returning soldiers, radicalized by the conflict, formed the Vietnam Veterans Against the War. In one of the most famous antiwar protests, this group organized a protest at the Capitol in Washington, D.C., in which several dozen decorated Vietnam veterans threw their medals away.[21]

Vietnam was not the first conflict to arouse significant antiwar opposition. It was the Civil War, not Vietnam, that witnessed the bloodiest and most destructive protests against the draft. But in a sense, the relative "consensus" that existed during the Second World War and the cold war encouraged government officials as well as much of the public to forget that most wars have engendered intense divisions among Americans.

Although the peace movement had an important impact on the course of the Vietnam War, it should not be overestimated. Until the Tet Offensive in 1968, many Americans associated the conflict with the image of the new model warrior of the cold war in the Third World, the men of the Green Beret. Although they did not play a major role in the war after the early 1960s, the exploits and heroism of the Green Berets were the subject of a best-selling novel and of a song that climbed the popular music charts to number one. The only Hollywood picture to deal with Vietnam during the 1960s featured John Wayne as the commander of a Green Beret unit. Wayne's movie, *The Green Berets,* depicted the war in stark, moralistic terms and portrayed it as a conflict between good Americans versus evil, treacherous Communists.[22]

In 1969 a monument was dedicated at Fort Bragg Army Base in North Carolina to members of the Green Berets who had died in service to their country in Vietnam and elsewhere. A bronze statue featured the image of a unit member carrying an automatic weapon and wearing the "distinctive headgear" identified with special forces. If the United States had "won" in Vietnam, would Green Beret statues dot the American landscape?[23]

But victory eluded America in Indochina. In 1968 the Tet Offensive dealt a crushing blow to American optimism, and both Lyndon Johnson and his successor, Richard Nixon, worked to reduce direct American military involvement. Before leaving office, Johnson opened negotiations with North Vietnam to end the war and placed restrictions on the use of American air power. In 1969 Nixon implemented a policy of Vietnamization in which American forces were withdrawn and replaced with South Vietnamese troops. To achieve victory, Nixon broadened the war by invading Cambodia in order to cut North Vietnamese and Vietcong supply lines.

Although his policy proved a disaster, both militarily and domestically, Nixon eventually succeeded in withdrawing the United States from Vietnam. In 1973 the United States signed an agreement with North Vietnam that formally ended American participation in the war.

For a time the Nixon administration tried to maintain the illusion that the United States had won a "peace with honor." When Richard Nixon signed a congressional resolution declaring that 29 March 1974 should be commemorated as Vietnam Veterans Day, he lauded the success of the Nixon Doctrine in providing Vietnam and other Southeast Asian nations the material assistance needed to defend themselves. The administration also staged an elaborate ceremony that included the participation of the South Vietnamese ambassador at a military base near Washington in which Nixon delivered an address that echoed these themes.[24]

Despite Nixon's rhetoric, however, a sense of defeat and loss pervaded efforts to commemorate Vietnam. The date, 29 March, had been selected because it marked the one-year anniversary of the return of the last U.S. prisoners of war from that conflict to the United States. The first anniversary of the "cease fire" ending the war, 29 January 1974, had been declared by Nixon to be National MIA (Missing in Action) Day in order to focus attention on the 1,100 American servicemen whose fate had not yet been accounted for. Nevertheless, the fall of South Vietnam in 1975 diminished the significance of both dates, and neither entered the national civic calendar and consciousness.

The missing in action issue loomed large in the public imagination, particularly after North Vietnam achieved a crushing victory in 1975. To many conservative Americans, the refusal of North Vietnam to account for the missing and to allow the United States to retrieve the remains of the war dead was despicable. Some suspected the worst, that this former enemy continued to hold U.S. servicemen as prisoners of war both as a way of punishing America and as a possible bargaining chip to be used at a later date.[25]

In 1983 the Reagan administration concluded that there was no evidence that any living American POWs remained in North Vietnam. Yet many conservatives and families of the MIAs refused to accept this conclusion. Some even held that there was a conspiracy on the part of the U.S. government to cover up the continued captivity of Americans. This theme was echoed in several films, the most notable being *Rambo*. In this film, Sylvester Stallone portrayed a Vietnam veteran who is sent on a mission to rescue captured American soldiers. After he succeeds in finding and liberating an American POW camp, he is allowed to fall into the hands of the enemy.[26]

The MIA issue developed into both a symbol of defeat and of the callous attitude of the federal government toward those who had served in Vietnam. Ironically, the United States military established during this conflict one of the most elaborate efforts in the history of warfare to retrieve the bodies of those who died in combat and return them to their hometowns. In contrast to the Korean War, where bodies of the fallen were temporarily interred in Asia, American soldiers seldom rested in South Vietnamese soil. Instead, they were immediately airlifted home for burial. The United States government's decision to return all the American war dead from Vietnam reflected, at best, the ambivalence the government and the public felt toward this Asian conflict. Defeat only heightened the need to return all the fallen service personnel to their homeland and to ensure that they rested among their friends.[27]

During the 1970s and early 1980s, many argued that the Vietnam veterans had been mistreated and that the conflict they fought had been forgotten. Critics accused the government of failing to meet the veterans' needs for medical care and educational assistance. Moreover, they often charged that American society had contributed to the alienation of the Vietnam veterans by failing to honor their service to the nation and by falsely stereotyping them as "baby killers." Often Vietnam veterans contrasted their experience with the elaborate "welcome home" celebrations Second World War veterans received.[28] Hollywood films and television movies of the 1970s and early 1980s frequently portrayed the "alienated" Vietnam veteran as a menace to society. The crazed, unstable veteran ready to commit murder, rape, and other horrible deeds was a stock character and an important symbol of the conflict. No doubt, it reflected American ambivalence regarding the conflict and those who participated in it.[29]

The fear of Vietnam veterans had ample precedents. In the aftermath of the American Revolution, civilian leaders wondered whether the Society of Cincinnati threatened to undermine republican institutions. After the Civil War, former Confederates in the Ku Klux Klan perpetrated violence against African Americans and attempted to subvert Reconstruction. Following the First World War, the National Civic Federation argued that the demobilized and unemployed soldiers returning from Europe could become easy prey to the organizing efforts of "Bolsheviki."[30]

The popular image of the crazed Rambo figure reflected an awareness by the public, albeit distorted, of the tremendous psychological toll caused by the Vietnam conflict. Many veterans of the Indochina conflict campaigned for recognition and treatment of post–traumatic stress syndrome by the Veterans Administration and greater understanding from the wider society. It was the First World War, not the Vietnam War, that first brought significant popular attention to the psychological casualties of war. The terms "shell shock" and "battle fatigue" entered the popular culture after this war and served as a staple of fictional accounts of the conflict. Even the image of the disordered veteran prone to commit violent crime had wide currency in the years immediately following the Second World War. In 1946, a Bill Mauldin cartoon satirized the spate of headlines that stereotyped the returning veteran as a dangerous psychopath.[31]

Did the veterans of Vietnam suffer from a greater sense of alienation than participants in earlier conflicts? To a large degree, the manner in which the United States prosecuted the Vietnam War contributed to the alienation experienced by veterans. Most soldiers of the world wars and of Korea traveled to and from the zones of battle with their units aboard troop ships. For these returning veterans, time spent in transit with their comrades allowed them an opportunity to reflect on their experiences. Moreover, the arrival and departure of troop ships in part provided the armed forces with an ideal public relations event, including elaborate welcome home parades. In the 1960s and 1970s, the U.S. armed forces required Vietnam combatants to serve only a one-year tour of duty. And because they were transported to and from Southeast Asia by air, few American soldiers went to or returned from Vietnam as part of a larger unit. After completing their 365 days of service, most veterans experienced a jarring transition back to their homes—the trip from Vietnam to the states only lasted a few hours. Some veterans later reflected that they arrived back in the States with the dirt from Indochina still underneath their fingernails.[32]

Why were there no victory parades for Vietnam veterans? In part, because of the conscious decision of the U.S. military to isolate the soldier from the community. In meeting the manpower needs of the war, the military wanted to frustrate any broad-based desire to "bring the boys home early" by using the draft to "selectively" draw a few men from each community. In contrast to the world wars and the Korean War, there was no wholesale mobilization of the National Guard, and members of the middle and upper classes frequently evaded the draft through college deferments or other means. As a result, groups of men from particular communities did not march off and return from Vietnam together as they had in these other wars. In addition, there was an effort by the Pentagon to "deritualize" the departure and arrival of troops from Vietnam, even at the war's conclusion.[33]

The reception of the POWs was, in one sense, the exception that proves the rule. When the American prisoners of war returned from Hanoi in 1973, the military staged elaborate welcoming ceremonies. President Nixon invited the POWs to the White House for a state dinner accompanied by entertainment from comedian Bob Hope. Moreover, there was widespread public sympathy for the returning POWs, and there were many gestures made to honor them as returning heroes. Many hometowns staged "welcome home" parades for them, and feature stories were written about them in local newspapers. One former prisoner of war recalled that for a year after his return to Massachusetts, he could not eat a meal in a restaurant without some stranger picking up the tab as a sign of gratitude.[34]

Many Vietnam veterans resented the apathy and hostility they received from the public. In oral interviews they frequently remained conscious that their homecoming differed from that of earlier generations. Many also believed that the federal government and older veterans organizations, such as the American Legion, failed to look after their interests. Although a substantial number of veterans joined the legion, the Veterans of Foreign Wars, and other veterans' organizations, a great many joined organizations open only to Vietnam veterans, such as the Vietnam Veterans of America, which was founded in 1978. Others avoided joining veterans' organizations altogether.[35]

The alienation expressed by many veterans at the lack of "welcome home" parades hints at the importance of ritual and tradition in "modern" American society. In a sense, the public and the federal government focused on the more palatable wars and events in the American past. A year after Vietnam fell in 1975, the United States witnessed a series of elaborate celebrations to mark the bicentennial of the Declaration of Independence and the American Revolution. After the fall of Saigon, the Vietnam War could not be portrayed as a U.S. victory. To commemorate this conflict it was necessary to focus on somber and difficult questions.

To a large degree, consumerism had reshaped American holidays, attenuating leisure and consumption. Suburbanization had diminished the crowds that in earlier times had watched huge parades marching down main city or town thoroughfares. Instead of attending commemorative services on Memorial Day or other civic holidays, most Americans went to the beach or went shopping. The demise of blue laws mandating the closing of stores on Sunday further contributed to this growing homogeneity of the American calendar. This secularization of Sunday suggests Americans' growing practice of treating no day of the week or year as distinct and divorced from the mundane world of commerce.[36]

The debates surrounding the creation of Monday holidays illustrates how American efforts to remember the war and other important civic occasions had been shaped by the rise of a consumer society. In 1968, Congress voted to change the date on which several holidays were observed—Washington's Day, Memorial Day, and Veterans Day—to ensure that they fell on a Monday each year so as to permit more three-day weekends. In the words of one sponsor, "Monday holidays" offered the opportunity to "improve the lot of all our citizens, smooth the paths of commerce, benefit the working man, save money for the country, and possibly lives, and it will not cost the government a penny." Three-day weekends allowed Americans greater opportunity to visit the extended family, take vacations, and visit tourist attractions connected with the nation's history. Federal agencies and employers could look forward to diminished absenteeism and factories could avoid costly midweek shutdowns. Labor Day holiday statistics indicated that fewer automobile fatalities took place on this already existing Monday holiday than on holidays celebrated during the midweek.[37]

Critics of the three-day holiday argued that they showed a flagrant disregard of national "traditions" and "sacred" days in order to promote the interests of the "money changers" and the "Almighty Dollar." The strongest objections came from veterans' groups and their supporters in Congress who insisted that tampering with Memorial or Veterans Day amounted to a rejection of America's "historic past."[38] In 1978 Congress responded to pressure from veterans' organization and changed Veterans Day back to 11 November, regardless of what day of the week it fell on. To a large degree, Congress heeded the call of the special interests of the veterans' organizations; much of the public was, in fact, apathetic. But in another sense, this action heralded a renewed interest in commemorating past wars and in underscoring their more tragic qualities.[39]

In contrast to Korea, Vietnam never came close to becoming a forgotten war. Even in the 1970s scores of novels, memoirs, and Hollywood films appeared that documented American involvement in this conflict. In 1971 a father who lost his son in Indochina built the Vietnam Veterans Peace and Brotherhood Chapel in New Mexico designed to preserve the memory of those who had served in that war. In 1974 members of Congress and the American Battle Monuments Commission began to suggest proposals for a national Vietnam memorial.[40]

In contrast to most of the national monuments of the world wars built by the U.S. government, the Vietnam Veterans Memorial was sponsored by a private organization. After seeing *The Deer Hunter,* a 1979 Hollywood film that examined the Vietnam veteran's experience of homecoming, Jan Scruggs, a Vietnam veteran and federal civil servant, decided that it was time to build a national Vietnam War memorial in order to help heal the divisions in American society caused by this conflict. Scruggs began his one-man crusade for a memorial, quickly garnering support from other veterans, the Congress, and the business community.[41]

Like the war it commemorated, the Vietnam memorial provoked controversy. It had to overcome the objections of members of the Interior Department and Congress, who resisted Scruggs's efforts to mandate that the memorial be constructed on a site near the Lincoln Memorial in Washington, D.C. After Scruggs managed to gain a congressional charter for the organization he founded and authorization to build a memorial after raising the necessary funds, disputes developed regarding the design of the monument. Congress mandated that Scruggs's committee build a memorial that included the names of all those who had died in Vietnam. Maya Lin, a Yale University architectural student, won the memorial design competition sponsored by the committee. She proposed building two stark black walls that touched at a 125-degree angle and sloped into the ground.[42]

The administration of Ronald Reagan forced changes in the Vietnam memorial proposed by Lin. President Reagan's first secretary of the interior, James Watt, refused to grant his approval to the project unless both a "traditional statue" and a flag pole were included. Grudgingly, the monument committee, Maya Lin, and the Commission of Fine Arts accepted these requirements. Ironically, the statue the committee selected for the memorial, after another open competition, also differed from what the conservatives had in mind. Designed by sculptor Frederick Hart, it portrayed three infantrymen who reflected the weariness of the battlefield.[43]

Although the Vietnam Veterans Memorial sparked debate, one must not overlook the considerable consensus that subsequently developed regarding it and the war it commemorated. When Jan Scruggs first proposed building a national Vietnam memorial in 1979, he rapidly garnered remarkable political support. In signing the legislation authorizing the memorial, President Jimmy Carter noted in 1980 that in a rare act of unanimity, all one hundred members of the Senate had cosponsored it.[44]

Although some conservatives, and some liberal magazines such as the *Nation*, attacked Lin's design, many supported the idea or at least went along with it. Despite the controversy surrounding the memorial, Scruggs's committee managed to raise more than $10 million for the monument, much of the money coming from small contributors, including many former veterans. In addition, organizations such as the American Legion, the Veterans of Foreign Wars, and many individuals, including H. Ross Perot, a Dallas financier, and Republican Senator John W. Warner of Virginia, contributed to the memorial and assisted in raising funds for it. Although the federal government provided no more than a site for the memorial, the memorial committee completed the monument with unprecedented speed. In 1980 Congress authorized the project; two years later the memorial was dedicated. In contrast, the American overseas memorials in the First and Second World Wars took fifteen to twenty years before they were finished. Nearly a decade elapsed before an agreement could be reached on the memorial for the Tomb of the Unknown Soldier. And it was not until 1986 that Congress finally authorized the erection of a national Korean War memorial by the American Battle Monuments Commission—more than thirty-five years after the conflict had ended.[45]

The Vietnam Veterans Memorial ultimately won unprecedented praise from veterans, conservatives, liberals, and the general public. Conservatives such as public affairs moderator John McLaughlin and James J. Kilpatrick, a syndicated newspaper columnist, praised it. Indeed, during the 1980s the Vietnam Veterans Memorial became one of the most visited monuments in Washington. It evoked a response not found at the typical "tourist" attraction, or even at the average American war memorial. At the memorial, silence or the muffled sounds of crying can often be heard. Frequently, visitors—usually veterans, friends, or family members of those who died in Vietnam—deposit various objects at the wall to symbolize their grief and to honor the dead.[46]

The continuing powerful response evoked by the Vietnam Veterans Memorial remains remarkable given the history of other memorials. The American Battle Monument Commission had often expressed concern and dismay over the lack of interest Americans had shown in their overseas memorials. Sometimes interest itself presented a problem. In the 1920s the

A snow-covered Veterans Day ceremony at the national Vietnam Veterans Memorial in 1987. This monument is the most visited war memorial in American history. (Photograph courtesy Smithsonian Institution Archives)

American Legion and the White House decided that a guard was needed at the Tomb of the Unknown Soldier because visitors failed to conduct themselves properly at this sacred shrine.[47]

Why has the Vietnam memorial differed from earlier memorials and why has it served to evoke such a continuing outpouring of emotion? In one sense, early conservative critics of the Vietnam War were correct in suggesting that this monument has a subversive quality about it. To begin with, it represents a total departure from the classical styles that had been the hallmark of the Commission of Fine Arts and the American Battle Monuments Commission. By discarding classical imagery and by focusing the visitors' attention on the names of those who died in the war, it emphasizes the loss and suffering the war caused. Thus it generates a type of emotion different from that evoked by heroic-style statuary.

Still, the Vietnam Veterans Memorial was not the first monument to focus on the sacrifice and service of the common soldier. After the Civil War both northern and southern communities built scores of bronze sentinels to Billy Yank and Johnny Reb, and beginning with that war, the federal

government accepted the responsibility of maintaining permanent cemeteries for all those who died in service of the nation. After each world war
the American Battle Monuments commission incorporated the names of
each missing soldier into several memorials. For instance, in New York City
the Commission erected a series of huge granite walls in a city park, within
sight of the Statue of Liberty, that listed names of all those who died and
were buried at sea in the Atlantic zone of operations during the Second
World War.

Although the average citizen-soldier received some of his due in earlier
struggles, their leaders had their fame preserved for posterity. Civil War
commanders, Union and Confederate, had monuments and, in the case of
Lincoln, Lee, and Davis, state holidays dedicated to their memory. After
World War I the American Battle Monuments Commission took upon itself the task of building a permanent memorial in Washington, D.C., to
General John J. Pershing and the American Expeditionary Forces. In the
1970s the commission finally completed a statue of Pershing with flanking
plaza walls bearing maps depicting the battles of this conflict and an inscription by the late commander paying tribute to his troops. When General Douglas MacArthur died in 1964, he received an elaborate state
funeral and was buried in the former Norfolk County courthouse. The old
courthouse not only contained his grave but also served as a museum—
some said a shrine—dedicated to the general's life and accomplishments.[48]

Although local and state communities have, since the 1980s, shown
greater interest in building memorials to the Vietnam War, few have sought
to honor the civilian or military leadership of this conflict. Memorials
honor Presidents John F. Kennedy and Lyndon Johnson, but not as war
leaders. As for William Westmoreland, the general most identified with the
Vietnam War, he lost a bid for the U.S. Senate and sued CBS television
over a documentary that stated he lied to his superiors about American
battlefield successes in Vietnam. During the 1980s few talked of building
a statue to Westmoreland or of naming a square or city street after him.
Instead, the general battled in court to defend his reputation and the case
was settled before it went to the jury.[49]

In a sense the common soldier became the central focus of the Vietnam
War because the leadership of this conflict remained so discredited. Many
conservatives, most notably Ronald Reagan, maintained that the Vietnam
War had been a noble cause and that the United States had come close to
winning and would have won if the war effort had not been subverted by
liberals and radicals. Other conservatives, as well as some liberals, affirmed

that the United States could have succeeded in Vietnam, but had needed a more effective leadership and better strategy. Conversely, to many on the Left, American involvement in Indochina is remembered merely as morally repugnant.[50]

Americans continued to disagree over the "lessons" to be drawn from the Vietnam War, but they agreed that a future conflict of this nature must be avoided. Liberals argued that the United States must limit its military involvement in the Third World, and some insisted that it consider aligning itself with authentic wars of national liberation. The American military has cautioned against the use of force in settling international disputes and insisted that any future war the United States enters must first have the full support of the American people. Conservatives declared that the United States must never fight a war it was not determined to win. The administrations of Ronald Reagan and George Bush demonstrated American military might by invading Grenada and, later, Panama. Both conflicts proved brief and decisive. In contrast, both administrations had limited American involvement in Afghanistan, Nicaragua, and El Salvador and relied on proxies to advance perceived American interests. To a large extent, both administrations responded to the lukewarm support Americans gave to intervening in any long and protracted conflict that might result in large-scale loss of American lives.

Although lessons learned from Vietnam shaped public policy in the 1970s and 1980s, Vietnam War memorials often avoided portraying these lessons in an overt way. Sponsors stressed that Vietnam memorials must avoid proclaiming any ideological message regarding the war. Few monuments explain why or how the United States entered this conflict. Instead, they emphasized the need to honor and remember the war dead and the veteran. During the 1980s, several cities held belated "welcome home" parades. To the dismay of the *National Review*, many former doves could be found among the marchers in New York City's ticker tape parade held for "returned" veterans in 1985.[51]

This emphasis on the average soldier and veteran paralleled the treatment of the war in fictional accounts and in Hollywood films. Most dwelt on the initiation and experiences of American soldiers or military advisors in Vietnam. Few explored why the United States entered the conflict and also usually ignored the Vietnamese people, friend or foe. Vietnam and its people remained anonymous, shadowy, or one-dimensional. In contrast, the best fictional accounts often portrayed American characters as complex, ambivalent, and tragic.[52]

America's effort to commemorate and remember the Vietnam War shows many remarkable similarities to American efforts to remember the Civil War in the aftermath of Reconstruction. In the late nineteenth century, in an attempt to promote reconciliation, elites in both regions of the country emphasized the need to honor the sacrifice of those who had fought in the Civil War. By focusing on the battlefields, they hoped to gloss over the causes of the conflict.[53] Although the battlefield remained a central focus of efforts to remember the Civil War, and to a large extent the world wars, the Vietnam monuments differed from earlier conflicts in their heightened ambiguity. In order to encourage reunion after the Civil War, the brutal and terrible nature of the combat was by and large forgotten. Except by a few novelists, the dissension, brutality, alienation, and anger of the war was forgotten or ignored by creators of Civil War memorials. Instead, the classically inspired monuments and ceremonies portrayed the Civil War as one in which the qualities of loyalty, valor, duty, and comradeship reigned supreme. Although the common soldier received his due, the officer retained an honored place in the pantheon of heroes.

Classicism had fallen out of vogue by the time of the Vietnam monuments. A number of memorials to the Indochina war, especially state-sponsored ones, were influenced by the simplicity and starkness of the somber walls designed by Maya Lin. Most dwelt on loss and pain; invariably they listed the names of the war dead and focused the viewer's attention on them. The New York City memorial did not list the names of those who served in Indochina, but placed on opaque glass quotations from letters Vietnam soldiers had written home to loved ones and friends. When memorials tended in the direction of realism, they frequently portrayed soldiers as harried, tired, and, in some cases, wounded. Often they followed the example of the "Three Fighting Men" statue at the Vietnam Veterans Memorial and included an African American figure to signify the multiracial composition of the American army in Vietnam. For instance, a Wilmington, Delaware, memorial completed in 1983 shows a distraught African American soldier carrying a fallen white comrade. Three years later citizens of San Antonio, Texas, dedicated a memorial that reversed the imagery and portrays a saddened white soldier aiding a wounded black comrade who was lying on the ground.[54]

In a sense, America turned inward as a result of the Vietnam War and remained unsure of its role—particularly its military role—in the world. But at the same time, efforts to commemorate the war entailed a far greater willingness to acknowledge a pluralistic vision of American nationhood. In many ways the Vietnam War marked the first war in which African American soldiers were viewed as vital participants in the struggle. Until the Vietnam era most war memorials remained "lily white"; few war memorials sponsored by the American Battle Monuments Commission even depicted a black soldier. Fictional accounts and Hollywood films tended to portray the American army in Vietnam as a biracial one, although they seldom made the black soldier the center of the story. The monument at the Vietnam Veterans Memorial, however, made a direct statement by making one of the soldiers an African American.

Such pluralism went from race in the 1970s to gender in the 1980s. Toward the end of the decade, women veterans demanded recognition for their service in Vietnam. A spate of oral histories and autobiographies appeared documenting their stories. Women also demanded that they be represented fully at the Vietnam memorial by the addition of a statue depicting a woman nurse. J. Carter Brown, chairman of the Commission of Fine Arts, opposed the addition of another figure to the memorial, citing the precedent it would establish. According to Brown, if a statue were added to commemorate the role of women, other groups and branches of the service would be encouraged to make similar demands. Despite his objections, in 1989 Congress decided that a statue depicting army nurses would be added to the memorial. It was unveiled on Veteran's Day 1993.[55]

In some ways the decision to add a statue commemorating the service of women followed an earlier pattern of remembering war. After the Civil War and the First World War, Arlington National Cemetery became the home of several memorials commemorating the service of women, particularly in their role as nurses. In 1913, Congress authorized construction of the national headquarters of the Red Cross, to be built with federal funds as a memorial to the services of both northern and southern women in the Civil War. After the First World War, Congress granted the national Red Cross permission to erect a statue to Jane Delano, a nurse killed in 1918, as a memorial to all nurses who lost their lives in World War I.[56]

But in an important way, by avoiding the overt allusions to motherhood, the woman's statue selected for the Vietnam memorial reflected a break from earlier memorials commemorating the wartime service of women. For instance, the Jane Delano memorial commissioned by the Red Cross in 1932 depicted a maternal figure dressed in a long flowing gown with arms outstretched. In contrast, the statue at the Vietnam memorial is of three women wearing military uniforms and caring for a wounded serviceman whose figure, by lying across sandbags, suggests that this scene took place during or soon after combat. The male figure is tended by one nurse; the other two nurses survey the distance. By placing this statue in the same symbolic space as the Hart's infantrymen, the memorial declared that the status and contribution of women was equal to that of men. In sum, efforts to remember the Vietnam War witnessed the acceptance of a more pluralistic vision of nationhood and the willingness to accord greater equality of recognition to African Americans and women.

This pluralism influenced the design of the Korean War Veterans Memorial proposed for Washington, D.C., by the American Battle Monuments Commission in 1989. To ensure that all ethnic groups and military units were honored, the commission called for a memorial that featured thirty-eight bronze soldiers. It would depict not only the diversity of American society, but also represent the participation of South Korean troops. At a White House ceremony in 1989 to announce the selection of the memorial design, the *Washington Times* noted that the four veterans who unveiled the design included "a female nurse, a double amputee, a black colonel, and a Hispanic man in a wheelchair."[57]

The Korean War Veterans Memorial was an attempt by the American Battle Monuments Commission to surpass the Vietnam Veterans Memorial and to avoid the somber imagery common to Vietnam memorials. The commission deliberately avoided placing the names of those who had died in Korea on the memorial because it left the impression that they were "victims." From the beginning, the commission wanted the American flag and realistic statuary to be a central part of the monument's design.[58]

At the same time, this monument became embroiled in a series of controversies that delayed its completion for several years. To begin with, the Pennsylvania State University team of architects that won the competition for the memorial's design lost control of the project and sued for damages. The American Battle Monuments Commission ordered a number of changes to the design of the monument and hired a new team of Washington, D.C. architects, Cooper-Lecky, to execute it. Both the Commission of Fine Arts and the Capital Planning Commission forced Cooper-Lecky to reduce the size of the monument in order to limit its impact on the open spaces available on the Mall and in West Potomac Park. In addition, the Commission of Fine Arts mandated that the thirty-eight soldiers be scaled down to sixteen and that these figures be more idealized.[59]

During the debate surrounding the Korean War Veterans Memorial, J. Carter Brown, the chairman of the Commission of Fine Arts and director of the National Gallery of Art expressed concern that Washington, D.C., would acquire a case of "memorialitis" and took note of the number of war memorials proposed for different wars and groups. Brown's concerns were shared by Congress in 1986 when they passed the Commemorative Works Act that created a rigorous review process that made it difficult for private organizations to place monuments in the nation's capital.[60]

Can pluralism go too far in the direction of fragmentation and trivialization? For instance, one can make a legitimate claim for many of the causes proposed for commemoration, but should every ethnic group in American society have a monument in the nation's capital memorializing their military service? Should a proposed monument honoring canines who served in the military be placed in the same symbolic space as the Vietnam Veterans Memorial or Holocaust Memorial Museum?[61]

The original architects of the Korean War monument charged that the American Battle Monuments Commission and other agencies modified their designs in order to glorify war. No doubt, the Korean memorial that finally won approval represented an assault on the antimonument tradition represented by the Vietnam Veterans Memorial. Nonetheless, one must ask how effective was the antimonument in portraying the dreadful cost and inhumanity of war? Can any monument, no matter how widely applauded, hope to convey the true nature of war? The success of the Vietnam memorial encouraged scores of communities and states to imitate the monument. But one art historian has pointed out that by doing so, "potential local voices are silenced in deference to a profound centralized symbol."[62]

Even though the antimonument idea won widespread acceptance in the 1980s, Americans remained ambivalent about the role played by the peace movement. In 1977 former peace activists failed to stop the construction of a gymnasium by Kent State University on the site where National Guardsmen killed four students during an antiwar protest in 1970. Both the Ohio Historic Site Preservation Advisory Board and the Carter Administration refused to declare part of the Kent State campus either a state or a national historic site, in order to prevent the building of the gymnasium.[63]

In the 1980s efforts to build a memorial at Kent State faced hostility or apathy in many quarters. The Ohio American Legion denounced efforts by Kent State to honor "terrorism" and defended the actions of the National Guard. The university, unable to raise the necessary funds to build a planned $1.3 million memorial, scaled back its plans and settled for a far more modest monument costing $200,000. Some of the parents of the slain students and those wounded by the guard objected to the modernist design that featured four pylons, and one deemed the monument dedicated on the twentieth anniversary of the slayings as nothing more than "a glorified sidewalk." They were particularly distressed that the monument failed to list the names of those who had been slain.[64]

This pattern was not unique to the Vietnam War. Although Americans are willing to recognize the tremendous cost and sacrifice of the common soldier, they often pay little attention to the peacemakers. Neither the anti-monuments of the Vietnam War nor the remembrance of the victims at Kent State served to halt American involvement in the Persian Gulf War. The Vietnam War, particularly the memory of the peace movement, cast a long shadow over American prosecution and commemoration of the Persian Gulf conflict. As the United States moved closer to war in the fall of 1990, a vigorous peace movement emerged that opposed waging war against Iraq in order to liberate Kuwait. In January 1991, a debate ensued in the Congress and a substantial number of members opposed granting the president authority to wage war. The Second World War, and also the Vietnam War, figured in the rhetoric of President George Bush in explaining the need for American involvement. On the eve of the conflict, Bush compared Saddam Hussein to Adolf Hitler and stressed the need to repel unprovoked aggression. When U.S. forces attacked, he insisted that military leaders, in a thinly veiled reference to Vietnam, would not have to fight with one arm tied behind their back.[65]

The Persian Gulf War ended quickly and the United States lost relatively few American service people. Moreover, most American service people went over with their unit and returned in the same manner. This clear beginning and end encouraged and made easier efforts to organize elaborate victory parades.[66] Vietnam cast a long shadow over the "welcome home" parades given the returning heroes from the Persian Gulf. The two largest parades, in New York City and Washington, D.C., included veterans from Vietnam and other earlier conflicts. Many journalists and commentators expressed the sense that the victory parades accorded the returning Persian Gulf veterans were designed to atone for the "neglect" shown the servicemen from Indochina.[67]

The Persian Gulf War failed to produce any immediate interest in building permanent memorials. In part, this stemmed from the fact that despite the epic scale of American involvement, few American lives were lost. The decisive military victory against Iraq alleviated the initial misgivings of many Americans. Although Saddam Hussein remained in power, the war produced lower gasoline prices and brought relative stability to the Middle East.

In a decisive break with the commemoration of the Vietnam War, the Persian Gulf conflict heralded the return of the hero general. Both Colin Powell and Norman Schwarzkopf received adulation akin to that received by Eisenhower and MacArthur after the Second World War. In 1991, they headed victory parades, received medals, attended testimonial dinners in their honor, and were mentioned as possible presidential candidates. They offered an opportunity for the American military leadership to restore its tarnished image. Although both generals achieved fame in the Persian Gulf, they also had served as junior officers in the Vietnam War.[68]

Powell declared in a Memorial Day address in 1991 before the Vietnam Veterans Memorial that the veterans of Indochina had fought with honor, and he explicitly linked their conflict with the Persian Gulf War. Powell's address and the victory parades suggest that many national leaders, especially in the Bush administration and U.S. military, tried to use America's most recent war to rehabilitate further the image of Vietnam and the veterans who fought in it.

If memorials are built to the Persian Gulf conflict, it is likely that they will commemorate Powell. Powell represents acceptance of a more pluralistic definition of the American identity. As the first African American to serve as chairman of the Joint Chiefs of Staff, Powell will probably be remembered more as a pioneer in the struggle for racial equality than as a war leader. At the same time, the honoring of Powell would also serve to acknowledge the disproportionate representation of African Americans in the U.S. military, especially in the army.[69]

The end of the cold war has not diminished American involvement in world affairs. In a sense, the Persian Gulf conflict signifies the continued willingness of the United States to intervene abroad and does not represent a radical shift in American foreign policy. But if the United States were to turn inward, this conflict would be remembered as the "last hurrah" of a fading world power. Although its memory would lack the sense of loss and mourning that has characterized the remembrance of Vietnam, it would still be tinged with melancholy.

# 6

# CONCLUSION

Can a modern nation-state exist without national rituals and monuments, particularly those memorializing its wars? In the early Republic many Americans thought ceremonies commemorating the Revolution were vital symbols ensuring that republican principles would endure in the young nation. Others maintained that a republican society should avoid monuments and ceremonies associated with the monarchical regimes of Europe. At the same time, there was substantial opposition to the efforts by former military officers to place the memory of the Revolution in the domain of small, privileged, "aristocratic" elites, such as the Society of Cincinnati. Both Federalists and Jeffersonian Republicans considered themselves the principal heirs of the Revolution's memory, and each contested the claims of the other over it. As a result, Independence Day ceremonies in many communities fragmented as opposing groups held separate celebrations.

The War of 1812, the demise of the Federalist Party, and the passing of the revolutionary generation had a profound impact on the American pattern of remembering war. Beginning in the 1820s and 1830s, the commemoration of the Revolution no longer aroused the partisan passions found in the opening years of the new Republic. National and local leaders portrayed the struggle for independence as an epic period in American history, and the heroes of this period became, particularly in the case of Washington, larger than life. Monuments gained increasing favor in a number of communities during this time.

During the postrevolutionary period, the federal government built few national monuments. Although it purchased an occasional statue or painting for the Capitol, it relied on a private society to build a suitable shrine to George Washington. With few exceptions, it did little to assist local communities or organizations in their efforts to commemorate the Revolution or later wars. It grudgingly created a national cemetery for soldiers who had died in the Mexican-American War only after the place of their burial had become a city garbage dump. This limited federal role allowed individual communities, states, and private organizations to play an important role in shaping the national memory of war. Women's organizations often came to the rescue with the funds necessary to complete unfinished monuments originally started by men's organizations. Over the course of the nineteenth century, especially after the Civil War, women's role as patrons of memorials only increased. Ethnic groups, especially in urban centers, started to use Independence Day ceremonies to assert an inclusive vision of nationhood that ran against nativist sentiments. Abolitionists and African Americans delivered Independence Day orations calling on Americans to realize the ideals of equality espoused by the Declaration of Independence.

During the Civil War, the Lincoln administration viewed memorials and rituals as playing an important role in prosecuting the war. It created an extensive series of national cemeteries for Union soldiers killed in the struggle, in part as consolation to the next of kin. In his famous Gettysburg Address, Lincoln made clear that the "hallowed dead" offered inspiration to carry on the struggle for Union. The national cemeteries marked the beginning of the expanded role the federal government would play in commemorating past wars. After the Civil War, it funded a series of memorials in Washington, D.C., not only to Union generals but also to revolutionary figures. Eventually Congress provided the funds to purchase many Civil War and revolutionary battlefields in order to foster a remembrance of the epic struggles that had taken place at these sites. For the first time Congress enacted legislation that created national holidays for the District of Columbia and, later, for all federal employees.

Even after the Civil War, the federal government continued to foster a vision of nationalism that represented an amalgam of different sectional, ethnic, gender, and economic divisions within American society. For instance, the government permitted monuments to Confederate soldiers and units within national cemeteries and battlefields. As a result, the veterans of many ethnic regiments created monuments to their units, especially at Gettysburg. In the 1880s and 1890s, business interests in the North supported sectional reconciliation in order to promote their interests in the South. Southern commercial elites and professionals wanted northern capital, but also wanted regional autonomy over race relations and an affirmation that the Lost Cause was a legitimate struggle over the meaning of nationhood. With the passage of time, Union veterans, especially after they were granted generous pensions, proved far more willing to accept a vision of the Civil War that honored the military service of their adversaries.

To foster reconciliation between the North and South, the federal government, veterans' organizations, and public and private monument committees chose to view the Civil War primarily as a struggle to preserve the Union, and they obscured the role African Americans played in their own liberation. African American leaders, most notably Frederick Douglass, countered this effort by reminding the nation that the Civil War had been above all a struggle for freedom.

By the closing decades of the nineteenth century, artists and sculptors became more strident in asserting a professional role regarding the commemoration of war. By creating public-art commissions, artists and their allies encouraged, and sometimes forced, ethnic and veterans' monuments to conform to prevailing definitions of good public art. In the 1910s and 1920s, for instance, the U.S. Commission of Fine Arts succeeded in making most monuments built in Washington, D.C., conform to the classically inspired style of the beaux-art movement. In a few major urban communities, most notably New York City, public-art commissions gained significant power to shape monumental art. Nonetheless, the professional art community usually expressed dismay, particularly after the Civil War and the First World War, in their inability to stop the construction of mass-produced commercial monuments.

The tremendous controversies surrounding the creation of memorials in the 1920s to the First World War cannot be ignored, yet these images gained acceptance with most Americans because they offered ambiguity. National leaders conceived of the overseas cemeteries and monuments, the Tomb of the Unknown Soldier, and Armistice Day ceremonies as a way of mythologizing America's first European war as a time when Americans of all regions, classes, and ethnic groups united behind a common goal. At the same time, they offered a message that stressed peace and assured Americans that this conflict was a "war to end all wars."

The dominant American view is that war is an aberration; thus, most Americans have resisted seeing it as an inevitable part of life. To endure, memorials and ceremonies must take into account the tremendous loss of life experienced during war and must offer the promise of peace. In many ways the decline of memorial building during the cold war signified the problematic nature of that conflict. Unlike earlier conflicts, the cold war prevented successive presidential administrations from promising a quick victory and a return to "normalcy."

Efforts to commemorate the Vietnam War offer insights into the vital importance rituals and memorials play in American society. In many ways the federal government, by neglecting rituals and memorials, contributed to the alienation of those who fought in this struggle. Moreover, it permitted a vacuum of authority to emerge that increased the ability of non-elite groups to shape the memory of the conflict. Although after the world wars the American Battle Monuments Commission built many of the principal national memorials, in the case of Vietnam, a private organization created the Vietnam Veterans Memorial. Eventually, Vietnam veterans created their own belated parades. More than in any other war, visual images, particularly from television and motion pictures, shaped the memory of the Vietnam War.

The federal government has recently sought to gain control over efforts to commemorate the Korean War. In 1986 Congress decided that America's most recent "forgotten" war should be commemorated with a memorial in Washington, D.C. Although Congress insisted that funds for this monument be raised through private contributions, it vested responsibility for overseeing the design and construction of the memorial in the American Battle Monuments Commission. The Korean War Veterans Memorial differs from its Vietnam counterpart in that it emphasizes the American flag and consciously seeks to avoid viewing the dead of this conflict as "victims." Nonetheless, it remains very much in the new tradition of the Vietnam-era memorial in that it offers a vision of nationalism that emphasizes pluralism.

The American tradition of remembering war remains malleable, subject to constant change. Although the memory of some wars, such as the Revolution and Civil War, continue in the national consciousness, others, such as the Spanish-American War and First World War, have faded. In many ways this flexibility may have contributed to the end of the cold war between the United States and Soviet Union. The hostility, anger, and frustration that marked this conflict and the limited wars that were spawned by it—the Korean War and the Vietnam War—may with the passing of the Vietnam generation fade in the American imagination.

There exists a distinctive American pattern of remembering war that can be seen when one compares it with the way some other societies commemorate past conflicts. Even in the twentieth century, limits have been placed on the role of the federal government to shape the public memory of wars. By contrast, in most European countries the central government plays a far more active role in shaping the remembrance of war. When local communities in France wanted to erect a war memorial after the First World War, they first had to have proposed memorials approved by the national government. The British government mandated that all the war dead killed in battle would be buried in national cemeteries, regardless of the wishes of the next of kin. Although the United States proved willing to grant veterans generous benefits, Britain provided only meager aid to former soldiers. In fact, members of Parliament feared during the First World War that returning Tommies would imitate American Civil War veterans and form organizations to lobby for benefits.[1]

German efforts to commemorate the First World War, according to George Mosse, expressed a vision of nationhood that wanted to obliterate individual identity and link it with the nation. In building cemeteries after this conflict, British and American governments stressed the need for uniformity in headstone design and placement, but both countries emphasized the importance of marking each grave with a headstone. In contrast, in Germany a number of cemeteries were built that intentionally obliterated individual grave markers and instead replaced them with a collective physical memorial—a wall or series of large Crosses—that listed the names of the fallen. Some of their war cemeteries, including the Totenburgen, "cities of the dead," reflect the starkest form of this effort to obliterate personal identity. Devoid of most Christian symbolism, the Totenburgen are huge stone buildings modeled after medieval castles. Inside the structures, altars, usually large stones, stand atop mass crypts containing the fallen. Except for listing the names of the war dead on the inside walls, nothing disturbs the image of nationhood that stressed the need for the individual to give up his identity and for the nation to remain vigilant against outside threats.

Furthermore, although American and European memorials to the First World War often used imagery that obscured the horrors of modern warfare, no country rivalled Germany in presenting a "cult of the battlefield" to portray war as a positive good. For instance, imagery that even hinted at the suffering and cost of war aroused controversy and was dismantled when the Nazis assumed power. The British government wanted flowers, particularly poppies, to grow in British cemeteries; but in Germany's case, flowers were banned both to minimize the costs involved in caring for cemeteries and to ensure that attention was not diverted from the heroic and tragic quality of dying for one's country. Few American, British, or even French memorials allude to the enemy or emphasize the need for vengeance, but this theme can be found in a number of German monuments. In the United States countless "living memorials" were built during the interwar years; but in Germany, the idea remained almost unthinkable, and only a few living memorials were proposed or completed. Even during the Weimar years, German efforts to memorialize the First World War conceived of, and even promoted, war as a positive good. George Mosse's examination of the German pattern of remembering war points to the importance of ritual and tradition. In his view, the way Germany commemorated the First World War helped pave the way for the second.[2]

Should all war memorials focus on suffering and loss? Would they thus help prevent future conflicts? Since 1945, Japan has memorialized the tremendous hardships on its citizens caused by the Second World War. The use of nuclear weapons against Japan serves as a central event in the national memory of this conflict. In 1949 the national diet of Japan created a peace park in Hiroshima. Over the course of the 1950s and 1960s, a series of monuments built in the park memorialized the victims and the destruction caused by the atomic attack. Each year, on the anniversary of the bombing of Hiroshima, solemn observances take place throughout Japan marking this tragic event.[3]

In postwar Japan, Hiroshima emerged as a powerful symbol of the need to avoid future wars. The memory of the Second World War as an event of epic loss has had a lasting impact on Japanese military and foreign policy. A new constitution drafted after the war placed strict limits on the overseas deployment of Japanese forces and renounced military force as an instrument of national policy. Although Japan emerged in the 1970s and 1980s as a major economic power, it refused to build a comparable military establishment. During the Persian Gulf War, Japan provided money, but delayed the deployment of even a token force to the region until the fighting had stopped.

Nonetheless, the focus on loss and suffering has limited the Japanese memory of the Second World War. The Japanese consider themselves victims of the conflict and thus absolve themselves of any sense of guilt. Although support for expansionist policies enjoyed significant public support in the 1930s, the postwar Japanese government tried to blame them solely on the evil designs of a small clique of war criminals. Despite international pressure from other Asian governments, Japan refused to acknowledge fully the suffering it inflicted on China and other nations. Even though many Korean workers died in the Hiroshima blast, official memorials ignored them. At the fiftieth anniversary of the surprise attack on Pearl Harbor, Japanese officials and the public expressed surprise, dismay, and even anger that such an event still loomed so large in the American imagination.[4]

Some historians have feared that the way Japan has commemorated the Second World War has ensured that the memory of this conflict will dim over time. Can a new generation of Japanese identify with a memory of the Second World War that stresses the fate of the Japanese victims of this conflict? What will happen when all the victims have passed away? On the other side of the world, the question of memory has haunted those who have tried to preserve the memory of the Holocaust. In oral interviews, survivors express a gnawing fear that their experiences will be forgotten by future generations. This fear is not baseless: a fringe group of Nazi sympathizers and white supremacists have denied that the Holocaust ever took place.

After the Second World War, a number of nations built memorials to the Holocaust. In the former communist states of Eastern Europe and the Soviet Union, Holocaust memorials tended to remember all the victims of Nazi Germany. Often, memorials and museums ignored the fact that Jews remained the principal victims of the death camps. In East Germany, concentration-camp museums stressed the resistance and fate of communist opponents to Hitler. In Poland, a memorial erected in 1948 commemorated the 1944 uprising in the Warsaw Ghetto. The communist government of Poland preserved the most infamous of the death camps of the Nazi era, most notably Auschwitz, but the Poles viewed the Holocaust as aimed not simply at the Jews but as part of larger Nazi effort to destroy the Polish people. Although the Holocaust eliminated virtually the entire Jewish community in Poland, anti-Semitism continued to thrive in postwar Poland.[5]

To West Germany, the Holocaust had a far more ambiguous meaning. In contrast to East Germany, the Federal Republic of Germany accepted responsibility for the deeds of the Third Reich and granted compensation to survivors of the death camps. The West German government turned the concentration camps of Dachau and Bergen-Belsen into historic sites and created museums to recount the Holocaust. Stark modernistic monuments at both camps remembered those who had died at the hands of the Nazis. At Bergen-Belsen a series of small memorial tablets mark the mass graves of thousands.[6]

In the early 1980s, West Germany remained torn and divided over the continued relevance of the Holocaust to the German national memory. The decision by Chancellor Helmut Kohl and President Ronald Reagan to place wreathes at the Bitburg cemetery fostered a debate within both West Germany and the United States over how German participation in the Second World War should be remembered. Many Germans maintained that virtually the entire German nation, even the soldiers who served in the armies of the Third Reich, should be remembered as victims of Nazi oppression. Others declared that honoring the fallen soldiers of Bitburg served to debase and obscure the memory of the Holocaust.

For Israelis, the memory of the Holocaust has served as the central event in explaining the existence of the state of Israel. In contrast to Holocaust memorials and museums in Europe and the United States, Holocaust memorials in Israel commemorate an event fixed in the larger web of Jewish history. For example, the principal Israeli museum at Yad Vashem not only documents the destruction wrought by the Nazis but also traces how Israel served as a place of refuge and rebirth for the shattered remnants of European Jewry. In 1959 Israel observed its first annual Holocaust memorial day. It remains secular in context, stressing the importance of remembering not only the victims of the Holocaust but also the heroism displayed by those who resisted it.[7]

What will happen to the memory of the Holocaust after the last survivors have died? Even when the Holocaust was a recent event, different nations created different memorials and monuments to commemorate this horrible event. In the former communist states of Eastern Europe, memorials focused on all the victims of Nazi oppression. But in Israel and the United States, the Holocaust has been remembered as a central event in Jewish history. In the case of the United States, remembrance of the Holocaust has served to affirm the incorporation of Jews into an American national identity and underscored the "justness" of the Second World War.

Has the importance of ritual and tradition faded with the advent of television? In some ways, a case can be made that the rise of the mass media in the United States and in many parts of the world since 1945 has served to diminish the role of both. Television can almost instantaneously transmit powerful images and symbols to an entire nation. At times television, together with motion pictures, can have a subversive quality that, in the case of the Vietnam War, often served to raise doubts about official rituals and symbols. Although the antiwar bias of the American media has been greatly exaggerated, the uncensored television and print images produced during the Vietnam War made it difficult to portray it in stark, moralistic terms and suggested ambiguity, particularly after the Tet Offensive of 1968.

Still, the rise of the mass media has not annihilated ritual and monuments; in fact, it has served to inspire and to further nationalize them. As a result of television, an entire nation could watch, if not participate in, the funeral services held for national heroes such as Generals Douglas MacArthur and Dwight D. Eisenhower. Even in the case of Vietnam, television and motion pictures have inspired and encouraged efforts to commemorate this conflict with monuments. Jan Scruggs, the leader behind efforts to build the Vietnam Veterans Memorial, decided that such a monument was needed after seeing the movie *The Deer Hunter.* As a result of television network news, millions could immediately witness scenes from the unveiling of this memorial and learn of the powerful impact it had on individuals.

Thus it seems certain that rituals and monuments will continue to endure in the United States, and in most other nations of the world, for the foreseeable future. Consequently, both scholars and the wider public need a better understanding of their history. In the American context, particularly since 1945, rituals and symbols designed to remember war have played a central role in forging a national identity that has embraced ethnic and religious pluralism and inclusion. Rituals and memorials have often declared that the avoidance of war should serve as the principal guide in shaping American foreign policy. But in other countries, most notably Germany in the 1920s and 1930s, rituals and symbols have sown the seeds of hatred and helped encourage another conflict. In short, it is at our peril that we ignore the role that ritual and tradition have played in the life of the modern nation-state.

# NOTES

### INTRODUCTION

1. "Stop That Monument," *National Review,* 18 September 1981, 1064; and Christopher Hitchens, "Minority Report," *Nation,* 13 November 1982, 486.

2. Michael G. Kammen, *Mystic Chords of Memory: The Transformation of Tradition in American Culture* (New York: Alfred A. Knopf, 1991) provides an insightful, almost encyclopedic, account of the history of memory and tradition in American society. Although Kammen's work argues for the primacy of war in shaping the national memory, he devotes little attention to the decisive shift that took place after the First World War in the federal government's efforts to foster an official remembrance of this and later conflicts. Furthermore, Kammen contends that Vietnam remains the most controversial war of the twentieth century for the United States, but this book will show that the debates surrounding the commemoration of the First World War during the interwar years make the disagreements surrounding the remembrance of the conflict in Indochina pale by comparison. These quibbles aside, I would be remiss if I did not acknowledge the intellectual debt I owe to Kammen's pathbreaking work on the memory of the American Revolution: *A Season of Youth: The American Revolution and the Historical Imagination* (New York: Alfred A. Knopf, 1978).

3. John Bodnar, *Remaking America: Public Memory, Commemoration, and Patriotism in the Twentieth Century* (Princeton, N.J.: Princeton University, 1992) views national elites as seeking to shape and construct a more simplistic and official vision of the past and to impose it on more ambiguous vernacular traditions. Although I do not want to minimize the power of business, financial, political, and professional elites in shaping the national memory, I will nonetheless argue that such sharp distinction between the official and the vernacular often does not exist. Many elite-sponsored rituals, holidays, monuments, and cemeteries created to

remember war succeed because of their ambiguity and their ability to strike responsive popular chords within the wider public. Elite efforts to brazenly stifle dissent or ignore popular consent have often provoked apathy and opposition. Despite some of my disagreements, I want to acknowledge the great value of Bodnar's study, particularly the chapters examining ethnic and regional patterns of remembrance. I also appreciate his kind offer to share his manuscript with me before its publication. Several historians see the First World War era and the interwar years as a crucial period for the "Americanization" of southern and eastern European immigrants. They emphasize the complexity of this process and note that the Left, particularly the Communist Party, embraced an American identity in the 1920s in order to foster working-class unity. See James R. Barrett, "Americanization from the Bottom Up: Immigration and the Remaking of the Working Class in the United States, 1880–1930, *Journal of American History* 79 (December 1992): 996–1020; and David Montgomery, "Nationalism, American Patriotism, and Class Consciousness among Immigrant Workers in the United States in the Epoch of World War I," in *"Struggle a Hard Battle": Essays on Working-Class Immigrants,* ed. Dirk Hoerder (De Kalb, Ill.: Northern Illinois University Press, 1986), 327–51.

4. Edward Tabor Linenthal, *Sacred Ground: Americans and Their Battlefields* (Urbana, Ill.: University of Illinois Press, 1991), provides a wealth of interesting material on the commemorative activity that has taken place at the battlefields of Lexington and Concord, the Alamo, Gettysburg, Little Big Horn, and Pearl Harbor. Nonetheless, this work suffers from many of the limitations of any case study. Linenthal's study often fails to provide a wider context for understanding the process of memorialization taking place at these battlefields and ignores other centers of memory that exist in commemorating past wars. For instance, he fails to explain why efforts to commemorate the attack on Pearl Harbor lagged far behind efforts to memorialize the flag raising at Iwo Jima. Or why, for example, did the fortieth anniversary of Pearl Harbor evoke hardly a whimper of controversy, whereas the fiftieth anniversary produced a flurry of debate and disagreement? For a further critique of Linenthal's work, see David Glassberg, "Patriotism from the Ground Up," *Reviews in American History* 21 (1993): 1–7.

5. W. Kendrick Pritchett, *The Greek State at War,* pt. 4 (Berkeley and Los Angeles: University of California Press, 1985), 94–259; Graham Webster, *The Roman Imperial Army of the First and Second Centuries A.D.,* 2d ed. (London: Adams and Charles Black, 1979), 271–73; George L. Mosse, *Fallen Soldiers: Reshaping the Memory of the World Wars* (New York: Oxford University Press, 1990); and *The Nationalization of the Masses: Political Symbolism and Mass Movements in Germany from the Napoleonic Wars through the Third Reich* (New York: Howard Fertig, 1975). For a superb work considering the role of heritage and memory in Western society, see David Lowenthal, *The Past Is a Foreign Country* (Cambridge, England: Cambridge University Press, 1985).

6. In seeking to understand the question of popular participation in the shaping American culture, I am heavily indebted to two works by Lawrence W. Levine: "The Folklore of Industrial Society: Popular Culture and Its Audiences," *American Historical Review* 97 (December 1992): 1369–99; and *Highbrow/Lowbrow: The Emergence of Cultural Hierarchy in America* (Cambridge, Mass.: Harvard University Press, 1988).

7. My definition of the importance of rituals has been influenced by Clifford Geertz, *The Interpretation of Cultures* (New York: Basic Books, 1973).

8. Until recently, the study of rituals has been left to the domain of anthropologists and antiquarians. Among the scholars who consider the role of ritual in modern society, see: Robert Bocock, *Ritual in Industrial Society: A Sociological Analysis of Ritualism in Modern England* (London: Allen and Unwin, 1974); David I. Kertzer, *Ritual, Politics, and Power* (New Haven, Conn.: Yale University Press, 1988); Lowenthal, *Past Is a Foreign Country;* and Wilber

Zelinksy, *Nation into State: The Shifting Symbolic Foundations of American Nationalism* (Chapel Hill, N.C.: University of North Carolina Press, 1988). Among the first historians to study the role of ritual as an agent of historical change, see: George L. Mosse, "National Cemeteries and National Revival: The Cult of Fallen Soldiers in Germany," *Journal of Contemporary History* 14 (1979): 1–20; Eric Hobsbawm and Terence Ranger, eds., *The Invention of Tradition* (New York: Cambridge University Press, 1983); and John R. Gillis, *For Better, For Worse: British Marriages, 1600 to the Present* (New York: Oxford University Press, 1985).

9. See, for example, Edmund Wilson, *Patriotic Gore: Studies in the Literature of the American Civil War* (New York: Oxford University Press, 1962); Daniel Aaron, *The Unwritten War: American Writers and the Civil War* (New York: Alfred A. Knopf, 1973); Paul Fussell, *The Great War and Modern Memory* (New York: Oxford University Press, 1975); and Susan D. Moeller, *Shooting War: Photography and the American Experience of Combat* (New York: Basic Books, 1989).

10. Robert G. Athearn, *The Mythic West in Twentieth Century America* (Lawrence, Kans.: University Press of Kansas, 1986), 160–89; Jules David Prown, Nancy K. Anderson, William Cronon, Brian W. Dippie, Martha A. Sandweiss, Susan Prendergast Schoelwer, and Howard R. Lamar, *Discovered Lands Invented Pasts: Transforming Visions of the American West* (New Haven, Conn.: Yale University Press, 1992); Richard Slotkin, *Regeneration through Violence: The Mythology of the American Frontier, 1600–1860* (Middletown, Conn.: Wesleyan University Press, 1973); and William H. Truettner, ed., *The West as America: Reinterpreting Images of the Frontier, 1820–1920* (Washington, D.C.: Smithsonian Institution Press, 1991).

11. Concerning Columbus Day, see Claudia L. Bushman, *America Discovers Columbus: How an Italian Explorer Became an American Hero* (Hanover, N.H.: University Press of New England, 1992) and Thomas J. Schlereth, "Columbia, Columbus, and Columbianism," *Journal of American History* 79 (December 1992): 937–68. On the American flag, see Scot M. Guenter, *The American Flag, 1777–1924: Cultural Shifts from Creation to Codification* (Rutherford, N.J.: Fairleigh Dickinson University Press, 1990).

12. John Whiteclay Chambers II, *To Raise an Army: The Draft Comes to Modern America* (New York: Free Press, 1987).

13. In contrast, a number of more recent works have traced the political and cultural agendas of both sculptors and patrons of public memorials. See, for example, Michele Bogart, *Public Sculpture and the Civic Ideal in New York City, 1890–1930* (Chicago: University of Chicago Press, 1989) and Karal Ann Marling and John Wetenhall, *Iwo Jima: Monuments, Memories, and the American Hero* (Cambridge, Mass.: Harvard University Press, 1991). For an overview of recent trends in art scholarship, see Wanda M. Corn, "Coming of Age: Historical Scholarship in American Art," *Art Bulletin* 70 (June 1988): 188–207.

## 1. THE MEMORY OF A NATION FORGED IN WAR

1. Charles Warren, "Fourth of July Myths," *William and Mary Quarterly*, 3d ser., 2 (July 1945): 254–59.

2. Fletcher Melvin Green, "Listen to the Eagle Scream: One Hundred Years of the Fourth of July in North Carolina, 1776–1876," in *Democracy in the Old South and Other Essays by Fletcher Melvin Green*, ed. J. Isaac Copeland (Nashville: Vanderbilt University Press, 1969), 112–16; Howard H. Martin, "Orations on the Anniversary of American Independence, 1777–1876" (Ph.D. diss., Northwestern University, 1955), 11–24; David G. Hackett, "The Social Origins of Nationalism: Albany, New York 1754–1835," *Journal of Social History* 21 (Summer 1988): 659–81; and Warren, "Fourth of July Myths," 255.

3. Peter Shaw, *American Patriots and the Rituals of Revolution* (Cambridge, Mass.: Harvard University Press, 1981), 14–15.

4. My view of the American Revolution has been influenced by the following: Bernard Bailyn, *The Ideological Origins of the American Revolution* (Cambridge, Mass.: Harvard University Press, 1967); Lance G. Banning, *The Jeffersonian Persuasion: Evolution of a Party Ideology* (Ithaca, N.Y.: Cornell University Press, 1978); Linda Kerber, *Women of the Republic: Intellect and Ideology in Revolutionary America* (Chapel Hill, N.C.: University of North Carolina Press, 1980); Gary B. Nash, *Race and Revolution* (Madison, Wisc.: Madison House, 1990); Mary Beth Norton, *Liberty's Daughters: The Revolutionary Experience of American Women, 1750–1800* (Boston: Little, Brown, 1980); Charles Royster, *A Revolutionary People at War: The Continental Army and the American Character, 1775–1783* (Chapel Hill, N.C.: University of North Carolina Press, 1979); Gordon S. Wood, *The Creation of the American Republic* (Chapel Hill, N.C.: University of North Carolina Press, 1969); and Alfred F. Young, *The American Revolution: Explorations in the History of American Radicalism* (De Kalb, Ill.: Northern Illinois University Press, 1976).

5. Richard H. Kohn, *Eagle and Sword: The Federalists and the Creation of the Military Establishment in America, 1783–1802* (New York: Free Press, 1975), 1–39; Paul K. Longmore, *The Invention of George Washington* (Berkeley and Los Angeles: University of California Press, 1988); and Barry Schwartz, *George Washington: The Making of an American Symbol* (New York: Free Press, 1987).

6. Minor Myers, Jr., *Liberty without Anarchy: A History of the Society of the Cincinnati* (Charlottesville: University Press of Virginia, 1983), 1–69.

7. Warren, "Fourth of July Myths," 259–60.

8. Benjamin Franklin, *Writings* (New York: Library of America, 1987), 1084–89.

9. Myers, *Liberty without Anarchy*, 48–67; William A. Benton, "Pennsylvania Revolutionary Officers and the Federal Constitution," *Pennsylvania History* 31 (October 1964): 419–35; and Carl E. Prince, *The Federalists and the Origins of the U.S. Civil Service* (New York: New York University Press, 1977).

10. David F. Epstein, "The Case for Ratification: Federalist Constitutional Thought," in *The Framing and Ratification of the Constitution*, ed. Leonard W. Levy and Dennis J. Mahoney (New York: Macmillan, 1987), 293–304; and Lawrence Delbert Cress, *Citizens in Arms: The Army and the Militia in American Society to the War of 1812* (Chapel Hill, N.C.: University of North Carolina Press, 1982), 75–109.

11. Cress, *Citizens in Arms*, 75–109.

12. Warren, "Fourth of July Myths," 259.

13. Kenneth R. Bowling and Helen E. Veit, eds., *The Diary of William Maclay and Other Notes on Senate Debates*, vol. 9, *Documentary History of the First Federal Congress of the United States of America* (Baltimore: Johns Hopkins University Press, 1988), 101–2.

14. Thomas P. Slaughter, *The Whiskey Rebellion: Frontier Epilogue to the American Revolution* (New York: Oxford University Press, 1986); *History of Allegheny County, Pennsylvania* (Chicago: A. Warner, 1889), 155–64; and Alfred Creigh, *History of Washington County* (Washington, Penn., 1870), 63–73.

15. Slaughter, *Whiskey Rebellion*, 205–21.

16. Theodore J. Crackel, *Mr. Jefferson's Army: Political and Social Reform of the Military Establishment, 1801–1809* (New York: New York University Press, 1987), 21–33.

17. On the political and ideological differences between Federalists and Jeffersonian Republicans, see Joyce Appleby, *Capitalism and a New Social Order: The Republican Vision of the 1790s* (New York: New York University Press, 1984); Jerald A. Combs, *The Jay Treaty: Political Battleground of the Founding Fathers* (Berkeley and Los Angeles: University of California Press, 1970); Eugene Perry Link, *Democratic Republican Societies, 1790–1800* (New York: Columbia University Press, 1942); and Drew McCoy, *The Elusive Republic: Political Economy in Jeffersonian America* (Chapel Hill, N.C.: University of North Carolina Press,

1980). My views regarding the intensity of divisions regarding the legacy of the American Revolution have also been shaped by an extensive reading of surviving newspapers from this period published in Newark and Morristown, New Jersey.

18. My views regarding the foreign policy and military history of the period have been shaped by Alexander DeConde, *The Quasi War: The Politics and Diplomacy of the Undeclared Naval War with France* (New York: Charles Scribner's Sons, 1966); Kohn, *Eagle and Sword,* 174–273; William J. Murphy, Jr., "John Adams: The Politics of the Additional Army, 1798–1800," *New England Quarterly* 52 (June 1979): 234–49; Thomas M. Ray, "'Not One Cent for Tribute': The Public Addresses and American Popular Reaction to the XYZ Affair, 1798–1799," *Journal of the Early Republic* 3 (Winter 1983): 389–412; and William Stinchcombe, *The XYZ Affair* (Westport, Conn.: Greenwood Press, 1980).

19. Len Travers, "Hurrah for the Fourth: Patriotism, Politics, and Independence Day in Federalist Boston, 1783–1818," *Essex Institute Historical Collections* 125 (April 1989): 129–61; Robert Pettus Hay, "A Jubilee for Freemen: The Fourth of July in Frontier Kentucky, 1788–1816," *Register of the Kentucky Historical Society* 64 (July 1966): 169–93; and Thomas Jefferson to James Madison, 10 May 1798, *The Papers of James Madison,* ed. William T. Hutchinson, Robert A. Rutland, Charles F. Hobson, William M. E. Rachal, and Jeanne K. Sisson (Charlottesville: University Press of Virginia, 1977–), 17:128–30.

20. *Centinel of Freedom* (Newark, N.J.), 17 April 1798.

21. Warren, "Fourth of July Myths," 261–64; *Centinel of Freedom* (Newark, N.J.), 10 July 1798.

22. *Centinel of Freedom* (Newark, N.J.), 10 July 1798.

23. Susan G. Davis, *Parades and Power: Street Theatre in Nineteenth-Century Philadelphia* (Philadelphia: Temple University Press, 1986; Berkeley and Los Angeles: University of California Press, 1988), 58–59.

24. James Madison to Thomas Jefferson, 12 February 1798, in Hutchinson et al, *Papers of James Madison* 17:80–81.

25. Benjamin Henry Latrobe to Robert Goodloe Harper, post–24 April 1800, *The Correspondence and Miscellaneous Papers of Benjamin Henry Latrobe,* ed. John C. Van Horne (New Haven, Conn.: Yale University Press, 1984), 1:160–61.

26. U.S. Congress, House, Representative Roger Griswold of Connecticut, Representative John Nicholas of Virginia, Representative Abraham Nott of South Carolina, and Representative Nathaniel Macon of North Carolina, *Annals of Congress,* 6th Cong., 2d sess., 5 December 1800, vol. 10, 799–803. See also Kirk Savage, "The Self-made Monument: George Washington and the Fight to Erect a National Memorial," *Winterthur Portfolio* 22 (Winter 1987): 227–28.

27. U.S. Congress, House, Representative John Randolph of Virginia, *Annals of Congress,* 6th Cong., 2d sess., 23 December 1800, vol. 10, 862–63. On the question of federal support for culture, see Sidney Hart and David C. Ward, "The Waning of an Enlightenment Ideal: Charles Willson Peale's Philadelphia Museum, 1790–1820," *Journal of the Early Republic* 8 (Winter 1988): 389–418.

28. *Newark Gazette,* 25 December 1798; John Adams to John Trumbull, 1 January 1817, *The Autobiography of Colonel John Trumbull,* ed. Theodore Sizer (New Haven, Conn.: Yale University Press, 1953), 311–12; and Blanche Linden-Ward, "Putting the Past Under Grass: History as Death and Cemetery Commemoration," *Prospects* 10 (1985): 279–314.

29. Benson J. Lossing, *The Pictorial Field-Book of the Revolution* (New York, 1851), 1:549; 2:177, 668.

30. U.S. Department of the Navy, *Naval Documents Related to the United States Wars with the Barbary Powers,* vol. 6, *Naval Operations* (Washington, D.C.: GPO, 1944), 362, 365–66, 384–85, 386, 497, 519, 580.

31. The Tripoli monument was moved from the Capitol grounds in 1860 to the United States Naval Academy, Annapolis, Maryland. See James M. Goode, *The Outdoor Sculpture of Washington, D.C.: A Comprehensive Historical Guide* (Washington, D.C.: Smithsonian Institution Press, 1974), 515–17.

32. *Newark Gazette,* 10 July 1804; and Hackett, "Social Origins of Nationalism," 668.

33. Robert A. Rutland, *The Presidency of James Madison* (Lawrence, Kans.: University Press of Kansas, 1990); and J. C. A. Stagg, *Mr. Madison's War: Politics, Diplomacy, and, Warfare in the Early American Republic, 1783–1830* (Princeton, N.J.: Princeton University Press, 1983).

34. Cress, *Citizens in Arms,* 173–77; Charles Royster, "Founding a Nation in Blood: Military Conflict and American Nationality," in *Arms and Independence: The Military Character of the American Revolution,* ed. Ronald Hoffman and Peter J. Albert (Charlottesville: University Press of Virginia, 1984), 40–43; and Steven Watts, *The Republic Reborn: War and the Making of Liberal America, 1790–1820* (Baltimore: Johns Hopkins Press, 1987).

35. John P. Resch, "Politics and Public Culture: The Revolutionary War Pension Act of 1818," *Journal of the Early Republic* 8 (Summer 1988): 139–50.

36. Cress, *Citizens in Arms,* 173–77; Marcus Cunliffe, *Soldiers and Civilians: The Martial Spirit in America, 1775–1865* (Boston: Little, Brown, 1968), 179–212; Robert Reinders, "Militia and Public Order in Nineteenth-Century America," *Journal of American Studies* 11 (1977): 81–101; John F. and Kathleen Smith Kutolowski, "Commissions and Canvasses: The Militia and Politics in Western New York, 1800–1845," *New York History* 63 (January 1982): 5–38; and J. Ritchie Garrison, "Battalion Day: Militia Exercise and Frolic in Pennsylvania Before the Civil War," *Pennsylvania Folklife* 26 (1976): 2–12. For an account of the honors bestowed on one aged veteran, see Alfred F. Young, "George Robert Twelves Hewes (1742–1840): A Boston Shoemaker and the Memory of the American Revolution," *William and Mary Quarterly* 38 (October 1981): 619–22.

37. Constance M. Greiff, *Independence: The Creation of a National Park* (Philadelphia: University of Pennsylvania Press, 1987), 35.

38. A. Levasseur, *Lafayette in America in 1824 and 1825,* trans. John D. Godman (Philadelphia: Carey and Lea, 1829; New York: Research Reprints, 1970), vol. 1; Sylvia Neely, "The Politics of Liberty in the Old World and the New: Lafayette's Return to America in 1824," *Journal of the Early Republic* 6 (Summer 1986): 151–71; and Fred Somkin, *Unquiet Eagle: Memory and Desire in the Idea of American Freedom, 1815–1860* (Ithaca, N.Y.: Cornell University Press, 1967), 131–74.

39. Merrill D. Peterson, *The Jefferson Image in the American Mind* (New York: Oxford University Press, 1962), 3–14.

40. Lossing, *Field-Book of the Revolution* 2:217.

41. Neil Harris, *The Artist in American Society: The Formative Years, 1790–1860* (New York: George Braziller, 1966), 188–98; Linden-Ward, "Putting the Past Under Grass," 300–307; and George Washington Warren, *The History of the Bunker Hill Monument Association* (Boston: James R. Osgood, 1877), 153–78.

42. J. Jefferson Miller II, "The Designs for the Washington Monument in Baltimore," *Journal of the Society of Architectural Historians* 23 (March 1964): 19–28; Robert L. Alexander, *The Architecture of Maximilian Godefroy* (Baltimore: Johns Hopkins University Press, 1974), 101–12; Ilene D. Lieberman, "Sir Francis Chantrey's Monument to George Washington: Sculpture and Patronage in Post-Revolutionary America," *Art Bulletin* 71 (June 1989): 254–68; and David C. Ward, "Celebration of Self: The Portraiture of Charles Willson Peale and Rembrandt Peale, 1822–27," *American Art* 7 (Winter 1993): 8–27.

43. U.S. Congress, House, Military Affairs Committee, *Monument to the Victims of the*

*Prison-Ships: Report*, 28th Cong., 2d sess., 1844, report no. 176; U.S. Congress, House, Select Committee, *Monument to Captain Nathan Hale: Report*, 26th Cong., 1st sess., 1840, report no. 713; and U.S. Congress, House, Select Committee, *Monument at York, in Virginia*, 24th Cong., 1st sess., 1836, report no. 82.

44. Theodor Sizer, ed., *The Autobiography of Colonel John Trumbull* (New Haven, Conn.: Yale University Press, 1953), 313; Lillian B. Miller, *Patrons and Patriotism: The Encouragement of the Fine Arts in the United States, 1790–1860* (Chicago: University of Chicago Press, 1966), 45–47; and U.S. Congress, House, Representative John Randolph of Virginia, *Gales and Seaton's Register*, 20th Cong., 1st sess., 9 January 1828, 4, pt. 1:942. See also Michael G. Kammen, *A Season of Youth: The American Revolution and the Historical Imagination* (New York: Alfred A. Knopf, 1978), 80.

45. Miller, *Patrons and Patriotism*, 133–55; Donald B. Cole and John J. McDonough, eds., *Witness to the Young Republic: A Yankee's Journal, 1828–1870, Benjamin Brown French* (Hanover, N.H.: University Press of New England, 1989), 130, 133; Harris, *Artist in American Society*, 100–101; and Gary Wills, "Washington's Citizen Virtue: Greenough and Houdon," *Critical Inquiry* 10 (March 1984): 420–41.

46. Savage, "Self-made Monument," 233; and Charles Warren, "How Politics Intruded into the Washington Centenary of 1832," *Proceedings of the Massachusetts Historical Society* 65 (December 1932): 37–62.

47. Savage, "Self-made Monument," 233–34; Robert Belmont Freeman, Jr., "Design Proposals for the Washington National Monument," *Records of the Columbia Historical Society* (1973–74): 151–86; and *New York Home Journal*, 17 April 1852, 2, in clipping file of Frederick Voss, National Portrait Gallery, Washington, D.C. I am indebted to Mr. Voss for providing me use of his files.

48. *New York Home Journal*, 28 October 1848, 2, and 24 April 1852, 2, in clipping file of Frederick Voss.

49. Savage, "Self-made Monument," 235. On nativism in the antebellum period, see David H. Bennett, *The Party of Fear: From Nativist Movements to the New Right in American History* (Chapel Hill, N.C.: University of North Carolina, 1988), passim.

50. "Appeal of 'The Ladies' Washington National Monument Society,'" [1860] and Margaret C. Brown, Tallahassee, Florida, to J. B. H. Smith, Treasurer of the Washington National Monument Society, 5 April [1861], box 1, Letters Received from the Ladies' Washington National Monument Society, 1859–61, Records of the Washington National Monument Society: Records of the Secretary, RG 42, National Archives.

51. Warren, *Bunker Hill Monument Association*, 285–314; and George Peck, *Wyoming: Its History, Stirring Incidents, and Romantic Adventures* (New York: Harper & Brothers, 1858), 376–87.

52. U.S. Congress, House, Representative Thomas Bayly of Virginia, *Congressional Globe*, 33d Cong., 1st sess., 15 December 1853, 28, pt. 1:52–54.

53. Wallace Evan Davies, *Patriotism on Parade: The Story of Veterans' and Hereditary Organizations in America, 1783–1900* (Cambridge, Mass.: Harvard University Press, 1955), 25–27.

54. Suzanne Lebsock, *The Free Women of Petersburg: Status and Culture in a Southern Town, 1784–1860* (New York: Norton, 1984), 195–236.

55. Lossing, *Field-Book of the Revolution* 2:427. On the feminization of American culture in the postrevolutionary period, see Ann Douglas, *The Feminization of American Culture* (New York: Alfred A. Knopf, 1977; New York: Doubleday, Anchor Press, 1988).

56. Lossing, *Field-Book of the Revolution* 1:366.

57. Lossing, *Field-Book of the Revolution* 2:103, 372; and Warren, *Bunker Hill Monument Association*, 195.

58. James Monroe to Albert Gallatin, 10 September 1816, *The Papers of Albert Gallatin,* microfilm, 46 reels (Philadelphia: Rhistoric Publications, 1969), 28:813.

59. Perhaps the clearest evidence that there exists a distinctive pattern to Independence Day ceremonies is the parodies and satires written by American critics of the orations given on this holiday. See Barnet Baskerville, "19th Century Burlesque of Oratory," *American Quarterly* 20 (Winter 1968): 726–43. For a racist parody of Independence Day ceremonies, see *Palladium of Liberty* (Morristown, N.J.), 3 September 1818.

60. Henry A. Hawken, *Trumpets of Glory: Fourth of July Orations, 1786–1861* (Granby, Conn.: Salmon Brook Historical Society, 1976), 136–59.

61. Davis, *Parades and Power,* passim; and Green, "Fourth of July in North Carolina," 126–27.

62. Philip S. Foner, *We, the Other People* (Urbana, Ill.: University of Illinois Press, 1976), 1–16; Mary Ryan, "The American Parade: Representations of the Nineteenth Century Social Order," in *The New Cultural History,* ed. Lynn Hunt (Berkeley and Los Angeles: University of California Press, 1989), 131–53; and Frederick Voss, "Honoring a Scorned Hero: America's Monument to Thomas Paine," *New York History* 68 (April 1987): 133–50.

63. *New York Herald,* 6 July 1845. See also Kathleen Neils Conzen, "Ethnicity as Festive Culture: Nineteenth-Century German America on Parade," in *The Invention of Ethnicity,* ed. Werner Sollors (New York: Oxford University Press, 1989), 45.

64. Hawken, *Trumpets of Glory,* 200–230.

65. Frederick Douglass, "What to the Slave is the Fourth of July?: An Address Delivered in Rochester, New York, On 5 July 1852," in *The Frederick Douglass Papers,* ser. 1, Speeches, Debates and Interviews, ed. John W. Blassingame (New Haven, Conn.: Yale University Press, 1978), 2:371.

66. Foner, *We, the Other People,* 77–83.

67. John William Ward, *Andrew Jackson: The Symbol for an Age* (New York: Oxford University Press, 1955); and George B. Forgie, *Patricide in the House Divided: A Psychological Interpretation of Lincoln and His Age* (New York: W. W. Norton, 1979), 70–77.

68. Roy P. Basler, ed., *The Collected Works of Abraham Lincoln* (New Brunswick, N.J.: Rutgers University Press, 1953), 1:226. On the reluctance of Americans to accept partisanship, see Richard Hofstadter, *The Idea of a Party System: The Rise of Legitimate Opposition in the United States, 1780–1840* (Berkeley and Los Angeles: University of California Press, 1969).

69. Allan Nevins, *Polk: The Diary of a President, 1845–1849* (London: Longmans, Green, 1952), 7–8; and Cole and McDonough, *Witness to the Young Republic,* 179–80.

70. U.S. Congress, House, Representative Jacob Collamer of Vermont, Representative John G. Palfrey of Massachusetts, Representative Thomas B. King of Georgia, and Representative Robert Schenck of Ohio, *Congressional Globe,* 30th Cong., 1st sess., 5 August 1848, vol. 18, 1045. See also, Vivien Green Fryd, "Sculpture as History: Themes of Liberty, Unity and Manifest Destiny in American Sculpture, 1825–1865" (Ph.D. diss., University of Wisconsin–Madison, 1984), 198–210.

71. U.S. Congress, House, Representative John Alexander McClernand of Illinois, *Congressional Globe,* 30th Cong., 1st sess., 5 August 1848, vol. 18, 1045.

72. Rosemary Hopkins, "Clark Mills: The First Native American Sculptor" (Master's thesis, University of Maryland, 1966), 43–98.

73. Frederick Merk, *Manifest Destiny and Mission in American History: A Reinterpretation* (New York: Alfred A. Knopf, 1963).

74. Paul D. Lack, *The Texas Revolutionary Experience: A Political and Social History* (College Station, Tex.: Texas A&M University Press, 1992).

75. Worthington Chauncy Ford, "Letters Responding to Sumner's Oration," *Proceedings of the Massachusetts Historical Society* 50 (April 1917): 249–307; Henry Adams, *The Writings of Albert Gallatin* (Philadelphia: J. B. Lippincott, 1879; New York: Antiquarian Press, 1960), 3:557–91; and John H. Schroeder, *Mr. Polk's War: American Opposition and Dissent, 1846–1848* (Madison, Wisc.: University of Wisconsin Press, 1973).

76. Merk, *Manifest Destiny*, passim.

77. Robert W. Johannsen, *To the Halls of the Montezumas: The Mexican War in the American Imagination* (New York: Oxford University Press, 1980).

78. Davies, *Patriotism on Parade*, 20; *The Constitution of the Aztec Club of 1847 and List of Members: 1893* (Washington, D.C., 1893); Cunliffe, *Soldiers and Civilians*, 70–75; and K. Jack Bauer, *Zachary Taylor: Soldier, Planter, Statesman of the Old Southwest*, Southern Biography Series, ed. William J. Cooper, Jr. (Baton Rouge, La.: Louisiana State University Press, 1985).

79. John C. Breckinridge, *An Address on the Occasion of the Burial of the Kentucky Volunteers* (Lexington, Ky., 1847); T. H. Bartlett, "Early Settler Memorials, XI," *American Architect and Building News* 22 (1987): 59–61; and R. P. Letcher to Daniel Webster, Secretary of State, 10 January 1852, file: Mexico City, 1851–1967, box 178, Agreements with Foreign Countries, Other Records Relating to Cemeteries and Memorials, Records of the American Battle Monuments Commission, RG 117, National Archives. See also John Porter Bloom, "With the American Army into Mexico, 1846–1848" (Ph.D. diss., Emory University, 1956), 157–62.

80. James W. Oberly, "Gray-Haired Lobbyists: War of 1812 Veterans and the Politics of Bounty Land Grants," *Journal of the Early Republic* 5 (Spring 1985): 35–58.

81. *Proceedings of the National Convention of the Soldiers of the War of 1812* (Philadelphia, 1854), 26.

82. *Proceedings of the Convention of the War of 1812 in the State of New York, Held at Schuylerville, Saratoga County, October 17, 1856* (Albany, N.Y., 1857), 7–26.

83. Although the Mexican-American War remains a largely forgotten struggle in the United States, this has not been the case in Mexico. This is most clearly suggested by the relative place given in the memories of the respective countries to the history of the Saint Patrick's Battalion, a unit of American deserters who fought for Mexico in this conflict. Although forgotten in the United States, Mexico has marked the service of this unit with commemorative medals and coins, monuments, and ceremonies. For a history of the Saint Patrick's Battalion and the commemoration of the Mexican-American War, see Robert Ryal Miller, *Shamrock and Sword: The Saint Patrick's Battalion in the U.S.-Mexican War* (Norman, Okla.: University of Oklahoma Press, 1989).

84. Susan Prendergast Schoelwer, *Alamo Images: Changing Perceptions of a Texas Experience*, DeGolyer Library Publications Series, vol. 3 (Dallas: DeGolyer Library and Southern Methodist University Press, 1985); Edward Tabor Linenthal, *Sacred Ground: Americans and Their Battlefields* (Urbana, Ill.: University of Illinois Press, 1991), 55–86; and Don Graham, "Remembering the Alamo: The Story of the Texas Revolution in Popular Culture," *Southwestern Historical Quarterly* 89 (1985): 35–66.

85. The role of slavery as a political and constitutional issue in the antebellum period has been examined by Don Edward Fehrenbacher, *The Dred Scott Case: Its Significance in American Law and Politics* (New York: Oxford University Press, 1978) and Eric Foner, *Free Soil, Free Labor, Free Men: The Ideology of the Republican Party Before the Civil War* (New York: Oxford University Press, 1970).

86. H. T. Tuckerman, "Holidays," *North American Review* 84 (April 1857): 334–63.

87. Ibid.

88. Basler, *Collected Works of Abraham Lincoln* 4:271.

## 2. THE DIVIDED LEGACY OF THE CIVIL WAR

1. "The Soldier's Grave," *New York Times,* 16 September 1861, 4; L. Thomas, Adjutant General, General Order No. 33, 3 April 1862, in U.S. Congress, House, *The War of the Rebellion: A Compilation of the Official Records of the Union and Confederate Armies,* by Fred C. Ainsworth and John W. Kirkley, 56th Cong., 1st sess., 1899, H. Doc. 118 (Washington, D.C.: GPO, 1899), ser. 3, vol. 2, 2–3; and War Department, "Annual Report of the Quarter-master-General, 1863," *Annual Reports of the Quartermaster-General from 1861 to 1866* (Washington, D.C.: GPO, 1880), 21, 48–51. For an overview of the Civil War, see James M. McPherson, *Battle Cry of Freedom: The Civil War Era* (New York: Oxford University Press, 1988).

2. David Charles Sloane, *The Last Great Necessity: Cemeteries in American History* (Balti-more: Johns Hopkins University Press, 1991), 113–15; and James J. Farrell, *Inventing the American Way of Death, 1830–1920* (Philadelphia: Temple University Press, 1980), 97–114.

3. Gary Wills, *Lincoln at Gettysburg: The Words that Remade America* (New York: Simon and Schuster, 1992). For a text of Everett's address, see pages 213–47.On the dedication of Gettysburg, see also John S. Patterson, "A Patriotic Landscape: Gettysburg, 1863–1913," *Prospects* 7 (1982): 315–33; and Frank L. Klement, "Benjamin B. French, the Lincolns, and the Dedication of the Soldiers' Cemetery at Gettysburg," *Historical New Hampshire* 42 (Spring 1987): 36–63.

4. Wills, *Lincoln at Gettysburg,* passim.

5. James F. Russling, "National Cemeteries," *Harper's New Monthly Magazine* 33 (August 1866): 310–22.

6. U.S. War Department, "Annual Report of the Quartermaster-General, 1866," *Annual Reports of the Quartermaster-General from 1861 to 1866* (Washington, D.C.: GPO, 1880), 18–19, 220–35.

7. U.S. War Department, *Report of the Quartermaster-General to the Secretary of War, 1868* (Washington, D.C.: GPO, 1868), 14. Although Montgomery C. Meigs, the quarter-master general, agreed that states and individuals should be permitted to build monuments in the national cemeteries, he maintained that the federal government must have full authority over these burial grounds. He opposed any effort to have state governments pay for perma-nent gravestones and declared: "The national government has taken charge of these sacred remains. They fell in the defense, not of the States, but of the nation, and the nation should make the expenditures necessary for their proper and tender preservation."

8. Quartermaster General Q. L. Meigs to Secretary of War John A. Rawlins, 7 August 1869; William W. Belknap, Secretary of War, to Governor of Virginia, 3 May 1870, copy; William Walker [?], Governor of Virginia, to Secretary of War, 5 May 1870, box 2, entry 569, Letters and Reports Received Relating to Cemeteries, 1865–70, Records of the Quartermas-ter General, RG 92, National Archives.

9. Michigan Civil War Centennial Observance Commission, *Michigan Civil War Monu-ments,* by George S. May (Lansing: Michigan Civil War Observance Commission, 1965); and George B. McClellan, *George B. McClellan's Letter of Acceptance Together with His West-Point Oration* (New York: E. P. Patten, 1864), 3–4. I am indebted to William Hoffmeister, a stu-dent at Rutgers University, for the material on McClellan.

10. Mildred C. Baruch and Ellen J. Beckman, *Civil War Monuments* (Washington, D.C.: Daughters of the Union Veterans of the Civil War, 1861–65, 1978); "Many Costly Monu-ments," *Boston Evening Transcript,* 14 November 1865, 2; "Dedication of the Soldiers' Mon-ument at Concord," *Boston Evening Transcript,* 19 April 1867; "A Soldiers' Monument in Boston," *Boston Evening Transcript,* 22 July 1867; and Calvin McCoy Hennig, "The Out-

door Public Commemorative Monuments of Syracuse, New York: 1885–1950" (Ph.D. diss., Syracuse University, 1983), 228–33.

11. Peggy McDowell, "Martin Milmore's Soldiers' and Sailors' Monument on the Boston Common: Formulating Conventionalism in Design and Symbolism," *Journal of American Culture* 11 (Spring 1988): 63–85; and *Dedication of the Soldiers' Monument at Worcester, Massachusetts* (Boston: Rockwell and Churchill, 1875).

12. Keith F. Davis, "'A Terrible Distinctness': Photography of the Civil War Era," in *Photography in Nineteenth-Century America,* ed. Martha A. Sandweiss (Fort Worth: Amon Carter Museum; New York: Henry N. Abrams, 1991), 131–79; and Alan Trachtenberg, *Reading American Photographs: Images as History, Mathew Brady to Walker Evans* (New York: Hill and Wang, 1989), 71–118.

13. Davis, "A Terrible Distinctness," 131–79.

14. Davis, "A Terrible Distinctness," 131–79; and Trachtenberg, *Reading American Photographs,* 71–118.

15. F. Lauriston Bullard, *Lincoln in Marble and Bronze* (New Brunswick, N.J.: Rutgers University Press, 1952); and J. C. Powers, *Abraham Lincoln: His Life, Public Services, Death and Great Funeral Cortege* (Chicago: H. W. Rokker, 1889), 11–63.

16. William S. McFeeley, *Grant: A Biography* (New York: W. W. Norton, 1983), 380–453, 518–22.

17. Peter Karsten, *Patriot-Heroes in England and America: Political Symbolism and Changing Values Over Three Centuries* (Madison, Wisc.: University of Wisconsin Press, 1978), 98–109.

18. Bullard, *Lincoln in Marble and Bronze,* 332–44; and David W. Blight, *Frederick Douglass' Civil War: Keeping Faith in Jubilee* (Baton Rouge, La.: Louisiana State University Press, 1989), 175–239.

19. Bullard, *Lincoln in Marble and Bronze,* 64–72.

20. "Oration in Memory of Abraham Lincoln, April 14, 1876," in *The Life and Writings of Frederick Douglass,* ed. Philip S. Foner, 5 vols. (New York: International Publishers, 1950–55, 1971), 4:309–19; Bullard, *Lincoln in Marble and Bronze,* 64–72; Blight, *Frederick Douglass' Civil War,* 227–28; and Waldo E. Martin, Jr., *The Mind of Frederick Douglass* (Chapel Hill: University of North Carolina Press, 1984), 266–67.

21. Michael E. McGerr, *The Decline of Popular Politics: The American North, 1865–1928* (New York: Oxford, 1986), 24–26.

22. Mary Dearing, *Veterans in Politics: The Story of the G.A.R.* (Baton Rouge, La.: Louisiana State University Press, 1952), 80–122; and Stuart McConnell, *Glorious Contentment: The Grand Army of the Republic, 1865–1900* (Chapel Hill, N.C.: University of North Carolina Press, 1992), 18–52, 206–7.

23. Dearing, *Veterans in Politics,* 175–90; Gaines M. Foster, *Ghosts of the Confederacy: Defeat, the Lost Cause, and the Emergence of the New South, 1865–1913* (New York: Oxford University Press, 1987), 42; and Frank Moore, *Memorial Ceremonies at the Grave of Our Soldiers: Saturday, May 30, 1868* (Washington, D.C.: William T. Collins, 1869).

24. Moore, *Memorial Ceremonies,* 9–31, 171–83.

25. Moore, *Memorial Ceremonies,* 33–35.

26. Dearing, *Veterans in Politics,* 113–47.

27. James E. Sefton, *The United States Army and Reconstruction, 1865–1877* (Baton Rogue: Louisiana State University Press, 1967; Westport, Conn.: Greenwood Press, 1980).

28. Dearing, *Veterans in Politics,* 185–218.

29. McGerr, *Decline of Popular Politics,* 24–26.

30. "Independence Day," *Charleston Daily Courier,* 4 July 1865, 2; "The Fourth of July,"

*Charleston Daily Courier,* 6 July 1866, 2; and "Independence Day," *Charleston News and Courier,* 5 July 1873, 4.

31. Stephen Davis, "Empty Eyes, Marble Hand: The Confederate Monument and the South," *Journal of Popular Culture* 16 (Winter 1982): 2–21; and Foster, *Ghosts of the Confederacy,* 36–46.

32. F. A. Porcher, *A Brief History of the Ladies' Memorial Association of Charleston, S.C.* (Charleston: H. P. Cooke, 1880), 9.

33. Foster, *Ghosts of the Confederacy,* 39–40. On the role of white southern women in the Civil War, see: Drew Gilpin Faust, "Altars of Sacrifice: Confederate Women and the Narratives of War," *Journal of American History* 76 (March 1990): 1200–28.

34. Foster, *Ghosts of the Confederacy,* 41–46.

35. Allen W. Trelease, *White Terror: The Ku Klux Klan Conspiracy and Southern Reconstruction* (New York: Harper and Row, 1971; Westport, Conn.: Greenwood Press, 1979); and George C. Rable, *But There Was No Peace: The Role of Violence in the Politics of Reconstruction* (Athens, Ga.: University of Georgia Press, 1984), 69–74, 91–100.

36. Mark C. Carnes, *Secret Ritual and Manhood in Victorian America* (New Haven, Conn.: Yale University Press, 1989).

37. Dearing, *Veterans in Politics,* 86–71; and Charles Reagan Wilson, Baptized in Blood: *The Religion of the Lost Cause, 1865–1920* (Athens, Ga.: University of Georgia, 1980), 111–14.

38. Foster, *Ghosts of the Confederacy,* 22–35; and Bertram Wyatt-Brown, *Southern Honor: Ethics, and Behavior in the Old South* (New York: Oxford University, Press, 1982), 454–58.

39. Eric Foner, *Reconstruction: America's Unfinished Revolution, 1863–1877* (New York: Harper and Row, 1988); William Gillette, *Retreat from Reconstruction, 1869–1879* (Baton Rogue: Louisiana State University Press, 1979); and C. Vann Woodward, *The Strange Career of Jim Crow,* 3d ed. (New York: Oxford University Press, 1974).

40. Stanley P. Hirshson, *Farewell the Bloody Shirt: Northern Republicans and the Southern Negro* (Bloomington, Ind.: Indiana University Press, 1962); and Foster, *Ghosts of the Confederacy,* 79–89.

41. Foster, *Ghosts of the Confederacy,* 112–59.

42. Foster, *Ghosts of the Confederacy,* 128–31.

43. B. A. C. Emerson, *Historic Southern Monuments* (New York: Neale Publishing, 1911); and Foster, *Ghosts of the Confederacy,* 133–44.

44. Foster, *Ghosts of the Confederacy,* 119–20, 128–31.

45. Robert Haven Schauffler, *Memorial Day,* American Holiday Series (1911; reprint, New York: Dodd, Mead, 1940).

46. Zonia Baber, *Peace Symbols* (Chicago: Women's International League for Peace and Freedom, n.d.), 46–47; Bullard, *Lincoln in Marble and Bronze,* 223–25; "Editorial," *San Francisco Daily Examiner,* 31 May 1886, 1–2; Patterson, "Patriotic Landscape," 328; and Dearing, *Veterans in Politics,* 448–54.

47. Foster, *Ghosts of the Confederacy,* 153–54; and *The Code of the Laws of the United States of America* (Washington, D.C.: GPO, 1935), 991.

48. U.S. Department of the Interior, National Park Service, *The Origins and Evolution of the National Military Park Idea,* by Ronald F. Lee (Washington, D.C.: GPO, 1973), 28–32.

49. Lee, *National Military Park Idea,* 28–32.

50. New York Monuments Commission, *Final Report on the Battlefield of Gettysburg,* 3 vols. (Albany, N.Y.: J. B. Lyon Printers, 1900).

51. Steve Walker and David F. Riggs, *Vicksburg Battlefield Monuments* (Jackson, Miss.: University Press of Mississippi, 1984), 42; and U.S. Department of Interior, National Park

Service, *Administrative History: Gettysburg National Military Park and National Cemetery,* by Harlan D. Unrau (Washington, D.C.: GPO, 1991), 95–96.

52. Edward Tabor Linenthal, *Sacred Ground: Americans and Their Battlefields* (Urbana, Ill.: University of Illinois Press, 1991), passim.

53. Thomas Sturgis, *Shall Congress Erect Statues at National Expense to Confederate Officers in Washington?* (New York, 1910).

54. Blight, *Frederick Douglass' Civil War,* 219–39; and William H. Wiggins, Jr., *O Freedom!: Afro-American Emancipation Celebrations* (Knoxville, Tenn.: University of Tennessee Press, 1987).

55. Albert Boime, *The Art of Exclusion: Representing Blacks in the Nineteenth Century* (Washington, D.C.: Smithsonian Institution Press, 1990), 15–19, 199–217.

56. Wilson, *Baptized in Blood,* 105–6; and U.S. Congress, House, Representative Charles M. Stedman of North Carolina, *Congressional Record,* 67th Cong., 4th sess., 9 January 1923, 64, pt. 2:1509.

57. Dearing, *Veterans in Politics,* 342–57; and Foster, *Ghosts of the Confederacy,* 154.

58. Kirk Savage, "The Politics of Memory: Black Emancipation and the Civil War Monument," in *Commemorations: The Politics of National Identity,* ed. John R. Gillis (Princeton, N.J.: Princeton University Press, 1994), 127–67. Efforts by African American leaders and organizations to remake the Lincoln Memorial into a symbol of the civil rights movement is superbly examined by Scott A. Sandage, "A Marble House Divided: The Lincoln Memorial, the Civil Rights Movement, and the Politics of Memory, 1939–1963," *Journal of American History* 80 (June 1993): 135–67.

59. Thomas L. Connelly, *The Marble Man: Robert E. Lee and His Image in American Society* (New York: Alfred A. Knopf, 1977), 99–140.

60. David M. Kahn, "The Grant Monument," *Journal of the Society of Architectural Historians* 41 (October 1982): 212–31; James L. Riedy, *Chicago Sculpture* (Urbana, Ill.: University of Illinois Press, 1981), 219–21; and George McCue, *Sculpture City: St. Louis* (New York: Hudson Hill Press, 1988), 36.

61. Max Lerner, ed., *The Mind and Faith of Justice Holmes: His Speeches, Essays, Letters and Judicial Opinions* (Boston: Little, Brown, 1943; Garden City, N.Y.: Halcyon House, 1948), 9–27.

62. Minnesota Monument Commission, *Report of the Minnesota Commission Appointed to Erect Monuments to Soldiers in the National Military Cemeteries* (St. Paul, 1916), 46.

63. Thomas C. Leonard, *Above the Battle: War Making in America from Appomattox to Versailles* (New York: Oxford University Press, 1978); Gerald F. Linderman, *Embattled Courage: The Experience of Combat in the American Civil War* (New York: Free Press, 1987); and McConnell, *Glorious Contentment,* 166–205.

64. Edmund Wilson, *Patriotic Gore: Studies in the Literature of the American Civil War* (New York: Oxford University Press, 1962); and Daniel Aaron, *The Unwritten War: American Writers and the Civil War* (New York: Alfred A. Knopf, 1973).

65. New York Andersonville Monument Dedication Commission, *A Pilgrimage to the Shrines of Patriotism* (Albany, N.Y.: J. B. Lyon, 1916), 125.

66. Gilbert Tapley Vincent, "American Artists and their Changing Perceptions of American History, 1770–1940" (Ph.D. diss., University of Delaware, 1982), 113.

67. Foster, *Ghosts of the Confederacy,* 172–79; and McConnell, *Glorious Contentment,* 200–238.

68. Thomas L. Connelly and Barbara L. Bellows, *God and General Longstreet: The Lost Cause and the Southern Mind* (Baton Rouge, La.: Louisiana State University Press, 1982).

69. "Symbols of Discontent," *Newark Star Ledger,* 19 November 1989, sec. 1:70; Peter

Applebome, "Enduring Symbols of the Confederacy Divide the South Anew," *New York Times,* 27 January 1993, A16; editorial, "Ms. Moseley Braun's Majestic Moment," *New York Times,* 24 July 1993, A18; and Douglas Lederman, "Old Times Not Forgotten," *Chronicle of Higher Education,* 20 October 1993, A50–52.

70. Thomas Cripps, *Slow Fade to Black: The Negro in American Film, 1900–1942* (New York: Oxford University Press, 1977), 24–41.

71. Cripps, *Slow Fade to Black,* passim; and Thomas Cripps, "African Americans and the Civil War and Reconstruction, film images from 1911 to 1989" (Paper presented at the War, Film, and History Conference, Rutgers Center for Historical Analysis, New Brunswick, N.J.,October 21, 1993).

72. Kirk Savage, "The Self-made Monument: George Washington and the Fight to Erect a National Monument," *Winterthur Portfolio* 22 (Winter 1987): 227–28; and Wallace Evan Davies, *Patriotism on Parade: The Story of Veterans' and Hereditary Organizations in America* (Cambridge, Mass.: Harvard University, Press, 1955), 44–53.

73. "The Fourth of July," *Charleston News and Courier,* 4 July 1885, 4.

74. Jefferson Davis, *The Address on the Mexican War and Its Results, As Delivered by the Honorable Jefferson Davis Before the Louisiana Associated Veterans of the Mexican War* (New Orleans: L. McGrane, 1876), 17–18.

75. McConnell, *Glorious Contentment,* 125–65; Michael B. Katz, *In the Shadow of the Poorhouse: A Social History of Welfare in America* (New York: Basic Books, 1986), 200; and Maris A. Vinovskis, "Have Social Historians Lost the Civil War? Some Preliminary Demographic Speculations," *Journal of American History* 76 (June 1989): 35–58.

76. Wallace E. Davies, "The Mexican War Veterans as an Organized Group," *Mississippi Valley Historical Review* 35 (1948): 221–38.

77. McConnell, *Glorious Contentment,* passim.

78. Davies, *Patriotism on Parade,* 74–104, 119–38; David Glassberg, "History and the Public: Legacies of the Progressive Era," *Journal of American History* 73 (March 1987): 957–80; Michael G. Kammen, *A Season of Youth: The American Revolution and the Historical Imagination* (New York: Alfred A. Knopf, 1978); Karal Ann Marling, *George Washington Slept Here: Colonial Revivals and American Culture, 1876–1986* (Cambridge: Harvard University Press, 1988); Michael Wallace, "Visiting the Past: History Museums in the United States," in *Presenting the Past: Essays on History and the Public,* ed. Susan Porter Benson, Steven Brier, and Roy Rosenzweig (Philadelphia: Temple University Press, 1986), 139–42; and James Michael Lindgren, "The Gospel of Preservation in Virginia and New England: Historic Preservation and the Regeneration of Traditionalism" (Ph.D. diss., College of William and Mary, 1984).

79. John Higham, *Strangers in the Land: Patterns of American Nativism, 1860–1925* (New Brunswick, N.J.: Rutgers University Press, 1955); and Merle Curti, *The Roots of American Loyalty* (New York: Columbia University Press, 1946).

80. Kathleen Neils Conzen, "Ethnicity as Festive Culture: Nineteenth Century German America on Parade," in *The Invention of Ethnicity,* ed. Werner Sollors (New York: Oxford University Press, 1989), 44–76; Public Law 120, 27 February 1903, Minutes, Pulaski Statue Commission, 22 March, 11 April 1905, Minutes, 1903–10, Records of the Pulaski Statue Commission; Augustus Saint-Gaudens to Secretary of War William Howard Taft, 28 March, 18 July 1905, and Saint-Gaudens to Fred W. Carpenter, 7 April 1905, tray 2, Letters Received by the Secretary of the Kosciusko and Pulaski Monument Commission; "Programme of Competition for the Pedestrian Statue of the late Commodore John Barry," 25 June 1908, tray 1, Correspondence and Other Records of the Executive and Disbursing Officer, 1907–17, Records of the Barry Statue Commission, Records of the Office of Building and Grounds, RG 42, National Archives. For the role of various ethnic groups in using ritual and memory

to define their identity, see John Bodnar, *Remaking America: Public Memory, Commemoration, and Patriotism in the Twentieth Century* (Princeton, N.J.: Princeton University, 1992), 41–77.

81. Joseph J. O'Brien, Corresponding Secretary, National Commodore John Barry Statue Association to Colonel William W. Harts, Executive Officer, Barry Statue Commission, 10 May 1914, enclosure, John J. O'Brien, "The History of the Commodore John Barry Statue," tray 5, Correspondence and Other Records of the Executive and Disbursing Officer, 1900–1917, Records of the Barry Monument Commission; Asa Gardiner [?], Secretary General, Society of Cincinnati to Colonel Spencer Cosby, Executive Officer, 11 April 1910, tray 1, Correspondence and Other Records Executive and Disbursing Officer, 1907–13, RG 42, National Archives.

82. Arthur S. Link, ed., *The Papers of Woodrow Wilson*, 65 vols. to date (Princeton, N.J.: Princeton University Press, 1966–), 30:34–36.

83. Michael E. Driscoll, "Commodore John Barry" (Washington, D.C.: GPO, 1904), 14.

84. G. W. Baird, President, Jonathan H. Moore, A. Howard Clark, District of Columbia Society of the Sons of the American Revolution to President of the United States, 13 October 1910, copy, tray 2, Letters Received by the Kosciusko and Pulaski Monument Commission, RG 42, National Archives.

85. Boston City Council, *A Memorial of Crispus Attucks, Samuel Maverick, James Caldwell, Samuel Gray, and Patrick Carr from the City of Boston* (1889; reprint, Miami: Mnemosyne Publishing, 1969); John McGlone, "Monuments and Memorials to Black Military History, 1775 to 1891" (Ph.D. diss., Middle Tennessee State University, 1985), 162–66; and Dennis P. Ryan, "The Crispus Attucks Monument Controversy of 1887," *Negro History Bulletin* 40 (January–February 1977): 656–57.

86. "Municipal Art Commission's Decision," *Monumental News* 15 (April 1903): 234.

87. Isabel McDougall, "Municipal Art," *Brush and Pencil* 3 (February 1899): 302–6.

88. Michael G. Kammen, *Mystic Chords of Memory: The Transformation of Tradition in American Culture* (New York: Alfred A. Knopf, 1991), 163–93.

89. Isabel McDougall, "Soldier Monuments," *Chicago Evening Post*, 16 July 1898, in *Brush and Pencil* 3 (August 1898): 217–21.

90. Michele Bogart, *Public Sculpture and the Civic Ideal in New York City, 1890–1930* (Chicago: University of Chicago Press, 1989), 17–66.

91. *Monumental News* 14 (September 1902): 525–27, quoted in Dennis R. Montagna, "Henry Merwin Shrady's Ulysses S. Grant Memorial in Washington, D.C.: A Study in Iconography, Content and Patronage" (Ph.D. diss., University of Delaware, 1987), 152–53.

92. James Barnes, "Soldiers Monuments," *Art and Progress* 1 (1910): 185–89.

93. "Monument Fight Ended," *Jersey City Journal*, 27 May 1898.

94. "To Bring Venus to Court," *New York Times*, 25 January 1898, 11; "No Greek Statue for Them," press clipping, National Sculpture Society Papers, reel 491:826, Archives of American Art, Smithsonian Institution, Washington, D.C.; "The Soldiers and Sailors' Monument for Jersey City," *Harper's Weekly* 42 (22 January 1898): 77–78; "Propriety of the Jersey City Soldiers' Monument Upheld," *American Architect and Building News* 60 (4 June 1898): 73; and "The Need for City Art Commission's," *Monumental News* 15 (April 1903): 234.

95. "Editorial," *Monument Retailer* 2 (November 1916): 17–19.

96. U.S. Commission of Fine Arts, *The Commission of Fine Arts: A Brief History, 1910–1976, with Additions, 1977–84*, by Sue A. Kohler (Washington, D.C.: GPO, 1985), 1–7; Lois Craig, *The Federal Presence: Architecture, Politics, and Symbols in United States Government Buildings* (Cambridge, Mass.: MIT Press, 1978), 210–15, 250–55; Philip C. Jessup, *Elihu*

*Root* (New York: Dodd, Mead, 1938), 284–86; and U.S. Congress, House, Representative James A. Tawney of Minnesota, Representative James R. Mann of Illinois, and Representative Michael E. Driscoll of New York, *Congressional Record,* 61st Cong., 2d sess., 9 February 1910, 45, pt. 2:1658–75.

97. U.S. Congress, House, Representative Driscoll, 1666.

98. George Gurney, *Sculpture and the Federal Triangle* (Washington, D.C.: Smithsonian Institution Press, 1985), 34–41.

99. Charles DeBenedetti, *The Peace Reform in American History* (Bloomington, Ind.: Indiana University, 1980), 59–78.

100. Peter Karsten, "Militarization and Rationalization in the United States, 1870–1914," in *The Militarization of the Western World,* ed. John R. Gillis (New Brunswick, N.J.: Rutgers University Press, 1989); and T. J. Jackson Lears, *No Place for Grace: Antimodernism and the Transformation of American Culture* (New York: Pantheon, 1981).

101. Gerald F. Linderman, *The Mirror War: American Society and the Spanish-American War* (Ann Arbor, Mich.: University of Michigan Press, 1974).

102. Bogart, *Public Sculpture,* 195.

103. Marjorie P. Balge, "The Dewey Arch: Sculpture or Architecture?" *Archives of American Art Journal* 22 (1983): 2–6.

104. Theodore Roosevelt, *The Works of Theodore Roosevelt,* vol. 11, *The Rough Riders and Men of Action,* national ed. (New York: Charles Scribner's Sons, 1926), 177, 343.

105. Robert L. Beisner, *Twelve Against Empire: The Anti-Imperialists, 1898–1910* (New York: McGraw Hill, 1968).

106. Stuart Creighton Miller, "The American Soldier and the Conquest of the Philippines," in *Reappraising an Empire: New Perspectives on Philippine-American History,* ed. Peter W. Stanley (Cambridge: Harvard University Press, 1984), 34; and "Admiral Dewey Honored," *New York Times,* 2 May 1899, 3.

107. U.S. Navy, Naval History Division, *How the Battleship Maine Was Destroyed,* by H. G. Rickover (Washington, D.C.: GPO, 1976), 75–91.

108. U.S. Navy, *Battleship Maine,* 79; and "Taft to Honor Maine Dead," *New York Times,* 23 March 1912, 6.

109. U.S. Congress, House, Representative Charles V. Fornes of New York, *Congressional Record,* 62d Cong., 2d sess., 4 April 1912, 48, pt. 5:4292.

110. James M. Mayo, *War Memorials as Political Landscape: The American Experience and Beyond* (New York: Praeger, 1988), 159–60; "Memorial Tablet from U.S.S. Maine Available for City," *Jerseyman* (Morristown, N.J.), 6 June 1919, 6; and "The Maine Sinks to Ocean Grave," *New York Times,* 17 March 1912, 1.

111. "Raising the Maine at Last," *New York Times,* 17 October 1910, 8; "What Will the Raising of the 'Maine' Disclose?" *Scientific American* 102 (4 June 1910): 454; "Destruction of the 'Maine' by a Low-Explosive Mine and Her Own Magazines," *Scientific American* 105 (23 December 1911): 578–79; and G. W. Melville, "Destruction of the Battleship Maine," *North American Review* 193 (June 1911): 831–49.

### 3. REMEMBERING THE WAR TO END ALL WARS

1. For an overview of the First World War and the interwar period, see: John Whiteclay Chambers II, *The Tyranny of Change: America in the Progressive Era, 1890–1920,* 2d. ed. (New York: St. Martin's Press, 1992); David M. Kennedy, *Over Here: The First World War and American Society* (New York: Oxford University Press, 1980); and Ellis Hawley, *The*

*Great War and the Search for a Modern Order: A History of the American People and Their Institutions, 1917–1933* (New York: St. Martin's Press, 1979).

2. U.S. Congress, House, Committee on Military Affairs, *American Purple Cross Association: Hearings*, 65th Cong., 1st sess., 5 September 1917, 14, 27; "American Purple Cross Society," *Casket* 42 (1 August 1917): 13–15; and "Bids Rejected By War Department," *Casket* (1 October 1917): 17–18.

3. U.S. Department of the Army, *Quartermaster Support of the Army: A History of the Corps, 1775–1939*, by Erna Risch (Washington, D.C.: GPO, 1962), 690–91.

4. "Brent Wants Dead to Stay in France," *New York Times*, 16 January 1920, 8; and "Objection to Bringing Home Soldier Dead," *New York Times*, 18 January 1920, sec. 8, p. 9.

5. Major H. R. Lemly to the Quartermaster General, 11 August 1919, memorandum, file 293.7 Cemeterial, copy, minutes, 21 November 1919, exhibit B, U.S. Commission of Fine Arts, Charles Moore to Henry White, Commissioner Plenipotentiary, Paris, 5 June 1919, White to Moore, 22 July 1919, file: American Cemeteries in Europe—World War I Graves, box 5, Project Files, Records of the Commission of Fine Arts, RG 66, National Archives; Adjutant General P. L. Harris to the Chief of Staff, 4 June 1919; untitled press release, 19 July 1919, file 293.8, box 566, central decimal file, 1917–1925, Records of the Adjutant General's Office, RG 407, National Archives.

6. V. J. Oldshue, "France Remembers," *American Legion Weekly*, 9 July 1920, 5; Elizabeth Hand, "American Graves in France," *New Republic*, 2 June 1920, 14–15; "French Pleas to Let Our Dead Rest," *Literary Digest*, 17 April 1920, 45; and Horace W. Scandlin, "How Mother France Honors the Gold Star American," *World Outlook*, September–October 1920, 32.

7. "A Solution Perhaps Acceptable," *New York Times*, 1 January 1919, 16.

8. "Plan to Bring Back Hero Dead Abroad," *Washington Times*, 26 November 1919, article, file: Headstones, World War I Graves, box 73, Project Files, RG 66, National Archives; Margaret Vascimini to Secretary of State Robert Lansing, 11 January 1920, central decimal file 351.116, box 4202, Records of the Department of State, RG 59, National Archives.

9. U.S. Congress, House, Representative Edward J. King of Illinois, Extension of Remarks, *Congressional Record*, 66th Cong., 2d sess., 11 February 1920, 59, pt. 9:8790; U.S. Congress, House, Representative Clement C. Dikinson of Missouri, *Congressional Record*, 66th Cong., 2d sess., 27 January 1920, 59, pt. 2:2132–33.

10. U.S. Congress, House, Representative John W. Rainey of Illinois, *Congressional Record*, 66th Cong., 2d sess., 6 February 1920, 59, pt. 3:2562–64; "Paris Director in League with Purple Cross (?)," *Embalmer's Monthly* 33 (January 1920): 10–11; and "Rid the Profession of Odium that Has Come to It," *Embalmer's Monthly* 33 (February 1920): 1.

11. "Bringing Our Dead Home from Russia," *New York Times*, 14 November 1919, 4; and "His Appeal Also Is to Sentiment," *New York Times*, 17 January 1920, 10.

12. Address, Charles Moore, Chairman, Commission of Fine Arts, Before the American Battle Monuments Commission, 2 October 1923, transcript, file: American Cemeteries in Europe—American Battle Monuments Commission, box 3, Project Files, RG 66, National Archives.

13. U.S. Commission of Fine Arts, *Ninth Report of the Commission of Fine Arts, July 1, 1919–June 20, 1921* (Washington, D.C.: GPO, 1921), 39–80; and "Resume of Decisions. War Memorials Council," 8 November 1920, copy, file: Headstones, World War I Graves, box 73, Project Files, RG 66, National Archives.

14. U.S. Congress, House, Committee on Foreign Affairs, *American Battle Monuments Commission: Hearings*, 67th Cong., 2d and 3d sess., 15–20 March, 28 November, 7–9 December 1922.

15. American Battle Monuments Commission, *Annual Report of the American Battle Monuments Commission: Fiscal Year 1925* (Washington, D.C.: GPO, 1926), 45–55; Record of Proceedings: 9th Meeting, 4 September 1924, American Battle Monuments Commission, Records of the American Battle Monuments Commission, RG 117, National Archives.

16. American Battle Monuments Commission, *Annual Report of the American Battle Monuments Commission: Fiscal Year 1926* (Washington, D.C.: GPO, 1927), 26–28.

17. Elizabeth G. Grossman, "Architecture for a Public Client: The Monuments and Chapels of the American Battle Monuments Commission," *Journal of the Society of Architectural Historians* 43 (May 1984): 119–43; and American Battle Monuments Commission, *Annual Report, 1925, Annual Report, 1926.*

18. Minutes, 2 December 1926, 12, U.S. Commission of Fine Arts, RG 66, National Archives.

19. H. P. Caemmerer, Secretary and Executive Officer, American Battle Monuments Commission to Charles A. Platt, 9 August 1928; Charles A. Platt to H. P. Caemmerer, 15 August 1928; Charles Moore to American Battle Monuments Commission, 9 October 1928, copy; Charles Moore to Charles A. Platt, 29 September 1928, file: American Cemeteries—Europe-Jewish Welfare Board—Tomb of the Unknown Soldier, box 6, Project Files, RG 66, National Archives; Grossman, "Architecture for a Public Client," 140–41.

20. U.S. Congress, House, Representative John Hill of Maryland, *Congressional Record,* 68th Cong. 1st sess., 14 March 1924, 65, pt. 4:4222–25; and Quartermaster General W. H. Hart to Assistant Secretary of War, 13 March 1924, memorandum, file 293.7, box 143, General Correspondence, subject file, 1922–35, RG 92, National Archives.

21. "Minutes of the Meeting of the Council of National Defense," 14 February 1918, 456, Records of the Council of National Defense, 1916–21, Microfilm Publication M–1069, RG 62, National Archives; Arthur S. Link, ed., *The Papers of Woodrow Wilson,* 65 vols. (Princeton, N.J.: Princeton University Press, 1966–), 48:24–27, 111, 117; Marguerite H. White, *American War Mothers: Fifty Year History* (Washington, D.C. American War Mothers, 1981); and "American Gold Star Mothers Constitution, Undated, ca. 1917 or 1918," Records of the American Gold Star Mothers, Inc., Library of Congress; "'A War Memorial,'" *Pencil Points* 11 (November 1930): 906.

22. U.S. Congress, House, Committee on Military Affairs, *To Authorize Mothers of Deceased World War Veterans Buried in Europe to Visit the Graves: Hearings Before the House Committee on Military Affairs,* 68th Cong., 1st sess., 19 February 1924, 20–21.

23. U.S. Congress, House, Committee on Military Affairs, *To Authorize Mothers and Unmarried Widows of Deceased World War Veterans Buried in Europe to Visit the Graves: Hearings before the House Committee on Military Affairs,* 70th Cong., 1st sess., 27 January 1928, 25–26.

24. Ibid., 10.

25. A. D. Hughes, "Pilgrims," *Quartermaster Review* (May–June 1931): 29–39.

26. Morris Frandin, "Gold Star Mothers and Widows End Pilgrimages," *Sunday Star* (Washington, D.C.), [5 November 1933], 10; "Gold Star Mother," *Mobile (Ala.) Register,* 16 August 1933; "War Department Studies Minutest Needs of Gold Star Mothers' Pilgrimage," *New York World,* 23 March 1930, file: Press Clippings, Mothers and Widows Pilgrimages to the Cemeteries of Europe, box 348, Correspondence Relating to the Gold Star Pilgrimage 1922–33, Central Records, 1917–54, General Records, RG 92, National Archives; John J. Noll, "Crosses," *American Legion Monthly,* September 1930, 14–17, 52–54; and Robert Ginsburgh, "This, Too, is America," *American Legion Monthly,* November 1933, 16–19, 49–52.

27. Secretary of War to Walter White, Secretary, National Association for the Advancement of Colored People, [5 June 1933], copy; Perry C. Thompson to Secretary of War

George H. Dern, 9 May 1933, copy, Secretary of War to Percy C. Thompson, Editor, *Chicago Review* [May 1933?], copy, file: Colored M & W, Correspondence Relative to Segregation, box 345; "Negro Gold Star Mothers Refuse Trip to Sons' Graves," *Washington Post,* 30 May 1930; "Gold Star Mothers' Segregation Creates Furor in New York," *Philadelphia Tribune,* 17 July 1930; "55 Negro War Mothers Cancel Trip, Write Hoover of 'Insult,'" *New York World,* 10 July 1930, file: Press Clippings, Mothers and Widows Pilgrimages to the Cemeteries of Europe, box 348, Correspondence Relating to the Gold Star Pilgrimage, 1922–32, RG 92, National Archives. See also: Donald J. Lisio, *Hoover, Blacks, Lily-Whites: A Study of Southern Strategies* (Chapel Hill, N.C.: University of North Carolina Press, 1985), 235–36.

28. George Peabody to Secretary of War Newton W. Baker, 18 September 1919, box 10, Newton D. Baker Papers, Manuscript Division, Library of Congress, Washington, D.C.; "The American Negro as a Soldier," *Literary Digest,* 27 June 1925, 14–15; Arthur E. Barbeau and Florette Henri, *The Unknown Soldiers: Black American Troops in World War I* (Philadelphia: Temple University Press, 1974), 164–74; and Hamilton Fish, Jr., to American Battle Monuments Commission, 26 May 1924; X. H. Price, Major, Corps of Engineers, Secretary to Representative William R. Wood, Chair, Subcommittee of House Committee on Appropriations, 17 January 1925, file: 369th Infantry, box 30, World War I Monument and Memorial files, Records Relating to Construction and Maintenance, Records of the American Battle Monuments Commission, RG 117, National Archives.

29. "Memorials that Serve Mankind—Theodore Roosevelt's Ideal," *American City* 20 (March 1919): 219; and "A Motive and a Method for American Reconstruction," *American City* 19 (November 1918): 347–52.

30. David Glassberg, *American Historical Pageantry: The Uses of Tradition in the Early Twentieth Century* (Chapel Hill, N.C.: University of North Carolina Press, 1990), 231–34.

31. Eugene Rodman Shippen, "Community Houses as Soldiers' and Sailors' Memorials," *American City* 20 (January 1919): 30.

32. Samuel Wilson, "The Community House—An Element in Reconstruction," *American City* 19 (December 1918): 467–73.

33. "World War Monuments," *Art World and Arts and Decoration* 10 (January 1919): 128.

34. Ernest Stevens Leland, "Permanent Soldiers' Monuments or Buildings," *Monumental News* 31 (February 1919): 103.

35. Celilia Beaux, "The Spirit of War Memorials," *American Magazine of Art* 10 (May 1919): 270–73.

36. "Art and War Memorials," *Advocate of Peace* 81 (February 1919): 38–39; and "Protecting America from the Atrocities of Art," *Current Opinion* 66 (March 1919): 187–88.

37. "War Memorials," *Bulletin of the Municipal Art Society of New York City* 17 (1st Quarter, 1919); Minutes, 30 January 1919, War Memorials Advisory Committee, American Federation of Arts, "War Memorials: Suggestion for their Treatment," 2 January 1919, box 3, American Federation of Arts, Archives of American Art, Washington, D.C.; and U.S. Commission of Fine Arts, "War Memorials: Suggestions as to the Forms of Memorials and the Methods of Obtaining Designers," 1919, file: World War Memorials—General, box 206, J. Templeman Coolidge, Secretary, "Report of the Secretary on the Meeting of January 7, 1919, Art Commissions of the United States," file: World War I Memorials—General, box 207, Project Files, RG 66, National Archives.

38. Because no comprehensive survey of World War I memorials exists, it is difficult to determine precisely the total number of commercial monuments purchased by communities. Sales brochures from the commercial monument industry and advertisements in *Monumental News* suggest a thriving industry. See, for example, "'Tyler' Bronze Tablets," file: World War I Memorials—General, box 206, Project Files, RG 66, National Archives. For a survey of war

memorials erected in one state, see Sarah Guitar, "Monuments and Memorials in Missouri," *Missouri Historical Review* 19 (July 1925): 555–603.

39. Weston Gladding Donehower, "Conflicting Interpretations of American Patriotism in the 1920's" (Ph.D. diss., University of Pennsylvania, 1982), 89–172.

40. William Pencak, *For God and Country: The American Legion, 1919–1941* (Boston: Northeastern University Press, 1989), 79–105, 209–34.

41. "In Memoriam: 1861–1865, 1898, 1917–1918," *American Legion Weekly*, 14 May 1920, 1; "To Keep a Buddy's Grave Green," *American Legion Weekly*, 18 May 1923, 5; and "Memorial Day, 1923," *American Legion Weekly*, 29 June 1923, 7.

42. A. P. Sanford and Robert Haven Schauffler, *Armistice Day*, Our American Holidays Series (New York: Dodd, Mead, 1927), 447–57.

43. *Philadelphia Inquirer*, 12 November 1932; *Chicago Daily Tribune*, 11 November 1925, 5; *Christian Science Monitor*, 11 November 1924, 1; Harry Emerson Fosdick, "My Account with the Unknown Soldier," *Scholastic* 27 (9 November 1935): 9–10; Edith Lovejoy Pierce, "Radio Speech," folder 5; Rabbi Ferdinand M. Isserman, "Suggestions for Dramatic Observance of Armistice Day: A Children's Armistice Day Parade as successfully carried out in St. Louis," folder 4; "Plays and Pageants Appropriate for Armistice Day," folder 5; "Disarmament Suggestions for Armistice Week," folder 6; Lincoln Wirt, "An Order of Service for Armistice Sunday," 11 November 1927; Daniel L. Marsh, "The Christian Use of Armistice Day," *Classmate*, 10 November 1928; Material for Armistice Day Programs for Church School and Community Celebrations," folder 6; Programs for Armistice Day, box 41, Education Department, 1921–40, National Council for the Prevention of War, Reel 41.31, Document Group 66, National Council for the Prevention of War, Swarthmore Peace Collection, Swarthmore, Pennsylvania.

44. "The Wilson Voice in the Campaign," *Literary Digest*, 24 November 1923, 10–11.

45. John Bennett, "Can Armistice Sunday be Saved?" *Christian Century*, 26 November 1930, 1444–45.

46. "President Places Wreath on Tomb of the Unknown Soldier," *Chicago Daily Tribune*, 12 November 1925, 4; and "College Pacifists Join in Parades on Armistice Day," *Christian Science Monitor*, 13 November 1933, 4.

47. *Chicago Daily Tribune*, 11 November 1929, 14.

48. "After Eighteen Years," *Philadelphia Inquirer*, 11 November 1936, 8; and Warren I. Cohen, *The American Revisionists: The Lessons of Intervention in World War I* (Chicago: University of Chicago Press, 1967).

49. Lewis J. Gorin, Jr., *Patriotism Prepaid* (Philadelphia: J. B. Lippincott, 1936), 100, 53, 98.

50. "The Saga of the Veterans of Future Wars," *Nassau Sovereign*, April 1941, 10–11, 28, 32.

51. Allan Greenberg, "Lutyens's Cenotaph," *Journal of the Society for Architectural Historians* 48 (March 1989): 5–23.

52. "Nameless Dead Soldiers Honored By England and France," *Literary Digest*, 11 December 1920, 54–59.

53. U.S. Congress, House, Committee on Military Affairs, *Return of Body of Unknown American Who Lost His Life During World War: Hearings Before Committee on Military Affairs*, 66th Cong., 3d sess., 1 February 1921, 17.

54. "A Request Wisely Refused," *New York Times*, 29 November 1920, 14.

55. "The Unknown Soldier," *New York Times*, 9 December 1920, 12; "The Unknown Soldier's Tomb," *New York Times*, 3 February 1921, 6; [F. W. Galbraith, Jr., National Commander] to General Leonard Wood, 3 December 1920, file: World War—Dead, Unknown Soldier, American Legion Library, Indianapolis, Indiana, and E. E. Davis, Executive Assistant,

GRS to the Quartermaster General, through Chief, Construction Service, 6 October 1922, file 293, box 2, Records Relating to the Construction of the Tomb of the Unknown Soldier, RG 92, National Archives.

56. F. W. Galbraith, Jr., to Hamilton Fish, Jr., 28 April 1921, file: World War—Dead, Unknown Soldier, American Legion Library, Hamilton Fish, Jr., to John W. Weeks, 9 March 1921, file 293.8, Tomb of the Unknown Soldier—Section 1: Legislation, box 563, central decimal file, 1917–25, RG 407, National Archives. See also U.S. Department of the Army, *The Last Salute: Civil and Military Funerals, 1921–1969*, by B. C. Mossman and M. W. Stark (Washington, D.C.: GPO, 1971), 3–18.

57. *Washington Post,* 11 November 1921.

58. *Washington Post,* 12 November 1921.

59. Rev. E. D. W. Jones, Minister, Union Wesley AME Zion Church, Washington, D.C., to Secretary of War John W. Weeks, 11 November 1921, file 293.8, box 565, central decimal file, 1917–1925, RG 407, National Archives.

60. *Washington Post,* 12 November 1921; Brigadier General William Lassiter, Assistant Chief of Staff, G-3 to Charles H. Brent, Bishop of Western New York, 4 October 1921, William Lassiter to Reverend Francis Kelly, 4 October 1921, William Lassiter to Rabbi Morris S. Lazaron, 10 October 1921, Charles Brent to William Lassiter, 21 October 1921, Charles Brent to Morris S. Lazaron, 1 November 1921, file 292.8, central decimal file, box 564, RG 407, National Archives.

61. *Washington Post,* 12 November 1921, 1; "'Unknown' Came from the Heart of America," *Philadelphia Inquirer,* 11 November 1921, 12; "The Unknown Soldier," *Chicago Daily Tribune,* 11 November 1921, 8; and "The Message of the Unknown," *Brooklyn Daily Eagle,* 11 November 1921, 6.

62. John Dos Passos, *Nineteen Nineteen,* in *U.S.A.* (Boston: Houghton Mifflin, 1930), 2:408.

63. Irving Lehman, President, Jewish Welfare Board to Charles Moore, 11 December 1923, box 23, Adler to Moore, 12 December 1923, telegram, file: Arlington National Cemetery—Tomb of the Unknown Soldier, box 23, Project Files, RG 66, National Archives.

64. *Washington Post,* 12 November 1921.

65. "November 11th as a Day of Prayer," *Literary Digest,* 24 September 1921, 28–29; and John Whiteclay Chambers II, *The Eagle and the Dove: The American Peace Movement and United States Foreign Policy, 1900–1922,* 2d ed. (Syracuse, N.Y.: Syracuse University Press, 1991), 179–98.

66. "No More War Parade: Headquarters for Committee on Decorations" [1934], file: Peace Parade Releases, 1934–36, subject file: Peace Parades and Rallies, 1924–, Swarthmore College Peace Collection, Swarthmore, Pennsylvania.

67. H. L. Chaillaux, Director, National Americanism Committee, undated circular letter with enclosure: John Haynes Holmes, "The Unknown Soldier Speaks," file: World War—Dead, Unknown Soldier, American Legion Library and Colonel W. K. Naylor, General Staff, Military Intelligence Division to the Chief of Staff, 11 December 1923, Records Regarding the Design and Construction of the Tomb of the Unknown Soldier, 1926–33, RG 92, National Archives.

68. The army also maintained that posting a guard would be counterproductive and create ill feelings among those who were assigned to do sentry duty. In the view of one general, the hardships imposed by this duty would create "feelings of irritation" that would be "transmitted from sentry to sentry" and that would "unquestionably detract from the respect and veneration in which the shrine is now held by our soldiers." H. H. Bandholtz, Brigadier General, U.S. Army to the Adjutant General, 23 October 1922, file: 293.8, box 565, central decimal file, 1917–25, RG 407, National Archives; Brigadier General S. D. Rosenback to the

Adjutant General, 19 March 1926, John Thomas Taylor to President Calvin Coolidge, 10 March 1926, file: 293.8, box 1271, Central Files 1926–29, Records of the Adjutant General's Office, RG 94, National Archives.

69. Charles Moore to Secretary of War John W. Weeks, 19 December 1923, copy in Minutes of the Commission of Fine Arts, 14 December 1923, 10–11, RG 66, National Archives; Secretary of War John W. Weeks, Secretary of the Navy Edwin Denby to Charles Moore, 11 February 1924, file: Arlington National Cemetery—Tomb of the Unknown Soldier, box 22, Project Files, RG 66, National Archives; and U.S. Commission of Fine Arts, *The National Commission of Fine Arts: Eleventh Report, January 1, 1926–June 1, 1929* (Washington, D.C.: GPO, 1930), 130–32.

70. Thomas Hudson Jones to Major General B. F. Cheatham, 2 January 1929, box 1, Records Regarding the Design and Construction of the Tomb of the Unknown Soldier, 1926–33, RG 92.

## 4. THE "GOOD WAR" AND MODERN MEMORY

1. John Morton Blum, *V Was for Victory: Politics and American Culture During World War II* (New York: Harcourt Brace Jovanovich, 1976); Paul Fussell, *Wartime: Understanding and Behavior in the Second World War* (New York: Oxford, 1989); and Lawrence Wells Cobb, "Patriotic Themes in American National Magazine Advertising, 1898–1945" (Ph.D. diss., Emory University, 1978).

2. John W. Dower, *War without Mercy: Race and Power in the Pacific War* (New York: Pantheon, 1986).

3. The different attitudes Americans had toward Germany and Japan were reflected in the way the enemy war dead from both countries were treated by the U.S. military. For example, General George S. Patton in early 1945 ordered Graves Registration Service units to accord German war dead the same care as their American counterparts, stating that "the enemy does one thing exceptionally well—and that is giving proper and adequate burial to his own Dead, and that he extends the same courtesy to our Dead, and to the Dead of our Allies." In the Pacific, the army and marines placed dead American soldiers in individual graves, according their Japanese counterparts mass burials. See U.S. Department of the Army, *The Quartermaster Corps: Operations in the War Against Germany,* by William F. Ross and Charles F. Romanus, United States Army in World War II Series (Washington, D.C.: GPO, 1965), 689–90; U.S. Department of the Army, *The Quartermaster Corps: Operations in the War Against Japan,* by Alvin P. Stauffer, United States Army in World War II Series (Washington, D.C.: GPO, 1956), 252.

4. Lucy S. Dawidowicz, "The American Jews and the Holocaust," *New York Times Magazine,* 18 April 1982, 47–48, 101–14; and David S. Wyman, *The Abandonment of the Jews: America and the Holocaust, 1941–1945* (New York: Pantheon Books, 1984).

5. Paul Boyer, *By the Bomb's Early Light: American Thought and Culture at the Dawn of the Atomic Age* (New York: Pantheon Books, 1985); Charles Beard, *President Roosevelt and the Coming of the War, 1941: A Study in Appearances and Realities* (New Haven, Conn.: Yale University Press, 1948); and John Toland, *Infamy: Pearl Harbor and its Aftermath* (Garden City, N.Y.: Doubleday, 1982).

6. R. Ernest Dupuy and Trevor N. Dupuy, *The Encyclopedia of Military History* (New York: Harper and Row, 1986), 990, 1198.

7. T. Bentley Mott to John J. Pershing, 26 December 1944, file 201, box 8, Pershing Correspondence, General Records, Records of the American Battle Monuments Commission, RG 117, National Archives.

8. "Should Our War Dead be Brought Home?" *Reader's Digest,* September 1945,

75–76; Blake Ehrlich, "Shall We Bring Home the Dead of World War II?" *Saturday Evening Post,* 31 May 1947, 25, 127–28, 130; and F. W. Graham, Jr., "Bring the War Dead Home?: No—Let Them Lie in the Ground They Hallowed," *Rotarian,* November 1946, 19–20.

9. Record of Proceedings: Forty-ninth Meeting, 13 February 1947, American Battle Monuments Commission, Records of the American Battle Monuments Commission, RG 117, National Archives.

10. Record of Proceedings: Fiftieth Meeting, 15 May 1947, American Battle Monuments Commission, RG 117; and Donald G. Glascoff, National Adjutant to Mancel B. Talcott, Chairman, Graves Registration and War Memorials Committee, 25 October 1946, file: Dead—Return of Bodies, American Legion Library, Indianapolis, Indiana.

11. Record of Proceedings: Forty-ninth Meeting, 13 February 1947, American Battle Monuments Commission, RG 117.

12. U.S. Commission of Fine Arts, *Report of the Commission of Fine Arts: July 1, 1948 to June 30, 1954* (Washington, D.C.: GPO, 1960), 33–40.

13. Record of Proceedings: Fifty-fifth Meeting, 24 May 1948, American Battle Monuments Commission, RG 117; Rabbi Hirsch E. L. Freund, Executive Director, Synagogue Council of America to Thomas North, Secretary, American Battle Monuments Commission, 7 February 1950, copy, RG 117, National Archives; North to Freund, 14 February 1950; Rabbi Aryeh Lev, Director, National Jewish Welfare Board to Graves Registration Section, Quartermaster General Office, 15 February 1950, copy; North to Lev, 27 February 1950; North, memorandum for Members of the Commission, No. 137, 13 March 1950, file 300.6, box 4, memorandums to the Commission, General Records and Reports, American Battle Monuments Commission, RG 117, National Archives.

14. U.S. Commission of Fine Arts, *Report: 1948–1954,* 33–40.

15. Ibid.

16. Kenneth C. Royall, Secretary of the Army, to Archibald B. Roosevelt, 25 March 1948, copy; Roosevelt to Thomas North, 17 March 1955, North to Roosevelt, 11 April 1955; file 293, box 180, Records Relating to Internments, Records Relating to Cemeteries and Memorials, American Battle Monuments Commission, RG 117, National Archives.

17. "President Designates Aug. 14, as Victory Day," *New York Times,* 4 August 1946, 44; "1945 V-J Day Now Only Memory," *New York Times,* 15 August 1946, 27; and Jane M. Hatch, ed., *American Book of Days,* 3d ed. (New York: H. W. Wilson, 1978), 754–45.

18. For instance, at a presidential press conference held on Armistice Day 1953, Dwight Eisenhower spoke wistfully of the meaning of the day for him. This veteran of both wars (although never seeing overseas service in the first) urged the reporters to grant him a favor and "make some mention in your stories that it is Armistice Day, and what Armistice Day really meant to us at one time." See U.S. President, *Public Papers of the President of the United States* (Washington, D.C.: Office of the *Federal Register,* National Archives and Records Service, 1960), s.v. Dwight D. Eisenhower, 1953, 757. During the interwar years, Eisenhower served as an army staff officer to the American Battle Monuments Commission and this no doubt strengthened the affinity he felt toward the holidays and symbols associated with the First World War. In 1968, Eisenhower appealed to President Lyndon B. Johnson to halt a proposal to disband the commission and collapse its functions into the Veterans Administration. In response, Johnson granted the request and tabled the plan. See Stephen E. Ambrose, *Eisenhower,* vol. 2, *The President* (New York: Simon and Schuster, 1984), 670–71.

19. U.S. Congress, House, Representative Edward Rees of Kansas, *Congressional Record,* 83d Cong., 2d sess., 15 March 1954, 100, pt. 3:3245; U.S. Congress, Senate, Committee on the Judiciary, *Changing Armistice Day to Veterans Day: Report,* 83d Cong., 2d sess, 17 May 1954, S. Rept. 1359; and U.S. Congress, House, Committee on the Judiciary, *Changing Armistice Day to Veterans Day: Report,* 83d Cong., 2d sess., 9 March 1954, H. Rept. 1333.

20. Kenneth Reid, "Memorials? Yes—But No Monuments!" *Pencil Points* 25 (May 1944): 35.

21. Archibald MacLeish, "Memorials Are for Remembrance," *Architectural Forum* 81 (September 1944): 111–12, 170.

22. For a sampling of articles in *American City*, see Walter D. Cocking, "'Community Institutes' as War Memorials," 59 (November 1944): 77–78; "Planning Memorial Community Buildings," 59 (June 1944): 113–14; "War Memorials," 58 (January 1944): 35–36; "War Memorials that Further Practical Democracy," 59 (October 1944): 72–75, 101; and Donald Wyman, "The Park as a Living War Memorial," 61 (April 1946): 92, 123. See also, "Let's Have Living Memorials," *Recreation* 39 (May 1945): 74, 109; Lucas Freeman, "Man on Horseback Fades Out," *Nation's Business* 33 (May 1945): 88; and "Parks for Memorials," *American Home* 31 (December 1943): 46–48.

23. "Thoughts on War Memorials," *Journal of the American Institute of Architects* 2 (November 1944): 221–22; James Earle Fraser, "Let Our New Monuments Inspire—and Endure," *Rotarian* 68 (February 1946): 24–25, 51–52; Margaret Cresson, "Memorials Symbolic of the Spirit of Man," *New York Times Magazine,* 22 July 1945, 14–15, 38; and Lewis Mumford, "Monuments and Memorials," *Good Housekeeping* 120 (January 1945): 17, 106–8.

24. The American Chamber of Commerce of the United States surveyed local chambers to determine war memorial plans in American communities. Out of the 265 chambers that replied, only 19 were erecting monuments. In contrast, 42 reported plans or completion of auditoriums, 20 of athletic stadiums, 19 of hospitals, 29 of recreation parks, 17 of community buildings, and 12 of American Legion buildings. "War Memorials—Planned or Completed," *American City* 63 (February 1948): 99–100; and "Living Memorials," *New York Times,* 5 January 1947, 10.

25. "The Famous Iwo Flag-Raising," *Life,* 26 March 1945, 17–18; and U.S. Congress, Senate, Senator Edwin Willis of Louisiana, *Congressional Record,* 79th Cong., 1st sess., 13 March 1945, 91, pt. 2:2079–80. See also: Lance Bertelsen, "Icons on Iwo," *Journal of Popular Culture* 22 (Spring 1989): 79–95; and Karal Ann Marling and John Wetenhall, *Iwo Jima: Monuments, Memories, and the American Hero* (Cambridge: Harvard University Press, 1991).

26. U.S. Congress, House, Representative Brooks Hays of Arkansas, *Congressional Record,* 79th Cong., 2d sess., 1 March 1946, 92, pt. 9:A1083–84.

27. Gilmore D. Clarke, Chairman, Commission of Fine Arts to Commission Members, 10 October 1947, copy; Lt. Cmdr. Wheeler Williams, USNR, inactive to James V. Forrestal, Secretary of the Navy, 28 February 1946, confidential memorandum, copy; Donald De Lue, President, National Sculpture Society, to Gilmore D. Clarke, Chairman, 15 August 1947, Clarke to Donald De Lue, 29 August 1947, copy; Clarke to General A. A. Vandergrift, Marine Corp Commandant, 2 December 1947, copy; Proceedings, Commission of Fine Arts, 28 August 1947, verbatim transcript, Marine Corp Monument file, box 100, Project Files, Commission of Fine Arts, RG 66, National Archives.

28. United States Marine Corp Memorial, 28 January 1954, Commission of Fine Arts Meeting, transcript, file: FAA, Statues, Monuments and Memorials—Marine Corp Memorial, box 62, Central Files, RG 66, National Archives.

29. Minutes, General Meetings of the National Sculpture Society, 10 April 1951, 3, file: National Sculpture Society, 1951–52, box 2, Adolph A. Weinman Papers, Archives of American Art, Washington, D.C.

30. Alice B. Louchheim, "Memorials to Our War Dead Abroad," *New York Times,* 15 January 1950, sec. 2, p. 10; Charlotte Devree, "Is this Statuary Worth More than a Million of Your Money?" *Art News,* April 1955, 34–37; and John Canaday, "Our National Pride: The World's Worst Sculpture," *New York Times,* 25 July 1965, reprinted in: *Culture Gulch:*

*Notes on Art and Its Public in the 1960s,* ed. John Canaday (New York: Farrar, Straus and Giroux, 1969), 96.

31. "Veterans Day: Old Holiday, New Accents," *Time,* 22 November 1954, 20–21; and "Veterans' Day," *New York Herald Tribune,* 11 November 1954, 22.

32. William Pencak, *For God and Country: The American Legion, 1919–1941* (Boston: Northeastern University Press, 1989), 144–69.

33. LeRoy Wolins, Vice Commander, Veterans for Peace, "Memo to Peace Activists and the Media Re: How Should We Celebrate the 40th Anniversary of Victory over Hitler's Germany?"; LeRoy Wolins, "U.C. Student 'on leave' Fights for UN 'peace oath' Approval," *Chicago Maroon,* 27 June 1950; "U.S. W.W. II Vet Buried in East Germany, *Stars and Stripes,* 27 November 1983, 42, file: Veterans for Peace, subject file, Swarthmore College Peace Collection, Swarthmore, Pennsylvania; and Mark Scott and Semyon Krasilshchik, *Yanks Meet Reds: Recollections of U.S. and Soviet Vets from the Linkup in World War II* (Santa Barbara, Calif.: Capra Press, 1988), 224.

34. Robert L. Tyler, "The American Veterans Committee: Out of a Hot War and into the Cold," *American Quarterly* 18 (Fall 1966): 419–36.

35. "Armistice Day," *New York Herald Tribune,* 11 November 1948, 26; "Preparedness Appeals Mark Armistice Day," *New York Herald Tribune,* 12 November 1948, 25; John Gregory, "Armistice Rites Honor Korean Dead," *Washington Post,* 12 November 1950, 1; "U.S. Pays Honor to War Veterans, Hears Pleas for Strength and Faith," *New York Times,* 12 November 1954, 12; and "San Diego Rejects 'Four Freedoms' Plaque; Standley Opposes 'Ideology' of Two Points," *New York Times,* 18 February 1950, 7.

36. T. B. Larkin, Major General to the Quartermaster General for the Secretary of the Army, memorandum [January 1949], copy in file: War Memorial Projects, National Sculpture Society, reel 490, Archives of American Art, Washington, D.C.

37. Minutes, 20 February 1950, Commission of Fine Arts, RG 66.

38. Ibid.

39. Harry H. Vaughan, Major General, U.S. Army (Ret.), Military Aide to the President to George C. Marshall, Secretary of Defense, 23 October 1990, file 293, central decimal file, July–December 1950, Correspondence Control Section, Office of the Administrative Secretary, Records of the Office of Secretary of Defense, RG 330, National Archives; U.S. Congress, House, Armed Service Committee, *Providing for the Burial in the Memorial Amphitheater of the National Cemetery at Arlington, VA., of the Remains of an Unknown American Who Lost His Life While Serving Overseas in the Armed Forces During the Korean Conflict: Report,* 84th Cong., 2d sess., 28 June 1956, H. Rept. 2503; and Jack Raymond, "Unknowns of World War II and Korea are Enshrined," *New York Times,* 31 May 1958, 1, 4.

40. "President Greets Nation's Heroes," *New York Times,* 31 May 1958, 1, 4.

41. A. E. Demaray, Associate Director, National Park Service, memorandum for the Regional Director, Region Three, 14 September 1945; Abe Fortas, Acting Secretary of the Interior, to Robert L. Patterson, Secretary of War, 21 September 1945, file 0-35, Site of the Atomic Bomb Proving Ground Part One, box 2982, Proposed National Monuments, Central Classified Files, 1933–49, Records of the National Park Service, RG 79, National Archives. On the role of the National Park Service in shaping the national memory through the preservation of historical places and structures, see John Bodnar, *Remaking America: Public Memory, Commemoration, and Patriotism in the Twentieth Century* (Princeton, N.J.: Princeton University, 1992), 169–205; and Michael G. Kammen, *Mystic Chords of Memory: The Transformation of Tradition in American Culture* (New York: Alfred A. Knopf, 1991), 448–73. I am particularly indebted to Bodnar's work for pointing me to the documents in the National Archives relating to the attempts to create an atomic bomb memorial at Los Alamos.

42. John J. Dempsey, Governor, New Mexico, to Newton B. Drury, Director, National Park Service, 22 September 1945, Site of the Atomic Bomb Proving Ground Part One,

43. Henry O. Roeske, Cuba, New York, to Harold L. Ickes, received 17 September 1945; Norman W. Clark to Harold L. Ickes, received 3 October 1945, Site of the Atomic Bomb Proving Ground Part One, RG 79.

44. "Crater of First A-Bomb Shown to U.S. Newsmen," *Los Angeles Times,* 12 September 1945, typescript copy, Site of the Atomic Bomb Proving Ground Part One, RG 79.

45. E. T. Scoyen, Acting Regional Director, 6 May 1946, memorandum for the Director, file 0-35, Proposed National Monuments, 1933–49, box 2982, RG 79, National Archives. In 1969 the Defense Nuclear Agency established a National Atomic Museum at Kirtland Air Force Base near Albuquerque, New Mexico, and in 1976 the Department of Energy later assumed control of it. The museum exhibited the empty casings that held a series of atomic bombs, including Little Boy and Fat Man, and displayed newsreels from the 1930s and 1940s dealing with the atomic bomb and nuclear energy. For a critique of this museum, see Kenneth Arnold, "The National Atomic Museum, Albuquerque, New Mexico: Where 'Weapon Shapes' Are Not Enough," *Technology and Culture* 30 (July 1989): 640–42.

46. B-29 "Enola Gay" Curatorial File, 1988, Department of Aeronautics, National Air and Space Museum, Washington, D.C.; Michael McMahon, "The Romance of Technological Progress: A Critical Review of the National Air and Space Museum," *Technology and Culture* 22 (April 1981): 281–96; and Samuel A. Batzli, "From Heroes to Hiroshima: The National Air and Space Museum Adjusts Its Point of View," *Technology and Culture* 31 (October 1990): 830–37. I am indebted to Dr. Michael J. Neufeld, Curator, Department of Aeronautics, National Air and Space Museum for the curatorial file on the *Enola Gay* and the citations regarding this airplane.

47. U.S. Department of the Interior, National Park Service, *Warships Associated with World War II in the Pacific: National Historic Landmark Theme Study, by Harry A. Butowsky* (Washington, D.C.: GPO, 1985).

48. Ibid.

49. Ibid.

50. U.S. Congress, House, Committee on Military Affairs, *Transfer of Certain National Military Parks,* 70th Cong., 2d sess., 31 January 1929.

51. C. R. Chandler, "World War II as Southern Entertainment: The Confederate Air Force and Warfare Re-Enactment Ritual," in *Rituals and Ceremonies in Popular Culture,* ed. Ray B. Browne (Bowling Green, Ohio: Bowling Green University Popular Press, 1980), 258–69.

52. Ibid.

53. Susan G. Davis, *Parades and Power: Street Theatre in Nineteenth Century Philadelphia* (Philadelphia: Temple University Press, 1986; Berkeley and Los Angeles: University of California Press, 1988), 64; Edward Tabor Linenthal, *Sacred Ground: Americans and Their Battlefields* (Urbana, Ill.: University of Illinois Press, 1991), passim; and *American Legion Weekly,* 22 October 1920, 14.

54. Chandler, "World War II as Southern Entertainment," 258–69.

55. Ibid.

56. "Join the March of Peace on World Peace Day 1948 (August 6th)," pamphlet, folder: International World Peace Day Committee, box 1, Records of the International Student Service, Collective Document Group A, Swarthmore Peace Collection, Swarthmore, Pennsylvania; Walter Sullivan, "Desert Rites Ask Ban on Atom War," *New York Times,* 7 August 1947, 2; Preston King Sheldon, "Prayers Will Note Bomb Anniversary," *New York Times,* 5 August 1950, 16; Charles DeBenedetti, *The Peace Reform in American History* (Bloomington, Ind.:

Indiana University Press, 1980), 138–64; and Gar Alperovitz, *Atomic Diplomacy: Hiroshima and Potsdam* (New York: Simon and Schuster, 1965).

57. "Forty Years after Battle, Smiles on Iwo Jima," *New York Times,* 20 February 1985, 1; "Remembering the Battle at Remagen," *New York Times,* 10 February 1985, 10; and Ralph Blumenthal, "Veteran Reunion Drawing Protests: Complaints Follow Disclosure of Meetings Exchanged by U.S. and SS Veterans," *New York Times,* 15 September 1985, 31.

58. President's Commission on the Holocaust, *Report to the President,* by Elie Wiesel, Chairman (Washington, D.C.: GPO, 1979). For a thorough discussion of Holocaust memorials in the United States, see James E. Young, *The Texture of Memory: Holocaust Memorials and Meaning* (New Haven, Conn.: Yale University Press, 1993), 283–350.

59. Ibid.

60. U.S. Holocaust Commission, *Days of Remembrance: 1983* (Washington, D.C.: GPO, 1983); *Days of Remembrance: 1987* (Washington, D.C.: GPO, 1987); and *Days of Remembrance, 1988: Planning Guide* (Washington, D.C.: GPO, 1988).

61. U.S. President, *Public Papers of the President of the United States* (Washington, D.C.: Office of the *Federal Register,* National Archives and Records Service, 1979), s.v. Jimmy Carter, 1978, 812–14.

62. U.S. Holocaust Commission, *Days of Remembrance: 1985* (Washington, D.C.: GPO, 1985).

63. Suzanne Garment, "The U.S. Builds A Memorial to the Unthinkable," *Wall Street Journal,* 4 February 1983, 24.

64. U.S. President, *Public Papers of the President of the United States* (Washington, D.C.: Office of the *Federal Register,* National Archives and Records Service, 1988), s.v. Ronald Reagan, 1985, 330–31.

65. For an overview of the Bitburg controversy, see Geoffrey Hartman, ed., *Bitburg: In Moral and Political Perspective* (Bloomington, Ind.: Indiana University Press, 1986).

66. Mayo, *War Memorials,* 244–45; and Herbert Muschamp, "How Buildings Remember," *New Republic,* 28 August 1989, 27–33.

67. Robert Reinhold, "Fifty Years after Attack, Survivors Are Told to Forget Animosity," *New York Times,* 8 December 1991, 1, 24; and George Bush, "Remarks to the Pearl Harbor Survivors Association in Honolulu, Hawaii, December 7, 1991," *Weekly Compilation of Presidential Documents* 27, no. 50 (16 December 1991): 1785–87.

68. Roberta Wohlstetter, *Pearl Harbor: Warning and Decision* (Stanford, Calif.: Stanford University Press, 1962).

69. Linenthal, *Sacred Ground,* 175–212.

70. Ibid, 179–81.

71. Ibid.

72. Ibid, 179–96.

73. "America-Bashing, Not all False," *New York Times,* 22 January 1992, 20.

74. "Rhode Island Takes a Holiday," *New York Times,* 7 August 1988, 39; and Robert Reinhold, "Fifty Years After Pearl Harbor, Reconciliation Is Still Elusive," *New York Times,* 1 September 1991, 1, 22.

5. FROM THE KOREAN WAR TO THE VIETNAM VETERANS MEMORIAL

1. For an introduction to American foreign policy during the cold war, see Stephen E. Ambrose, *Rise to Globalism: American Foreign Policy Since 1938,* 4th rev. ed. (New York: Penguin Books, 1985).

2. Russell F. Weigley, *The American Way of War: A History of United States Military Strategy and Policy* (New York: Macmillan, 1973).

3. For an overview of the Korean War, see Burton I. Kaufman, *The Korean War: Challenges in Crisis, Credibility and Command* (Philadelphia: Temple University Press, 1986).

4. For an introduction to Joseph J. McCarthy and McCarthyism, see David M. Oshinsky, *A Conspiracy So Immense: The World of Joe McCarthy* (New York: Free Press, 1983); and Athan Theoharis, *Seeds of Repression: Harry S. Truman and the Origins of McCarthyism* (Chicago: Quadrangle Books, 1971).

5. "U.S. Announces Program on Returning War Dead," *New York Times,* 9 March 1951, 2; Secretary of Defense George Marshall to Secretaries of Army, Navy, and Air Force, memorandum, Order on Reinternment, 1 March 1951, copy; M. B. Ridgway, Commander in Chief, Far Eastern Command to the Adjutant General, Department of the Army, 4 September 1951, file 293: Army Forces in Korea—Disposition of Unidentified Remains, box 651, miscellaneous file, 1939–54, General Correspondence, RG 92, National Archives.

6. "Homecoming," *New York Times,* 22 March 1951, 30.

7. Marshall S. Carter, Brigadier General, USA, Director, Executive Office, Department of Defense Directive, Number 110.04-3, 21 September 1951, Frank Pace, Jr., Secretary of the Army to Representative John R. Murdoch, Chairman, Committee on Interior and Insular Affairs, 18 December 1951, file 293.7, Armed Forces—Korea, box 506, miscellaneous file, 1939–54, General Correspondence, RG 92, National Archives; U.S. Congress, House, Representative Karl Stefan of Nebraska, *Congressional Record,* 82d Cong., 1st sess., 19 September 1951, 97, pt. 9:11664; U.S. Congress, Senate, Senator William F. Knowland of California, Senator Arthur V. Watkins of Utah, *Congressional Record,* 82d Cong., 1st sess., 21 September 1951, 97, pt. 9:11823–24; and U.S. Congress, House, Representative Harold Royce Gross of Iowa, *Congressional Record,* 82d Cong., 1st sess., 11 October 1951, 97, pt. 10:13016–17.

8. James Barron, "A Korean War Parade, Decades Late," *New York Times,* 26 June 1991, B3.

9. American Battle Monuments Commission, "Honolulu Memorial National Memorial Cemetery of the Pacific," Washington, D.C.: American Battle Monuments Commission, 1985.

10. James M. Mayo, *War Memorials as Political Landscape: The American Experience and Beyond* (New York: Praeger, 1988), 194–95, 284.

11. Record of Proceedings: Sixty-first Meeting, 24 October 1950, American Battle Monuments Commission, Records of the American Battle Monuments Commission, RG 117, National Archives.

12. U.S. Congress, Senate, Committee on Interior and Insular Affairs, *Creating a National Monument Commission,* 83d Cong., 2d sess., 30 July 1954, S. Rept. 2020; and "'Freedom Wall' Project Rouses Arlington Board," *Washington Evening Star,* 18 August 1957, "Speaking of Freedom," *Washington Evening Star,* 21 August 1957, "Fast Action Questioned on Freedom Monument," *Washington Evening Star,* 22 August 1957, "Sheppard Objection Stalls Monument Bill," *Washington Post,* 20 August 1957, A10, "Freedom Shrine Muddle," *Washington Evening Star,* 11 September 1957, "VFW Battles Freedom Wall," *Washington Evening Star,* 4 February 1958, "Again—The Freedom Shrine," *Washington Evening Star,* 19 March 1958, "Freedom Wall Killed in House, 195–169," *Washington Evening Star,* 28 March 1958, "'That Wall Again,'" *Washington Evening Star,* 15 June 1959, "Arlington Board Hits 'Freedom Wall' Again," *Washington Sunday Star,* 21 June 1959, "Monument Bill Appears Doomed," *Washington Post,* 23 May 1960, Ada Louise Huxtable, "Plan for a Freedom Shrine Introduced in Congress," *New York Times,* 3 June 1960, clippings in file: FAA, Statues, Monuments, and Memorials: Five Freedoms Memorials, 1954–61, Central Files, box 61, Records of the Commission of Fine Arts, RG 66, National Archives.

13. Leonard Carmichael, Secretary, Smithsonian Institution, memorandum, 31 January 1957, enclosure memorandum to the President, 30 January 1957 [Nelson Rockefeller, et. al.], box 92, Office of the Secretary Records, 1949–64, Record Unit 50, Smithsonian Institution Archives, Washington, D.C.

14. Nelson Rockefeller to Leonard Carmichael, 26 February 1959, John Nicholas Brown to Leonard Carmichael, 16 March 1959, box 92, Office of the Secretary Records, 1949–64, Record Unit 50, Smithsonian Institution Archives, Washington, D.C.

15. U.S. Congress, Senate, Committee on Rules and Administration, *Establishing a National Armed Forces Museum Advisory Board of the Smithsonian Institution and Authorizing Expansion of the Armed Forces Exhibits Therein: Report,* 87th Cong., 1st sess., 16 August 1961, S. Rept. 752.

16. "Preliminary Development Plan: National Armed Forces Museum Park," 1966, box 12, Colonel John H. Magruder to S. Dillon Ripley, 17 January 1967, John H. Magruder, "Summary of Mail Received by Smithsonian Institution Protesting National Armed Forces Museum Park," 13 January 1967, memorandum, box 2; press clippings and letters to the editor in box 12: "Military Park Planned on 610-Acre River Site, *Washington Post,* 21 September 1966, B1; "Militant Play," *Washington Post,* 28 September 1966, A24; "A Difficult Choice," *Washington Evening Star,* 29 September 1966, A18; "Military Museum," *Washington Evening Star,* 10 March 1967; "Is This Museum Necessary?" *Nation,* 23 January 1967; "Armed Forces Museum Park," *Boston Globe,* 17 January 1967; "Writer Deplores Creation of 'Disneyland of War,'" *(Newburyport, Mass.) News,* 24 January 1967, Eisenhower Institute for Historical Research Records, National Museum of American History, Accession No. T 89062, Smithsonian Institution Archives, Washington, D.C.

17. J. S. Hutchins to Colonel Magruder, 4 November 1969; Colonel Magruder to Members, National Armed Forces Museum Advisory Board, 19 January 1970, box 1, Eisenhower Institute for Historical Research Records, National Museum of American History, Accession No. T89062, Smithsonian Institution Archives, Washington, D.C.; "National Armed Forces Museum Advisory Board," *Smithsonian Year: 1975: Annual Report of the Smithsonian Institution for the Year Ended June 30, 1975* (Washington, D.C.: Smithsonian Institution Press, 1975), 189–90; and Interview, James Hutchins, Former Director, National Armed Forces Museum Advisory Board, 10 February 1990, Washington, D.C.

18. Charles Blitzer to Dillon Ripley, 26 September 1966, box 56, Assistant Secretary for History and Art, 1965–72, Record Unit 104, Smithsonian Institution Archives, Washington, D.C.

19. Gary O. Larson, *The Reluctant Patron: The United States Government and the Arts, 1943–1965* (Philadelphia: University Pennsylvania Press, 1983); and John Wetenhall, "The Ascendancy of Modern Public Sculpture in America" (Ph.D. diss., Stanford University, 1988), 41–68, 310–80.

20. For the best single volume survey of the Vietnam War, see George C. Herring, *America's Longest War,* 2d ed. (New York: Knopf, 1986). The literature documenting American involvement is reviewed in Christopher C. Lovett, "'We Had the Day in the Palm of Our Hand': A Review of Recent Sources on the War in Vietnam," *Military Affairs* 51 (April 1987): 67–72.

21. Charles DeBenedetti, *The Peace Reform in American History* (Bloomington, Ind.: Indiana University Press, 1980), 165–96; Mary Crawford, "Peg Mullen and the Military: The Bureaucracy of Death," *Ms.* 5 (January 1977): 70–73, 95; U.S. Congress, House, *A Bill to Prohibit Use of Names of Members of the Armed Forces Who Have Died as a Result of Combat Actions, and for Other Purposes,* 91st Cong., 1st sess., H. Rept. 15100, 1969; and Malcolm Thompson, "When They Read the Name of My Son . . . ," *Las Vegas Review Journal,* 16 October 1969, press clipping; Jack L. Higgons, Chairman, Americanism Committee, Depart-

ment of Nevada, American Legion to National Headquarters, American Legion, 22 October 1969, Mrs. Richard A. Evans, Independence, Missouri, to J. Milton Patrick, National Commander, American Legion, 18 February 1970, James S. Whitefield, Executive Director, American Legion to Evans, 26 February 1970; Representative Glenn Cunningham, Press Release on H.R. 150001, file: Vietnam—War Dead, Legion, American Legion Library, Indianapolis, Indiana.

22. John Hellmann, *American Myth and the Legacy of Vietnam* (New York: Columbia University Press, 1986), 53–66; and Albert Auster and Leonard Quart, *How the War Was Remembered: Hollywood and Vietnam* (New York: Praeger, 1988), 33–36.

23. Mayo, *War Memorials,* 199.

24. U.S. President, *Public Papers of the President of the United States* (Washington, D.C.: Office of the *Federal Register,* National Archives and Records Service, 1975), s.v. Richard Nixon, 1974, 40–44, 210–12, 325–27.

25. H. Bruce Franklin, *M.I.A. or Mythmaking in America* (Brooklyn, N.Y.: Lawrence Hill Books, 1992). Franklin traces the origins of the MIA myth to efforts by the Nixon administration to prolong the war and to score a propaganda victory against the North Vietnamese government.

26. Paul A. Gigot, "Lost or Merely Forgotten?" *National Review,* 17 August 1979, 1035–38; Thomas D. Boettcher and Joseph A. Rehyansky, "We Can Keep You . . . Forever," *National Review,* 21 August 1981, 958–62; Daniel A. O'Donohue, "Americans Missing in Southeast Asia," *Department of State Bulletin* 83 (January 1983), 19–20; and Paul D. Wolfowitz, "POW-MIAs and U.S. Policy Toward Southeast Asia," *Department of State Bulletin* 83 (September 1983): 55–57.

27. U.S. Department of the Army, *Logistic Support,* by Joseph M. Heiser, Jr., Vietnam Studies Series (Washington, D.C.: Department of the Army, 1974), 204–5.

28. *The Class that Went to War,* produced by American Broadcasting Company, 38 min., CRM McGraw-Hill Films, 1977, 16mm motion picture; *"How from Home": Veterans After Vietnam,* produced by Richard Ellison, Northern Lights Production, 30 min., 1985, 16mm motion picture; "Home from Vietnam," *U.S. News and World Report,* 12 February 1973, 21–23; Chuck Noell and Gary Wood, *We Are All POWs* (Philadelphia: Fortress Press, 1975), 55–57; quoted in Peter Karsten, *Soldiers and Society: The Effects of Military Service and War on American Life* (Westport, Conn.: Greenwood Press, 1978), 272–73; and Julius Duscha, "New Vets and the Old Legion, *Nation,* 13 August 1973, 103–6.

29. Auster and Quart, *Hollywood and Vietnam,* passim.

30. R. M. Easley to Colonel Richard Derby, Temporary Committee, April 26, 1919, box 19, General Correspondence, National Civic Federation, Manuscript and Rare Books Division, New York Public Library, New York.

31. Roger J. Spiller, "Shell Shock," *American Heritage* 41 (May/June 1990): 74–87; and Peter Karsten, *The Military in America: From the Colonial Era to the Present,* rev. ed. (New York: Free Press, 1986), 371.

32. William G. Pelfrey, "No Laurels for Legionnaires," *New Republic,* 21 November 1970, 18; and B. Drummond Ayres, Jr., "The Vietnam Veteran: Silent Perplexed, Unnoticed," in *The Vietnam Veteran in Contemporary Society: Collected Materials Pertaining to the Young Veterans, U.S. Veterans Administration, Department of Medicine and Surgery* (Washington, D.C.: GPO, 1972), vol. 4, pt. 52:5, pt. 5:11. For an example of the homecoming Korean veterans received, see "Session at Seattle," *Life,* 17 August 1953, 28–29.

33. D. Michael Shafer, "The Vietnam-Era Draft: Who Went, Who Didn't, and Why it Matters," in *The Legacy: The Vietnam War in the American Imagination,* ed. D. Michael Shafer (Boston: Beacon Press, 1990), 57–79.

34. "Home At Last!" *Newsweek*, 26 February 1973, 16–24; "An Emotional Exuberant Welcome Home," *Time*, 26 February 1973, 12–17; "The POW's Come Home: Unbounded Joy, But—," *U.S. News and World Report*, 26 February 1973, 21–23; U.S. President, *Public Papers of the President of the United States* (Washington, D.C.: Office of the *Federal Register*, National Archives and Records Service, 1975), s.v. Richard Nixon, 1973, 564–65; and Colonel Joseph E. Milligan, Lieutenant Colonel, Air Force (Ret.), interview by author, 18 May 1990, New Brunswick, New Jersey.

35. Richard Moser, "Talkin' the Vietnam Blues: Vietnam Oral History and Our Popular Memory of War," in *The Legacy: The Vietnam War in the American Imagination*, ed. D. Michael Shafer (Boston: Beacon Press, 1990), 104–21; and Peter Karsten, *Soldiers and Society: The Effects of Military Service and War on American Life* (Westport, Conn.: Greenwood Press, 1987), 263.

36. Catherine Albanese, "Requiem for Memorial Day: Dissent in the Redeemer Nation," *American Quarterly* 26 (October 1974): 386–98.

37. U.S. Congress, House, Representative Thomas J. Meskill of Connecticut, Representative Edward Boland of Massachusetts, and Representative Peter Rodino of New Jersey, *Congressional Record*, 90th Cong., 2d sess., 9 May 1968, 114, pt. 10:12583–12612.

38. U.S. Congress, House, Representative Edward Hutchinson of Michigan, Representative Basil Lee Whitener of North Carolina, Representative John D. Waggonner, Jr., of Louisiana, Representative James A. Burke of Massachusetts, and Representative Richard Roudebush of Indiana, *Congressional Record*, 90th Cong., 2d sess., 9 May 1968, 114, pt. 10:12583–12612.

39. U.S. Congress, House, Representative Patricia Schroeder of Colorado, Representative Samuel Stratton of New York, and Representative Edward Boland of Massachusetts, *Congressional Record*, 94th Cong., 1st sess., 9 September 1975, 121, pt. 22:28024–33.

40. Jerry L. Strait and Sandra S. Strait, *Vietnam War Memorials: An Illustrated Reference to Veterans Tributes throughout the United States* (Jefferson, N.C.: McFarland, 1988), 144–45; and Charles Hillinger, "Father Builds Mountain Chapel to Honor Son Killed in Vietnam," press clipping, Walter Douglas Westphall, "Vietnam Veterans Chapel Bulletin, July 1977," subject file: Vietnam Veterans Peace and Brotherhood Chapel, Swarthmore Peace Collection; Record of Proceedings, 94th Meeting, 1 May 1974, 95th Meeting, 14 November 1974, American Battle Monuments Commission, Washington, D.C.

41. For an overview of the Vietnam Veterans Memorial controversy, see Jan C. Scruggs and Joel L. Swerdlow, *To Heal a Nation: The Vietnam Veterans Memorial* (New York: Harper & Row, 1985) and Karal Ann Marling and Robert Silberman, "The Statue Near the Wall: The Vietnam Veterans Memorial and the Art of Remembering," *Smithsonian Studies in American Art* 1 (Spring 1987): 5–29.

42. U.S. Congress, House, Representative Lucien Nedzi of Michigan, Representative John P. Hammerschmidt of Arkansas, and Representative Phillip Burton of California, *Congressional Record*, 96th Cong., 2d sess., 20 May 1980, 126, pt. 9:11834–36; and U.S. Congress, House, *Vietnam Veterans Memorial: Conference Report*, 96th Cong. 2d sess., 25 June 1980, H. Rept. 96-1129. On the design of the Vietnam Veterans Memorial, see also Nicholas J. Capasso, "Vietnam Veterans Memorial," in *The Critical Edge: Controversy in Recent American Architecture*, ed. Tod A. Marder (Cambridge, Mass.: MIT Press, 1985), 189–202 and Vincent J. Scully, *Architecture: the Natural and the Manmade* (New York: St. Martin's Press, 1991), 362–67.

43. U.S. Commission of Fine Arts, *The Commission of Fine Arts: A Brief History, 1910–84, with Additions, 1977–84*, by Sue A. Kohler (Washington, D.C.: GPO, 1985), 125–35.

44. U.S. President, *Public Papers of the President of the United States* (Washington, D.C.:

Office of the *Federal Register,* National Archives and Records Service, 1982), s.v. Jimmy Carter, 1980–81, 1268–71.

45. "Honored at Last: A Memorial for Viet Nam Vets," *Time,* 14 July 1980, 23.

46. "That Vietnam Monument," *National Review,* 26 November 1982, 1461; Arthur C. Danto, "The Vietnam Veterans Memorial," *Nation,* 31 August 1985, 152–55; William Barry Furlong, "What Insiders Love about Washington, D.C.," *Discovery,* Spring 1990, 20–27; and Kurt Andersen, "A Homecoming at Last," *Time,* 22 November 1982, 44–46.

47. J. Mayhew Wainwright to John J. Pershing, 20 September 1936, Pershing Correspondence file, box 7, General Records and Reports, RG 117, National Archives.

48. U.S. Congress, Senate, Committee of Veterans' Affairs, *Annual Report of the American Battle Monuments Commission: Fiscal Year 1976,* 95th Cong., 1st sess., 1977, 10.

49. Renata Adler, *Reckless Disregard: Westmoreland v. CBS et al.; Sharon v. Time* (New York: Alfred A. Knopf, 1986); and Bob Brewin and Sydney Shaw, *Vietnam on Trial: Westmoreland vs. CBS* (New York: Atheneum, 1987).

50. George C. Herring, "Vietnam, American Foreign Policy, and the Uses of History," *Virginia Quarterly Review* 66 (Winter 1990): 1–16.

51. D. Keith Mano, "The Vietnam Veterans' Parade," *National Review,* 26 July 1985, 52–53.

52. Timothy J. Lomperis, *"Reading the Wind": The Literature of the Vietnam War* (Durham, N.C.: Duke University Press for the Asia Society, 1987), 101–13; and John Clark Pratt, "Bibliographic Commentary: 'From the Fiction, Some Truths,'" in Lomperis, *"Reading the Wind,"* 117–54.

53. Gaines M. Foster, "Coming to Terms with Defeat: Post-Vietnam America and the Post–Civil War South," *Virginia Quarterly Review* 66 (Winter 1990): 17–35.

54. Strait and Strait, *Vietnam War Memorials,* 34, 148–49, 193–94.

55. Elizabeth M. Norman, *Nurses in War: Female Military Nurses Who Served in Vietnam* (Ann Arbor, Michigan: UMI Press, 1986); Lynda Van Devanter, *Home Before Morning: The Story of an Army Nurse in Vietnam* (New York: Beaufort, 1983); Keith Walker, ed., *A Piece of My Heart: The Stories of 26 American Women Who Served in Vietnam* (Novato, Calif.: Presidio Press, 1986); Marie E. Ferrey, "Fight for Vietnam Women's Memorial Shifts to Senate," *Navy Times,* 30 November 1987, 10; Kara Swisher, "Reagan Signs Bill for Vietnam Women's Memorial," *Washington Post,* 17 November 1988, C4; Tom Kelly, "They Faced a Wall of Opposition," *Washington Times,* 8 March 1989, E1; and Eric Schmitt, "A Belated Salute to the Women Who Served," *New York Times,* 12 November 1993 A1, A29. See also, Karal Ann Marling and John Wetenhall, "The Sexual Politics of Memory: The Vietnam Women's Memorial Project and 'The Wall,'" *Prospects* 14 (1989): 341–72.

56. James M. Goode, *The Outdoor Sculpture of Washington, D.C.: A Comprehensive Historical Guide* (Washington, D.C.: Smithsonian Institution Press, 1974), 462–63.

57. Frank J. Murray, "The Korean War 'Silent Veterans' Will Get Memorial," *Washington Times,* press clipping in American Battle Monuments Commission, "Fact Sheet: Korean War Veterans Memorial to be Erected in the Nation's Capital" (Washington, D.C.: American Battle Monuments Commission, n.d.).

58. Ibid.

59. Bruce Cumings, *War and Television* (London: Verso, 1992), 269; Tim Weiner, "Design Fight Embroils Korean War Memorial," *Philadelphia Inquirer,* 24 October 1990, 1-A, 6-A; Sarah Booth Conroy, "The Korea Memorial's Slow March," *Washington Post,* 5 April 1991, B1, B3; and Benjamin Forgey, "The Korean Controversy," *Washington Post,* 2 February 1993, D1, D9.

60. Sarah Booth Conroy, "Korea Memorial Design Rejected," *Washington Post,* 29 June 1991, C1, 5.

61. "A Pet Cemetery Proposal To Honor the Dogs of War," *New York Times,* 11 August 1992, B6.

62. Nicholas Capasso, "Constructing the Past: Contemporary Commemorative Sculpture," *Sculpture* 9 (November/December 1990): 56–63.

63. Melissa Brown, "Memorials not Monuments," *Progressive Architecture* 66 (September 1985): 43–46; and Miriam Ruth Jackson, "We Shall Not Be Moved: A Study of the May 4th Coalition and the Kent State University Gymnasium Controversy of 1977" (Ph.D. diss., Purdue University, 1982).

64. Jennifer Stoffel, "Terrible Event Echoes in Dispute on How to Remember It," *New York Times,* 14 December 1988, A20; Linda Ellerbee, "Kent State Honors Slain Students, but Can't Lay to Rest Bitter Dispute," *New York Post,* 26 April 1990, 2; Robin Wilson, "As Kent State Prepares to Unveil Memorial, Critics of University Plan a Silent Protest," *Chronicle of Higher Education,* 2 May 1990, A31-2; and Jonathan Alter and Jennifer Stoffel, "Four Dead in Ohio Remembered," *Newsweek,* 7 May 1990, 27.

65. George Bush, "Address to the Nation Announcing Allied Military Action in the Persian Gulf," *Weekly Compilation of Presidential Documents* 27 (16 January 1991): 50–52.

66. Robert D. McFadden, "In a Ticker-Tape Blizzard, New York Honors the Troops," *New York Times,* 11 June 1991, A27, B4; Michael Wines, "Parade Unfurls Symbols of Patriotism in the Capital," *New York Times,* 9 June 1991, 20; and "Hometown Heroes," *Reno Gazette Journal,* 3 May 1991.

67. Sydney H. Schanberg, "A Great Parade, but the U.S. Can Do Even Better," *Newsday,* 11 June 1991, 85; and Anthony Lewis, "Not a Time to Celebrate," *New York Times,* 19 April 1991, A27.

68. H. Fineman, "Schwarzkopf for President?" *Newsweek,* 1 April 1991, 24; J. Ranelagh, "America's Black Eisenhower," *National Review,* 1 April 1991, 26–28; and B. B. Auster, "In the Footsteps of the Two Georges," *U.S. News and World Report,* 4 February 1991, 26–27.

69. "U.S. Senator Kasten Pushing Effort to Award Powell with Historic Fifth Star," *Jet,* 25 March 1991, 8.

### 6. CONCLUSION

1. Thomas W. Laqueur, "Memory and the Naming in the Great War," and Daniel J. Sherman, "Art, Commerce, and the Production of Memory in France After World War I," in *Commemorations: The Politics of National Identity,* ed. John R. Gillis (Princeton, N.J.: Princeton University Press, 1994), 150–67, 186–211; and Stephen R. Ward, "British Veterans' Organizations of the First World War" (Ph.D. diss., University of Cincinnati, 1969).

2. George L. Mosse, *Fallen Soldiers: Reshaping the Memory of the World Wars* (New York: Oxford University Press, 1990), 70–106.

3. James M. Mayo, *War Memorials as Political Landscape: The American Experience and Beyond* (New York: Praeger, 1988), 237–41.

4. Carol Gluck, "The Disappearing Past: Public Memory in Contemporary Japan" (Lecture presented at Rutgers University, New Brunswick, New Jersey, 18 April 1991); and Steven R. Weisman, "Pearl Harbor in the Mind of Japan," *New York Times Magazine,* 3 November 1991, 30–33, 42–47, 68.

5. James E. Young, "The Biography of a Memorial Icon: Nathan Rapoport's Warsaw Ghetto Monument," *Representations* 26 (Spring 1989): 69–104.

6. James E. Young, *Writing and Rewriting the Holocaust* (Bloomington, Ind.: Indiana University Press, 1988), 181–84.

7. Ibid., 184–87.

# INDEX

Page numbers in italics refer to illustrations.

227